SURVIVING
THE GLOBAL FINANCIAL AND
ECONOMIC
DOWNTURN

The **Institute of Southeast Asian Studies (ISEAS)** was established as an autonomous organization in 1968. It is a regional centre dedicated to the study of socio-political, security and economic trends and developments in Southeast Asia and its wider geostrategic and economic environment.

The Institute's research programmes are the Regional Economic Studies (RES, including ASEAN and APEC), Regional Strategic and Political Studies (RSPS), and Regional Social and Cultural Studies (RSCS).

ISEAS Publishing, an established academic press, has issued more than 2,000 books and journals. It is the largest scholarly publisher of research about Southeast Asia from within the region. ISEAS Publications works with many other academic and trade publishers and distributors to disseminate important research and analyses from and about Southeast Asia to the rest of the world.

The Cambodia Development Resource Institute (CDRI)

The GMS Development Series is an initiative of CDRI. Established in 1990, CDRI is Cambodia's leading independent development policy research institute. Its mission is to contribute to Cambodia's sustainable development, and the well-being of its people, through the generation of high quality policy-relevant development research, knowledge dissemination, and capacity development.

CDRI works to achieve this mission in partnership with Cambodian public institutions and civil society, and their regional and international development partners, with respect for the capacity of the Cambodian people and their institutions, for the value of local knowledge and experience, and for Cambodia's history and culture.

CDRI produces policy-relevant development research on:

- Economy, trade, and regional cooperation;
- Agriculture and rural development;
- Democratic governance and public sector reform;
- Natural resources and the environment;
- Social development;

with cross-cutting themes of inclusive growth, poverty reduction, sustainability, governance and institutional arrangements, gender equity, and conflict prevention and resolution.

Located in the Phnom Penh suburb of Tuol Kork, the CDRI has ninety-five staff members, including management, professional and technical staff, operations and support staff, of whom ninety-two are Cambodian. It also houses Cambodia's most extensive development research library and resource centre. Its publications, in both English and Khmer, are available as free PDF downloads from its website at <www.cdri.org.kh>.

The Greater Mekong Subregion Development Analysis Network (GMS-DAN)

The Greater Mekong Subregion Development Analysis Network (GMS-DAN) is a collaborative research network of leading development policy research institutes in Cambodia, Lao PDR, Thailand, Vietnam and Yunnan province of China. GMS-DAN's current core members are:

- The Cambodia Development Resource Institute (CDRI), Cambodia
- The National Economic Research Institute (NERI), Lao PDR
- General Department of Statistics, National Committee for Planning and Investment, (formerly National Centre of Statistics), Lao PDR
- Thailand Development Research Institute (TDRI), Thailand
- Central Institute for Economic Management (CIEM), Vietnam
- Institute of Economics, Vietnam Academy of Social Sciences, Vietnam
- ASEAN Regional and Industrial Development Research Centre, Faculty of Management and Economics, Kunming University of Science and Technology, Yunnan, China

The GMS-DAN has, with the support of the Rockefeller Foundation, undertaken collaborative research, and published research reports and associated publications, on the following topics:

- The Impact of the Asian Financial Crisis on the Southeast Asian Transitional Economies
- Labour Markets in Transitional Economies in Southeast Asia and Thailand
- Off-farm and Non-farm Employment in Southeast Asian Transitional Economies and Thailand
- The Cross-Border Economies of Cambodia, Laos, Thailand and Vietnam
- Pro-poor Tourism in the Greater Mekong Subregion
- Labour Migration in the Greater Mekong Subregion
- Agricultural Trade in the Greater Mekong Subregion
- Assessing China's Impact on Poverty Reduction in the Greater Mekong Subregion.

GMS Development Series 4
A CDRI Publication

SURVIVING
THE GLOBAL FINANCIAL AND
ECONOMIC
DOWNTURN
The Cambodian Experience

Hossein Jalilian,
Sothorn Kem, **Glenda Reyes** and **Kimsun Tong**

ISEAS
INSTITUTE OF SOUTHEAST ASIAN STUDIES
SINGAPORE

First published in Singapore in 2014 by
ISEAS Publishing
Institute of Southeast Asian Studies
30 Heng Mui Keng Terrace
Pasir Panjang
Singapore 119614

E-mail: publish@iseas.edu.sg
Website: bookshop.iseas.edu.sg

The responsibility for facts and opinions in this publication rests exclusively with the authors and their interpretations do not necessarily reflect the views or the policy of the publishers or their supporters.

ISEAS Library Cataloguing-in-Publication Data

Jalilian, Hossein.
    Surviving the global financial and economic downturn : the Cambodian experience / Hossein Jalilian, Sothorn Kem, Glenda Reyes, Kimsun Tong.
    1. Cambodia—Economic conditions—1979-
    2. Cambodia—Politics and government—1979-
    3. Global Financial Crisis, 2008-2009.
    4. Financial crises—Cambodia.
    5. Food prices—Cambodia.
    6. Food security—Cambodia.
    7. Poverty—Cambodia.
    I. Kem, Sothorn.
    II. Reyes, Glenda.
    III. Tong, Kimsun.
    IV. Title.
HC442 J26   2014

ISBN 978-981-4379-89-2 (soft cover)
ISBN 978-981-4459-66-2 (hard cover)
ISBN 978-981-4459-67-9 (E-book PDF)

Cover photo: Harvesting for export.
Source: CDRI.

Typeset by International Typesetters Pte Ltd
Printed in Singapore by Markono Print Media Pte Ltd

CONTENTS

LIST OF FIGURES

LIST OF TABLES

LIST OF ACRONYMS AND ABBREVIATIONS

3mma	3-month Moving Average
ADB	Asian Development Bank
AFP	Associated Fee Press
AFTA	ASEASN Free Trade Area .
ASEAN	Association of Southeast Asian Nations
ATC	Agreement on Textiles and Clothing
BFC	Better Factories Cambodia
CARD	Council for Agriculture and Development
CCSEAS	Canadian Council for Southeast Asian Studies
CDC	Council for the Development of Cambodia
CDRI	Cambodia Development Resource Institute
CMT	Cut-Make-Trim
CPP	Cambodian People's Party
CRDB	Cambodian Rehabilitation Development Board
CSES	Cambodia Socio-Economic Survey
DFID	Department for International Development (UK)
DTIS	Diagnostic Trade Integration Strategy
EBA	Everything But Arms Initiative
EIU	Economist Intelligence Unit
EU	European Union
FAO	Food and Agriculture Organisation
FCD	Foreign Currency Deposit
FDI	Foreign Direct Investment
FGD	Focus Group Discussion
FSN	Food Security and Nutrition

FUNCINPEC	Front Uni National pour un Cambodge Indépendant, Neutre, Pacifique, et Coopératif
GDCC	Government-Donor Coordination Committee
GDP	Gross Domestic Product
GFEC	Global Financial Economic Crisis
GHI	Global Hunger Index
GMAC	Garment Manufacturers Association of Cambodia
GNI	Gross National Income
GSP	Generalised System of Preferences
H1N1	Swine influenza virus
IFC	International Finance Corporation
IFPRI	International Food Policy Research Institute
ILO	International Labour Organisation
IMF	International Monetary Fund
IRRI	International Rice Research Institute
ISDR	International Strategy for Disaster Reduction
MAFF	Ministry of Agriculture, Forestry and Fisheries
MFA	Multi-fibre Arrangement
MFI	Microfinance Institutions
MoC	Ministry of Commerce
MoEF	Ministry of Economy and Finance
MoRD	Ministry of Rural Development
MoT	Ministry of Tourism
MPDF	Mekong Private Sector Development Facility
NBC	National Bank of Cambodia
NGO	Non-governmental Organisation
NIS	National Institute of Statistics
NPL	Non-performing Loans
NSDP	National Strategic Development Plan
OECD	Organisation for Economic Cooperation and Development
PDS	Poverty Dynamics Study
PFMRP	Public Financial Management Reform Programme
RCA	Revealed Comparative Advantage
RGC	Royal Government of Cambodia
RHS	Rural Household Survey
ROR	Rules of Origin Requirement
SAM	Social Accounting Matrices

SSI	Semi-structured Interview
TATA	Trade Agreement on Textiles and Apparel
UN	United Nations
UNCTAD	UN Conference on Trade and Development
UNDESA	UN Department of Economic and Social Affairs
UNESCAP	UN Economic and Social Commission for Asia and the Pacific
UNICEF	United Nations Children's Fund
UNSCN	United Nations Standing Committee on Nutrition
UNTAC	UN Transitional Authority in Cambodia
UNWTO	United Nations World Tourism Association
US	United States
USAID	United States Agency for International Development
USD	United States Dollar
USDA	United States Department of Agriculture
USEIA	United States Energy Information
US ITC	US International Trade Commission
VWS	Vulnerable Worker Survey
WB	World Bank
WDI	World Development Indicators
WEF	World Economic Forum
WEO	World Economic Outlook
WFP	World Food Programme
WHO	World Health Organisation
WTO	World Trade Organisation
y-o-y	Year-on-year

FOREWORD

Following a decade of strong economic growth, socio-economic development, and poverty reduction, the Global Financial Crisis (GFC) and associated regional economic downturn in 2008–09 had a severe impact on Cambodia's economy, exposing its vulnerability due to the narrowness of its economic base and its reliance on European and North American export markets. While annual GDP growth has now recovered to levels of 6–7 per cent, the vulnerability remains, with a shared imperative by the Cambodian government, the private sector, investors and development partners to work together for the diversification of the economy. The experiences of 2008–09, despite their severity, also provided useful lessons for policy-makers. I am pleased to introduce this volume which provides an independent analysis of the impact of the crisis on Cambodia and a deeper understanding of the Cambodian economy, its strengths and weaknesses, and policy challenges for the future.

Since 1993, the Cambodian economy has undergone a dramatic and rapid transformation. The traditional economy, based on agriculture, is now driven increasingly by the industrial and the tertiary sectors. With the return of peace and stability in the late 1990s, a sense of confidence and pride pervades the country. All Cambodians now share a common vision of sustained economic growth with employment and a secure future for all. The government's strategy is to help realize this vision by reinforcing Cambodia's comparative advantages both regionally and internationally. In the era of globalization the fortunes of all countries in the world are intertwined; autarchy is not an option for sustained high economic growth for a small sized economy as Cambodia. Hence Cambodia's continued economic success will depend on full market access for its products and the cooperation of its development partners.

Cambodia had to rebuild itself virtually from scratch after the defeat of the Khmer Rouge regime. At the very outset, the country had to face the harmful consequences of the international economic embargo imposed in 1979. The annual rate of economic growth did not exceed 3.4 per cent during 1988–91, even though average annual growth in the manufacturing sector reached 6.3 per cent. Growth has been particularly strong since the early 1990s, with the implementation of macroeconomic reforms and the normalization of economic and trade relations with countries in the region. An annual average rate of growth of 6.3 per cent was achieved during 1994–98, despite the upheaval caused by the Asian financial crisis of 1997–98.

It was only after the successful implementation of the "win-win" policy put forward by Samdech Hun Sen in 1998 that the government was able to dismantle the politico-military organization of the Khmer Rouge, thus re-establishing peace throughout the Kingdom and achieving the physical and political unification of the country. The government could then take steps to strengthen the spirit of national reconciliation. The elections of 1998 created conditions for political stability that allowed the government to focus on macroeconomic management.

Following the July 1998 elections, the government adopted the Triangular Strategy with the objective of promoting sustainable development in Cambodia. The strategy aimed at the restoration of peace and stability, as well as the maintenance of security for the country and its people. The strategy was by and large successfully implemented and the process of robust economic recovery initiated.

At the opening meeting of the Council of Ministers on 16 July 2004, Prime Minister Hun Sen launched the "Rectangular Strategy for Growth, Employment, Fairness and Effectiveness in Cambodia". The successful implementation of the strategy depends on establishing a conducive environment in four critical areas: (i) peace, political stability and social order; (ii) partnership for development, particularly partnership with the private sector, donor community and civil society; (iii) economic and financial stability; and (iv) integration of Cambodia in the region and in the world. The strategy was reviewed and reinforced after the elections of 2009 and is currently under implementation.

During the 1990s, the Cambodian economy was transformed from a centrally planned to a market economy. Reforms and policies intended to encourage private sector development were adopted in 1989–90. Government liberalized the economy by dismantling price controls and encouraged private sector development including foreign investment. Growth during this period was achieved mainly from the manufacturing and services sectors. Agricultural production, on average, remained lower than population growth. Since 1999, Cambodia has been working towards accelerating development based on market principles and private sector development. Growth was 11.9 per cent in 1999 and recorded annual average rate of 8.8 per cent during 1999–2003. Growth performance was consolidated further during 2004–08. In the decade ending 2010, GDP rose at an average annual rate of 9.3 per cent. Growth in the last decade was based on the strong performance of garments and tourism. From the policy side, sound macroeconomic management, in particular a prudent fiscal policy and tight monetary management supported by structural reforms, contributed to this performance.

In 2005 questions arose about the capacity of Cambodia to sustain high growth due to loss of competitiveness. The Multi-Fibre Agreement (MFA), which allowed World Trade Organization member countries, primarily China, to export clothing on a worldwide basis with no quotas imposed, expired in December 2004. It was anticipated that while the larger and more efficient textile manufacturers in Cambodia would be able to survive global competition, the smaller ones would perish as they would be unable to compete. The GFC had a crushing impact on Cambodia and growth slowed down sharply in 2009. The country had to rethink and reformulate its development strategy.

Moreover, the economic success of recent years has been accompanied by rural and agricultural stagnation, growing inequality between urban and rural sectors, social problems of landless farmers, and the growing pressure of finding productive employment for youth who are swelling the labour force day by day. Cambodia, with an annual per capita GDP of US$700 in 2010, remains a least developed country (LDC). Cambodia's economic future depends on how effectively it will be able to address the following challenges:

First, political stability, governance and respect for law and order must be strengthened and law enforcement must be guaranteed. Cambodia has adopted systems of governance appropriate for its culture and history. Elections are organized regularly and transparently. Individual and collective freedoms are assured. Political parties, labour unions, and the press function freely in this young democracy. Cambodia has also signed and ratified most of the international agreements on human rights protection. Education of citizens about their rights and responsibilities is an important area of government responsibility. However, the pursuit of political liberties should not derail political and social stability achieved after decades of turmoil and bloodshed by overstretching the capacity of the fragile political, social, and governance institutions of the nascent democracy. Also, the fruits of development must be shared equitably between the rich and the poor for preserving social stability.

Seccnd, much remains to be done to correct social injustices. The press, including the foreign press, enjoys great freedom in Cambodia and several non-government organizations, both national and foreign, are working in the country in diverse areas of social development. Although their activities have helped to increase awareness of social ills prevailing in the community, social equity remains a distant goal. In particular, human trafficking in women and children and the deprivation of landless farmers are serious concerns.

Third, the capacity to implement policy must be improved. Several institutional and policy reforms were undertaken during 1993–2010. Much more effort is needed to ensure that institutions function effectively, and that concrete actions follow approved strategies and policies. The top priorities are the implementation of an employment-oriented and market-responsive education policy along with the provision of technical and vocational training, improving access to good quality healthcare and swiftly propagating the latest advances in information and communications technology to the public to serve the cause of progress.

Fourth, protecting and developing natural resources will be crucial for sustaining development. Fair and equitable access to resources must be ensured to sustain social stability. Government policies and actions in technical, financial, cultural and academic sectors as well as in institutional coordination must reflect the political will to protect the environment. A transparent mechanism must be put in place to implement the sub-decree on social concessions to address the problem of landless farmers.

Fifth, in the area of capital accumulation, emphasis must be put on domestic resource mobilization and the selection of efficient investment projects. For augmenting human capital, human resource development at all levels should be encouraged. Skilled entrepreneurs and administrators and technical knowledge are key factors of production and no less important than physical capital. Cambodia's business community needs to improve its institutional and technical capacity. Investments for raising labour productivity and the introduction of improved technology should be given priority. A middle class has emerged in recent years; this welcome development will contribute to social stability. The middle class should strengthen Cambodia's capacity to benefit fully from the opportunities of development.

Sixth, Cambodia needs to attract private investment and mobilize broad-based international support for its development effort. In particular, international cooperation must be enhanced in the areas of (i) official development assistance; (ii) direct foreign investment; and (iii) foreign trade. The activities and outcomes of the Cambodian Development Forum (CDF), cooperation with the Asian Development Bank, International Monetary Fund, World Bank, and other donors of bilateral funds, along with deliberations in ASEAN, ASEAN Plus Three, and the World Trade Organization will provide important policy inputs to the government. Cambodia is committed to cooperating with these agencies.

The GFC had a largely indirect impact on the Cambodian economy. Cambodia's commercial banks did not have direct exposure to subprime loans, and the banking sector, while small, has grown healthily through responsible governance by the National Bank of Cambodia. However the crisis severely impacted on the real sectors, particularly export of garments. Cambodia's GDP growth fell from 10.2 per cent in 2007 to 6.7 per cent in 2008 and 0.1 per cent in 2009, but bounced back to 6 per cent in 2010 and is projected at 6.4 per cent in 2011. The Cambodian economy is expected to grow at about 7–8 per cent per annum over the next several years, but growth will likely accelerate after oil production commences on a commercial scale, expected in 2012. The high growth seen in the last decade was partly a post-conflict "catch up" phenomenon. As Cambodia confronts stiffer competition from globalization, the high cost of doing business — characterized principally by high energy and transport costs — could also become a binding constraint. As a result growth could become less buoyant. In the near term, the economy will likely continue to be led by tourism, garment industry, and construction, with agriculture providing periodic but volatile spurts of growth depending on weather conditions. However, there are already promising signs that investors from the Asian region, China, Japan and South Korea are leading the way in the diversification of the economy through investment in light industrial manufacturing and agri-business.

This volume not only makes a timely and useful contribution to analysis of the past and present challenges faced by Cambodia and its economy, but also reflects the valuable role played by CDRI as Cambodia's leading independent development policy research institute, widely respected by government, the private sector, the research community and civil society for the quality and objectivity of its research. CDRI's initiation of the GMS Development Series in partnership with ISEAS Singapore provides an important new platform for the dissemination of quality development policy research on Cambodia and Its Greater Mekong Subregion.

HE Dr Hang ChuonNaron
Secretary of State, Ministry of Economy and Finance &
Permanent Vice Chairman, Supreme National Economic Council,
Royal Government of Cambodia

ACKNOWLEDGEMENTS

This study is based on research projects funded by the World Bank (Cambodia office), Department for International Development (DfID) of the UK, and the Food and Agriculture Organisation (FAO) of the UN (Regional Office, Bangkok). The Rockefeller Foundation (Regional Office, Bangkok) funded the publication of this study. The significant contributions of all of them to this study are gratefully acknowledged.

LIST OF AUTHORS

Hossein Jalilian   Reader, University of Bradford, UK; Former Research Director, CDRI

Socheth, Hem   Research Fellow, CDRI

Sothorn, Kem   Research Associate, CDRI

Pide, Lun   Research Associate, CDRI

Glenda Reyes   Researcher, CDRI

Chan Hang, Saing   Research Associate, CDRI

Sovannarith, So   Research Fellow, CDRI

Vuthy, Theng   Research Fellow and Programme Coordinator, CDRI

Kimsun, Tong   Research Fellow and Programme Coordinator, CDRI

1

TRIPLE CRISES IN POST-CONFLICT MILIEU

Hossein Jalilian and Glenda Reyes

1.1 EXOGENOUS TRIGGERS, ENDOGENOUS INFLUENCES

The global financial and economic shock of 2007–09 is the third major economic crisis to have buffeted Cambodia in its post-conflict period, coming in the wake of the food crisis of 2007–08 and just a decade after the Asian financial crisis of 1997–98 (the "triple crises"). Cambodia's post-conflict history can be divided into two periods: 1991–98, referred to as the early phase of transition during which the first of the triple crises, the Asian financial crisis, occurred; and 1998 to the present, the late phase of transition during which the food and economic shocks transpired. A stocktake of the developments in Cambodia's post-conflict history suggests that the country has come a long way in reinstituting the foundations of a capitalist economic and procedural democracy but has yet to make significant headway in economic sophistication and substantive democracy.

The triple crises were different, yet had similar characteristics. They were all exogenously-driven shocks with their own specific causes but their effects were shaped by the country's situation at the time. In terms of magnitude of impact, the global financial and economic downturn was the worst of the three crises. That it caused the first ever growth contractions in the post-conflict period was sufficient rationale for the series of studies that substantiate this book. Like the two shocks that preceded it however, the way it impacted on Cambodia cannot be understood in isolation from the overall post-conflict milieu. The thesis here is not that endogenous factors caused the crisis. Country circumstances would hardly be able to account for that which is international in origin (Rose and Spiegel 2009). It is simply that endogenous factors shaped the impact of the crisis and a historical, as opposed to a static, analysis better illuminates the nature of the impact. For instance, the growth contractions cannot be explained outside of Cambodia's post-conflict growth pattern while any poverty effect was most likely due to the cumulative impacts of the global economic slump and the hike in food prices. By the same token, sustainable recovery from the downturn rests on deeper reforms affecting major economic and political aspects of the country's post-conflict milieu.

This book is an in-depth comprehensive examination of the impact of the global financial and economic crisis on Cambodia. It probes into the effects of the shock at macro, sectoral and micro levels using qualitative and quantitative techniques. This first chapter gives some background, linking the nature of crisis transmission with broader post-conflict developments. This approach is integrated in the conceptual framework on the crisis transmission presented in Chapter 2 and reflected in the policy directions advanced in the final chapter. The characterization of the milieu during the early and late phases of transition starts by discussing the broader growth and poverty trends and then key growth facilitators, bearing in mind their relevance in shaping crisis contagion, after which the transmission of the Asian financial crisis and the food and economic shocks are briefly discussed. Chapter 2 explores the macroeconomic and sectoral effects of the global financial and economic crisis based largely on the conceptual framework introduced in this chapter. It builds on previous papers written by CDRI researchers (Jalilian et al. 2009, 2010; Jalilian and Reyes 2010). Chapters 3 and 4 investigate the micro-level impacts and give substance to the so-called human face of the crisis. Chapter 3 capitalizes on the quantitative approach, particularly a panel dataset generated from surveys conducted before and over the period of the crisis. Chapter 4 makes use of the qualitative approach, particularly the results of the focus group discussions (FGDs) and semi-structured interviews (SSIs) conducted during the crisis. Chapters 3 and 4 draw on research and reports by Tong et al. (2009a, 2009b), Tong and Pon (2009a, 2009b, 2010), Theng and Kem (2009), So (2009a, 2009b), Kem (2009, 2010), all of whom are researchers at the Cambodia Development Resource Institute (CDRI). Chapter 5 draws on research conducted by Jalilian et. al. (2010) addressing the impact of unprecedented food price increases that took place in 2007. Combined with the GFEC that followed shortly afterwards, the two crisis had considerable impact on the level of poverty and prosperity in the country. The final chapter discusses the nature of the rebound, and the risks, opportunities and directions that could underpin a recovery that is resilient to the factors that heighten the country's vulnerability to shocks and is thus more sustainable.

1.2 EARLY TRANSITION PERIOD ONTO THE ASIAN FINANCIAL CRISIS

1.2.1 Fragile Milieu, Fragile Growth

Post-conflict countries have a fair chance of reverting to a state of war within ten years of the termination of conflict (Collier 2000). The combination of several colossal challenges common to post-conflict countries heightens this possibility and makes the development needs of recovering countries quite different from the others. Cambodia faced such challenges after coping with a three-decade civil war[1] spanning the U.S. bombing campaign till the 1970s, the Khmer Rouge regime of 1975–79, the Vietnamese occupation between 1979 and 1991, and the United Nations Transitional Authority in Cambodia (UNTAC) and post-UNTAC period of 1992–98. These challenges were: obliterated physical infrastructure; decimated human capital; high physical insecurity and recurrent violence; macroeconomic instability and uncertainty; weak rule of law and protection of property rights; severed access to markets, public services, credit and financial services; and highly fragile state-society relations due to lack of trust and low government legitimacy. Coming from a communist tutelage, the transition was not only post-conflict but also post-communist. It faced the challenge of economic rehabilitation towards capitalism, albeit a private economy already subsisted under the communist regime[2] and market reforms were underway in the 1980s[3] (Curtis 1993; Irvin 1993; Quinn 2008).

The year 1991, with the signing of the Paris Peace Agreements and the deployment of the United Nations (UN) Mission in Cambodia, marked the beginning of Cambodia's post-conflict history, termed the "peace onset".[4] The following year witnessed the institution of the UNTAC, which was given responsibility for major aspects of the country's immediate post-conflict rehabilitation.[5] At best, the UNTAC had mixed success in fulfilling its mandate. Recovery in the peace onset period was in reality at the mercy of contending parties — the Khmer Rouge, the Royalists which constituted the FUNCINPEC,[6] the Cambodian People's Party (CPP),[7] and the Buddhist Liberal Democratic Party — and was no more than that manifested in the ceasefire violations, failures in demilitarization, and the political impasse during and after the 1993 elections that the UNTAC was powerless to avert. The CPP refused to acquiesce to the electoral results which showed that it had lost to FUNCINPEC. A power sharing agreement was eventually brokered but, overall, it was a fragile and potentially explosive situation.

In brief, the nature of economic growth during the embryonic phase of Cambodia's post-conflict transition reflected the overall milieu at that time — that is, fragile. In the first decade of peace, the economic growth of post-conflict countries generally follows an inverted U-shaped curve. The economy rebounds in the first two or three years at rates below the pre-conflict growth average, gains momentum and grows at above average rates in the fourth to seventh years before cooling off to expand at a self-sustaining pace (Collier and Hoeffler 2002; USAID 2009). Cambodia's conflict history is not so straightforward and does not quite fit this growth pattern (see Figure 1.1). The three decades of civil war spanned the U.S. bombing campaign, the Khmer

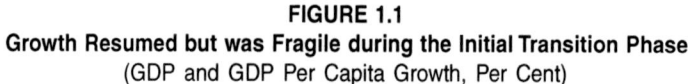

FIGURE 1.1
Growth Resumed but was Fragile during the Initial Transition Phase
(GDP and GDP Per Capita Growth, Per Cent)

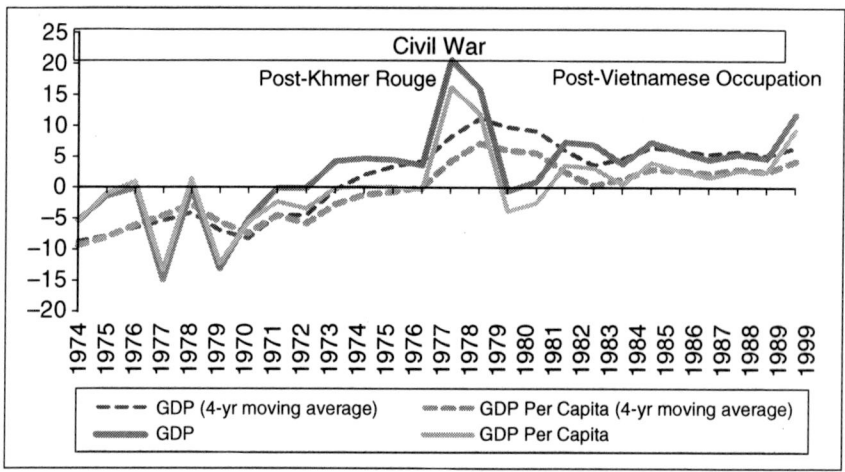

Source: Authors' calculations based on UNESCAP data.

Rouge regime, and the Vietnamese occupation. Heavily influenced by external forces, the civil war had an international dimension. Moreover, despite the international economic embargo and internal military incursions, a significant amount of political and economic rebuilding took place under the communist government, enough to restore 1960s paddy production and life expectancy levels by 1990 and re-establish the administrative, health and education sectors (World Bank 1992; Curtis 1993). Growth trends after the Khmer Rouge era did to some extent follow the inverted U-shaped growth curve as shown in Figure 1.1. In the first three years after the Khmer Rouge period, Cambodia's real gross domestic product (GDP) and GDP per capita experienced smaller contractions, but this still suggests a frail economy compared to that of the period 1961–65.[8] By the fourth to the seventh year, both GDP and GDP per capita had swelled. Growth trends after the communist regime did not follow the inverted U-shaped curve. One reason for this is that economic reconstruction had already significantly progressed under communist rule. In fact, with the drying up of Soviet Union aid and the initial inability of Western and multilateral donors to resume their development assistance (World Bank 1992), Cambodia's annual real GDP growth tumbled from an average of 10.3 per cent between 1988 and 1990 to an average of 5 per cent between 1991 and 1993, while its per capita output growth fell from 6.4 to 1.5 per cent over the same periods. With the eventual inflow of massive development aid, both its annual real GDP grew at the higher average rate of 6.1 and 2.9 per cent, respectively, between 1994 and 1997. The dividends from this growth significantly reduced the country's poverty rate. Cambodia emerged from its communist experience as one of the poorest in the world. National poverty headcount[9] stood at 45–50 per cent in 1993–94. The majority of the poor resided in rural areas and though economic growth slashed the poverty rate by 9–14 percentage points, its concentration in urban areas translated to less improvement in rural poverty reduction (World Bank 1999, 2009b). This urban bias of growth and rural bias of poverty have prevailed up to the present.

1.2.2 The Underpinnings of Economic Growth and Transformation

Immediate post-conflict growth in general rests on three factors: physical security or "negative peace", donor consumption, and donor investment (USAID 2009). This was true in the case of Cambodia. However, another factor — rebound in private investment and trade — also served as a key growth facilitator particularly towards the end of the first phase of transition. These four factors and their consequences had significant implications for the impact of the triple crises in Cambodia.

Negative Peace

There are two known types of peace: negative peace which refers to the absence of armed conflict, and positive peace which refers to the absence of the conflict's structural causes.[10] As advanced by the grievance thesis, relative deprivation and inequality are key root causes of conflict.[11] The restoration of negative peace during the country's initial phase of transition was enough to jump start reforms and resuscitate market activity, but this negative peace was neither complete nor stable. In 1997, the CPP, under Hun Sen, launched a coup against FUNCINPEC in a bid to consolidate power. This suspended the entry of Cambodia into the Association of Southeast Asian Nations (ASEAN). The Asian financial crisis was just as much about the impact of this coup as it was about the impact of the financial blow-out in Thailand.[12] It was not until after 1998 when complete negative peace was attained — the results of the next parliamentary elections gave CPP a clear victory, Khmer Rouge rebels defected to the government, and Pol Pot died — that comprehensive and coordinated economic programming could be realized.

The attainment of positive peace on the other hand cannot be reasonably expected in the initial phase of transition. Post-conflict countries, saddled as they have been by the near absence of rule of law, weak social cohesion and infighting for political power, have been especially vulnerable to state capture and grand corruption in general. Economic liberalization has come with multiple openings for corruption (UNDESA 2007; Hellman et al. 2000; Hellman and Kauffman 2001). In Cambodia, opportunism exploiting the lucrative rent-seeking unleashed by the transition proliferated during the early phase of transition. This was particularly evident in relation to the privatization of state industries and natural resources. Absent or inadequate legal framework, political power, connection and money enabled the misappropriation of public assets and land. Economic reforms in the immediate post-conflict period are said to have served one primary purpose: the maximization of political power (Hughes undated; Quinn 2008). This was not conducive to eliminating relative deprivation, a prerequisite for positive peace, and can be blamed for the limited extent of the poverty reduction achieved. The persistence of negative peace has continued to be a central feature of Cambodia's post-conflict milieu, shaping the nature of its growth. Some schools of thought refuse to label this political incident as a coup. See for instance Springer (2005).

Consistent with the experience of other post-conflict countries, Cambodia's immediate post-conflict growth was heavily donor-financed. Such aid dependence has continued to be a key characteristic of the country's post-conflict milieu and helped determine the impact of the triple crises. Yearly aid as per cent of gross national income (GNI) swelled from an average of 2.5 per cent in 1987–90 to 10.9 per cent in 1991–98 (see Figure 1.2). It financed, on average, 88 per cent of annual gross capital formation in 1991–98 compared to only 27 per cent in 1988–90 (see Figure 1.3). Overall budget deficit stood at 4 per cent per year on average in 1991–98 (see Figure 1.4), the bulk of which was financed by official grants and concessional loans. Given the mixed progress in implementing the Paris Peace Agreements, donor investment was mostly tied to longer term projects, not rehabilitative activities (Curtis 1993). The sequence and purpose of aid have been considered critical in optimizing aid effectiveness in post-conflict situations. Historically, post-conflict aid in general tended to spike in the initial post-conflict phase then taper out by the end of the first post-conflict decade. This is apparent in Cambodia's experience. Such pattern of aid flows has been criticized, even called a paradox, inasmuch as the spike occurs just when the absorptive capacity of the recovering country is low and the decline happens just when the absorptive capacity of the country is higher.[13]

FIGURE 1.2
Cambodia Depended on Aid for Capital Formation
(Aid as Per Cent of Gross Capital Formation)

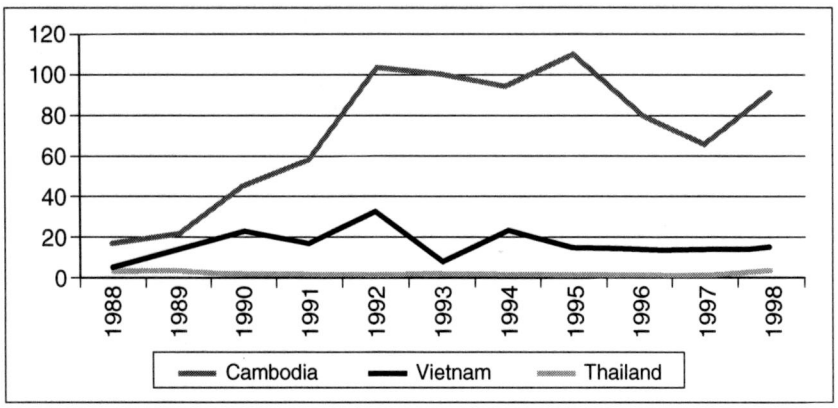

Note: No available comparable data for Lao PDR.
Source: World Bank WDI CD-ROM.

FIGURE 1.3
Aid Was Significantly Depended On for Budget Financing
(Budget Deficit as Per Cent of GDP)

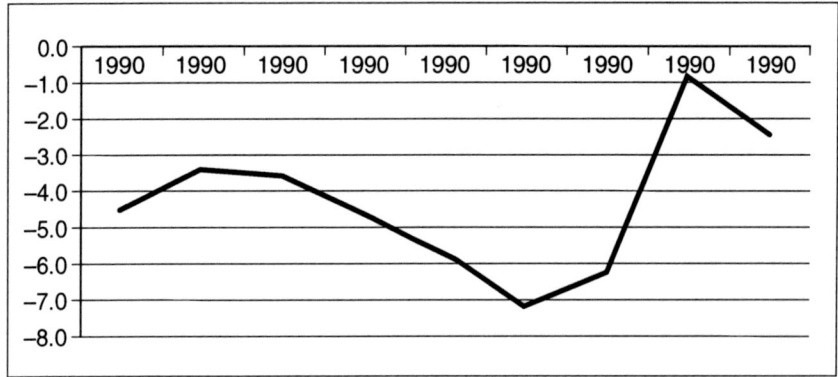

Source: ADB (2010).

FIGURE 1.4
Trade Openness Improved but Remained Modest
(Trade Openness Index of Selected Developing Asian Countries)

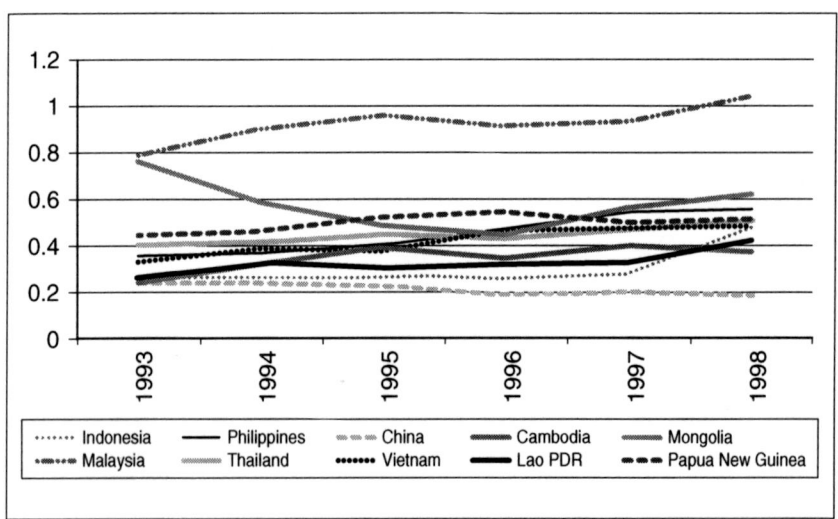

Note: The index is calculated by dividing the sum of exports and imports by two and then by GDP. A higher index means greater trade openness.
Source: Authors' calculations based on data from World Bank WDI Online.

Aid-induced Expenditure Shock

In whatever case, donor consumption and investment were vital in catalysing economic rebound in the peace onset period. UNTAC, with some 22,000 military and civilian personnel, caused an "expenditure shock". This shock stimulated trade, employment and construction. The beginnings of the structural transformation of the Cambodian economy can be traced to the establishment of the garment industry and the surge in construction during the country's initial phase of transition. Having grown at double-digit rates, the share of construction in real GDP steadily rose from 6.7 per cent in 1991 to 10.4 per cent in 1996 while the government's capital expenditure, mostly donor-financed, leapt from 0.4 to 6.5 per cent of GDP over the same period (World Bank 1997).

Substantial external assistance can engender three macroeconomic challenges, namely inflation, Dutch Disease and dollarization. Inflation did escalate during the peace onset period in Cambodia. It averaged 130.5 per cent per year in 1990–93 before plunging to an annual average of 9 per cent in the next four years. A combination of factors — deficit monetization, influx of donor consumption and investment, elimination of price controls — largely caused the price spikes (World Bank 1996; Irvin 1993; Carnahan et al. 2005).[14] Concerning Dutch Disease,[15] country studies on whether aid induces it report mixed results (Nkusu 2004). In the case of Cambodia, some increases in real effective exchange rate were seen during the first phase of transition. These increases were particularly notable following the sharp depreciation of the riel as a reaction to the high inflation in 1993 and the political crisis in 1997–98.[16] These episodes of appreciation, however, would not have necessarily resulted in Dutch Disease effects.[17] Dollarization proved to be most enduring impact of aid that flowed to Cambodia during the initial phase of its transition. Supply-side dynamics coupled with the lack of confidence in the riel caused the near complete dollarization of Cambodia in its first phase of transition. The foreign currency deposit (FCD) ratio[18] was nearing 70 per cent by 1997 (de Zamaróczy and Sa 2002; Jalilian and Reyes 2010). This dollarization helped determine the impact of the economic shocks and the ability of the government to respond to them.

Investment and Trade Bias

The pick-up in economic activity due to the restoration of negative peace, donor financing, and government interventions encouraged increasing flows of investment and rapid growth of trade. The Law on Investment passed in 1994 was liberal by international standards. On top of the tax and duty exemptions, a number of ad hoc exemptions benefited the then major exports of logs, timber and rubber. Most non-tariff barriers were removed and there were no quantitative restrictions on imports. The pricing and exchange rate systems were liberalized (World Bank 1996, 1997). Another factor that was central to the surge in investment and trade by the mid to late 1990s was the Generalized System of Preferences (GSP) status granted by European countries and the United States (U.S.). This preferential access was critical to the establishment of the country's current leading export industry and growth sector, garments. On the downside, continuing major business constraints, including degraded infrastructure, sluggish revenue mobilization and low administrative capacity which affect the level of complementary public investments, shortage of skilled human capital, and weak legal framework and enforcement, still kept trade and investment levels comparatively low.

A significant increase occurred in both the country's trade and financial openness during its initial phase of transition, albeit at comparatively low levels having come from a very low base. Trade openness ratio rose from 0.24 in 1993 to 0.39 in 1997 (see Figure 1.4). In both years, the ratio was well below the average for developing East Asia.[19] The flush of external capital not only comprised aid, private transfers mainly in the form of foreign direct investment (FDI) also poured in. The lack of portfolio investment helped shield the country from the first round effects of financial shocks. Net FDI ballooned from US$54 million in 1993 to US$203 million in 1997. Net FDI inflows as a percentage of GDP climbed from 2.1 to 5.9 per cent over the same period (see Figure 1.5). The ratio was well below the average for developing East Asia in 1993 but had surpassed the average by 1997.[20] It could have been higher if it were not for the impact of the Asian financial crisis. Official remittance inflows increased from nil to US$120 million by 1998, reflecting the

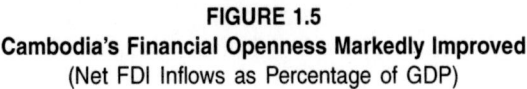

FIGURE 1.5
Cambodia's Financial Openness Markedly Improved
(Net FDI Inflows as Percentage of GDP)

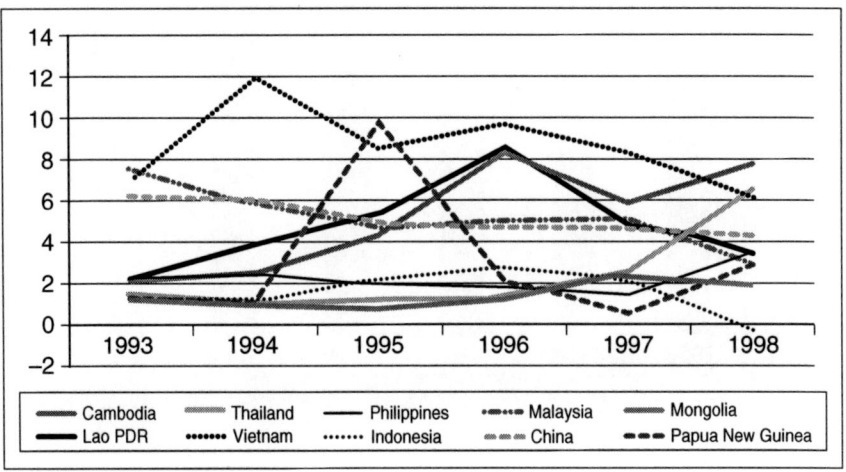

Source: World Bank WDI Online.

intensification of labour export. The influx of foreign capital supported financial deepening. The banking industry dominated and continues to dominate the financial sector. The envisioned two-tier system was finally realized with the privatization of several state-owned banks in 1997. Financial intermediation and reach remained low, however, affording Cambodia protection against the first round effects of the financial crises.

The vast improvement in openness paved the way for the beginnings of Cambodia's economic structural transformation. This restructuring rode on the back of the garments, construction and tourism sectors. The take-off of the garment sector was largely catalyzed by the GSP status granted to Cambodia and the inward FDI that followed. The signing of the Agreement on Textiles and Clothing (ATC) in 1995, which curtailed garment imports from the then already established garment manufacturers, enabled the fourth production shift in the global garment business. This benefited latecomers to the industry, including Cambodia (Jalilian and Reyes 2010).[21] In 1997, prospects for the domestic garment industry significantly perked up with the grant

FIGURE 1.6
Industry Expanded, Largely due to Construction and Garment Sectors

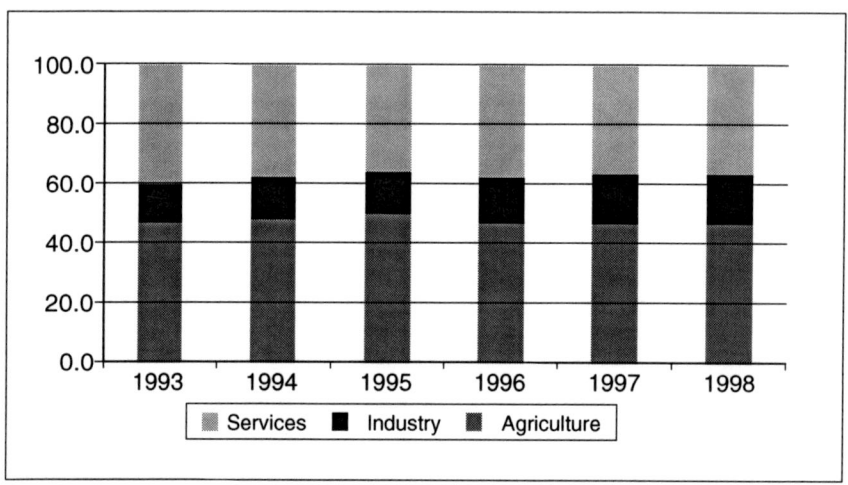

Source: World Bank WDI Online (2010*a*,*b*).

of GSP status to Cambodia by the U.S. The boom in garment production expanded the export base (formerly dominated by natural resource-based products) and diversified the export market (formerly dominated by ASEAN member countries, Singapore, Thailand and Vietnam). Garment export values experienced a thousand fold increase from US$24 million in 1995 to US$359 million in 1998. Cambodia's export share of the U.S. garment market soared from 2 to 81 per cent. However, the country's export base remained narrow.

Due to the outstanding growth in construction and garments, the contribution of the industrial sector increased from about 13 per cent of the total output in 1993 to 17 per cent in 1998. The benefits of industrial growth were mostly felt in urban areas. The contribution of agriculture, though it remained dominant, stagnated at about 46 per cent on average (see Figure 1.6). This was largely due to the erratic growth of rice and fisheries output. Government spending on agriculture had risen steadily but often fallen short of the programmed budget. Defence expenditure accounted for the bulk of current spending and frequently overran budget targets (World Bank 2009). This feature of the budget continues up to the present and has restrained the government's response to crisis. The urban bias of industrial expansion, stagnation in agricultural growth, and gap in agricultural spending were all unwelcome news for poverty reduction efforts given the concentration of poverty among rural farming households. It marked the beginning of the non-inclusive growth which was to become a central feature of Cambodia's post-conflict milieu. The output share of the services sector changed little (see Figure 1.6). Wholesale and retail trade expanded but with the transition, government services decreased. Meanwhile, the tourism sector significantly benefited from the expenditure shock caused by the UNTAC operations and was poised for take off.

1.2.3 The Political and the Financial Crises

The most defining element of the Asian financial crisis was the rapid and large-scale reversal of the foreign capital inflows that catalyzed Asia's emerging economies. The Asian financial crisis was thus dubbed the "crisis of success" (Radelet and Sachs 1998). In Cambodia, both this "crisis of economic success" and "crisis of political failure" underpinned the economic slide in 1997–98. Compared to those experienced by its neighbouring countries, this setback was modest. Cambodia was mostly spared the first round effects of the Asian financial crisis due to its underdeveloped financial sector and FDI-dominated investment portfolio. Even so, the country's economy was arrested by political upheaval featuring the overthrow of the FUNCINPEC leadership by the CPP under Hun Sen in July 1997. This shattered the negative peace, one of the key immediate post-conflict growth facilitators. Donor support, another growth facilitator was truncated by the political crisis. Donors, including the U.S., Japan and the EU, either suspended or cut back financial assistance. This caused serious shortfalls in revenue, in turn squeezing out capital expenditures in particular. Investor confidence also waned as a result of the political turmoil and more so when the second-round effects of the Asian financial crisis swept through Cambodia.

Somewhat mirroring the transmission mechanism for the global financial and economic shock, the second-round impact of the Asian financial crisis infiltrated Cambodia via investment and, to a lesser extent, trade channels. Net FDI fell sharply from US$293 million in

1996 to US$203 million in 1997, then recovery in the second-half of 1998 saw FDI increase to US$223 million by the end of the year. As a result of the decline in official and private capital flows, the capital account position deteriorated. The brunt on the real sector was moderated by the strength of garment exports, which were mostly destined to countries unruffled by the crisis, and the heavy dollarization of the economy, which mitigated the impact of the riel's depreciation against other currencies. Agricultural exports declined, but this was equally about other factors.[22] Imports on the other hand dropped, reflecting the slowdown in the implementation of donor and FDI-funded projects. In the end, the current account balance showed a surplus in 1997 and a lower deficit in 1998 relative to 1996 (IMF 1998). The reversal in capital inflows triggered a contraction in FCD, thus a liquidity squeeze. This in turn caused a credit crunch that was however modest relative to that witnessed in other affected countries. FCD growth plunged year-on-year from 57 to nearly zero per cent while private credit growth declined year-on-year from about 48 to 3 per cent between end of 1996 and 1998 (see Figure 1.7). The revenue shortfall precipitated

FIGURE 1.7
Liquidity and Credit Squeeze Was Experienced
(Per Cent Growth)

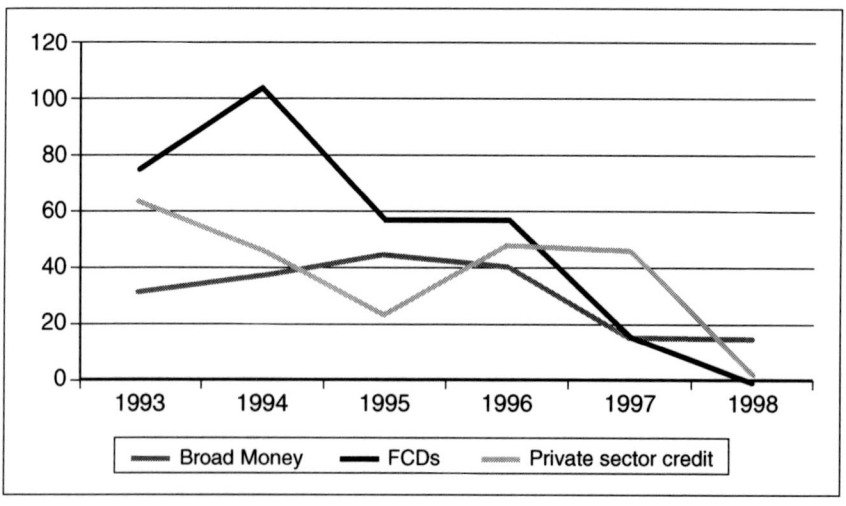

Source: World Bank (1997); IMF (1999).

by the tightening of aid was exacerbated by the slowdown in the real sector. Total revenues as per cent of GDP dropped from 9.1 per cent in 1996 to 8.5 per cent in 1998. Helped by the prioritization of defence spending, capital expenditure as per cent of GDP fell from 6.4 to 3.6 per cent over the same period.

In the end, the decline in real output was restrained, growing by 5 per cent in 1998 which was not far off the 5.4 per cent growth in 1996. Although construction activity slackened, the industrial sector was kept strong by the surge in garment exports. In contrast, services experienced a slowdown as the political instability dampened tourism. The number of international visitor arrivals by air dropped by roughly 28 per cent in 1998 relative to 1996 (IMF 1998). The agricultural sector put on strong growth of 6 per cent, helping prop up the economy (see Figure 1.8). Agriculture's role as a buffer was likewise observed during the global financial and economic crisis.

FIGURE 1.8
Industry and Agriculture Remained Strong while Services Slackened
(Sectoral Growth, Per Cent)

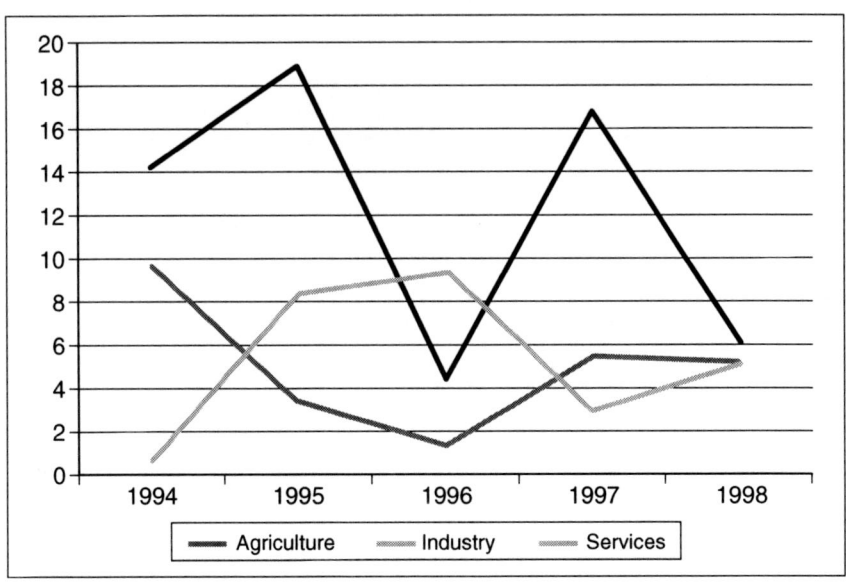

Source: World Bank WDI Online (2010*b*).

1.3 LATE TRANSITION PERIOD ONTO THE FOOD AND GLOBAL FINANCIAL AND ECONOMIC CRISES

1.3.1 Stable Milieu, High but Non-inclusive Growth

The period following the 1998 elections held much promise. The restoration of stability allowed comprehensive economic programming and the realization of enduring peace. The threat of war can be safely said to have passed with the last of the Khmer Rouge rebels having surrendered, defected or been caught. The reintegration of Cambodia into the international community was also clinched by the country regaining its seat in the UN in 1998[23] and its entry into ASEAN the following year. Growth performance reflected the fruits of this new era. Real GDP growth averaged nearly 10 per cent per year between 1999 and 2007, the highest annual average for the early transition period. This later post-conflict growth also made the Cambodian economy one of the fastest growing in the world. Between 1999 and 2007, world output grew only by 3 per cent on average while that of the low-income countries as a whole grew by nearly 4 per cent and that of developing East Asia and the Pacific, by about 9 per cent (see Figure 1.9).

FIGURE 1.9
Cambodian Economy Was One of the Fastest to Grow
(Real GDP Growth, Per Cent)

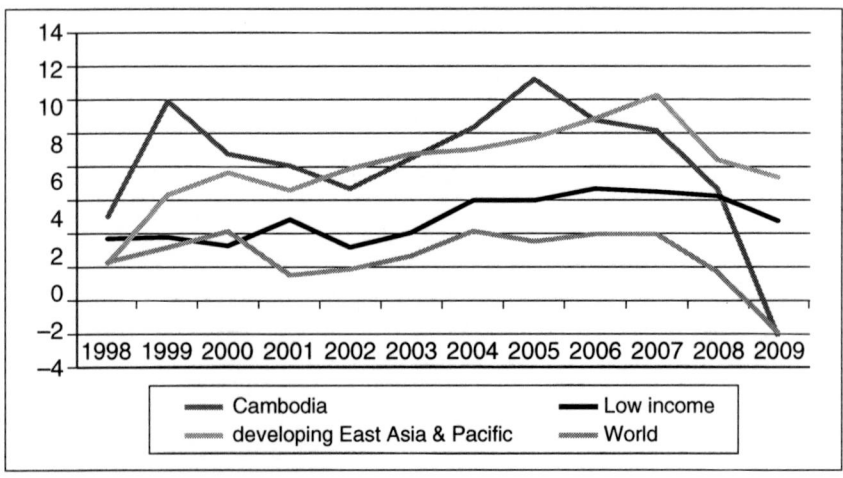

Source: World Bank WDI Online (2010b).

The high growth in the second phase of transition was not enough to lift Cambodia from its low-income status. The country's GNI per capita may have doubled to US$560 between 1998 and 2007, surpassing the average for the entire low income cluster; however, it stayed well below the lower limit (US$996) for the GNP per capita of the lower middle income group (see Figure 1.10). Also, growth dividends did not rebound to the equal benefit of everyone. The country's poverty headcount dropped from 36 to 30 per cent between 1997 and 2007 (World Bank 1999, 2009b). Thus, while output grew at about 9 per cent per year on average during said period, the poverty rate declined by only 0.5 per cent per year. Poverty remains concentrated in rural Cambodia, the rural poverty headcount standing at 34.7 in 2007. The poverty rate for the capital, Phnom Penh, in the same year was estimated at a mere 0.8 per cent.

FIGURE 1.10
High Capital Was Not Enough to Progress from Least Income Status
(GNI Per Capita, US$)

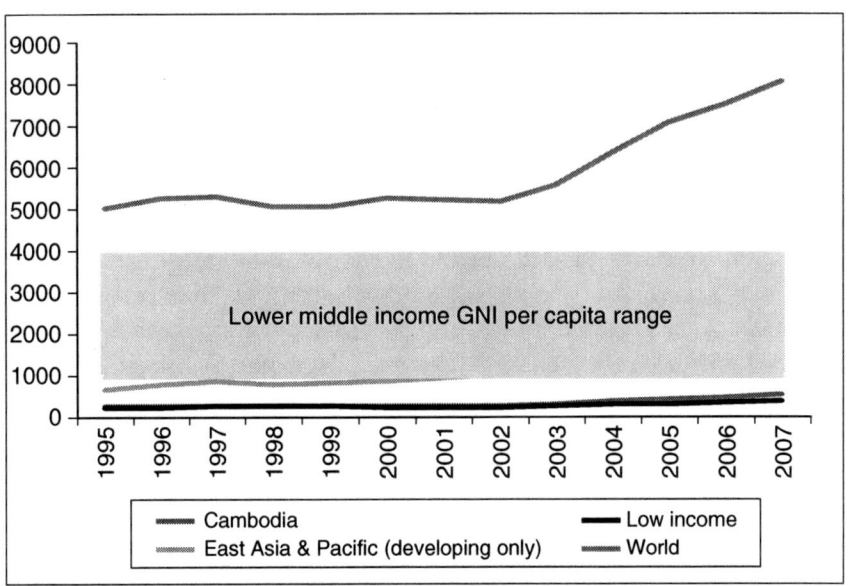

Source: World Bank WDI Online (2010b).

Economic growth is a necessary but not a sufficient condition for poverty reduction. The growth elasticity of poverty is conditioned by the nature of growth and other context-specific factors. Differences in economic and non-economic circumstances have generated and will generate differentiated effects on poverty and inequality.[24] The characteristics of economic growth and poverty status in turn shape the impact of economic shocks. The sectoral make-up of output, trade and financial openness were the growth determinants found to have chiefly shaped the impact of the crisis.[25] Meanwhile, countries with dire poverty, which is a function of inequality, risked greater exposure to the crisis at micro-level given that there are fewer coping mechanisms available to poorer groups in general.[26] The next section discusses the growth facilitators mentioned earlier in closer detail to explore relevant growth and poverty characteristics and how they have progressed from the first to the second phase of Cambodia's post-conflict transition.

1.3.2 Continuance of Economic Transformation and Non-inclusiveness

Elusive Positive Peace

There has been no internal armed conflict in Cambodia since the political coup of 1997. This has prompted countless pronouncements that stability and order finally reign in the country. The legacy of the Khmer Rouge is confined to museums and the ongoing trial of alleged former senior leaders of the regime. The quality of the prevailing stability has of course been put into question. Also, it has been sporadically interrupted by border skirmishes between Cambodia and Thailand[27] which aggravated the impact of the global financial and economic crisis on tourism. Nonetheless, negative peace has largely prevailed, enabling a more decisive implementation of reform and the achievement of high economic growth. The role of stability in enhancing the country's growth has been well established on both theoretical and empirical fronts.[28]

Positive peace by contrast has remained beyond reach. This translates to the continuation of serious inequality. Available data show that Cambodia's GINI index worsened from 39 per cent in 2004 to

43 per cent in 2007. Changes in the average consumption of the poorest fifth and richest fifth of the population were markedly different (8 versus 45 per cent in 2004). The greater disparity was largely accounted for by the increase in inequality in rural Cambodia. Meanwhile, assessments have honed in on the problematic state of governance. The country's scores on key governance indicators, with the exception of political stability, barely changed or even worsened between 1996 and 2008 (Kauffman et al. 2009). Good governance is one of the factors forging positive links between economic growth and poverty eradication.[29]

Fiscal Dependence: Less on Aid, More on Internal Revenues

Dependence on aid has remained high, albeit lower than that during the initial phase of transition. Aid flows continued to increase rapidly as non-traditional bilateral donors and non-governmental organizations (NGOs) contributed greater financial assistance. However, their shares in GNI and gross capital formation fell as internal revenue mobilization played an increasing role in meeting the country's budgetary requirements (see Figure 1.11). Together with social sectors and transport infrastructure, agricultural and rural development dominated the sectoral composition of aid. Aid flows benefiting agriculture showed signs of stagnation however, mirroring global trends.[30,31]

Seriously weak revenue generation during the first phase of transition, due to the small revenue base and feeble collection efforts, made the country extremely vulnerable to the withdrawal of donor funds following the coup and constrained the government's response to the Asian financial crisis. Reforms in revenue administration have made significant headway since then. The revenue base was widened with the introduction of new taxes such as the Value Added Tax, auction of garment export quotas, removal of most ad hoc tax exemptions, and more rigorous and transparent collection among others. Under the umbrella of the ten-year Public Financial Management Reform Programme (PFMRP) implemented in 2004, considerable progress in enhancing budget credibility, the first of the four platforms of the PFMRP, has been made.[32] Other major revenue-enhancing reforms implemented under the programme included the rolling

FIGURE 1.11
Aid Dependence Remains High, Though Less So

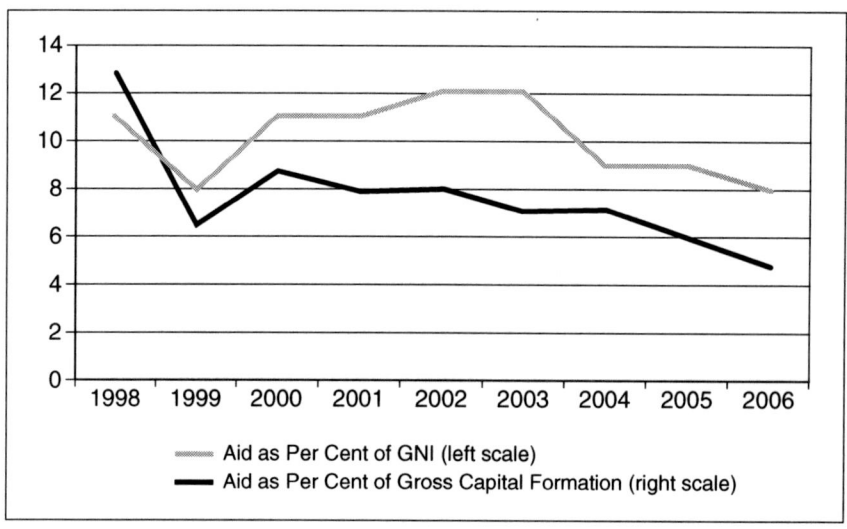

Source: World Bank WDI (2010a).

out of the Automated Systems for Customs Data, deconcentration of public procurement, greater use of the banking system for revenue collection, introduction and review of relevant laws, and strengthening of institutional capacity.[33] Helped tremendously by these reforms, total revenues as per cent of GDP swelled from 9 per cent in 1999 to 11.9 per cent in 2007. Total tax revenues went up from 6.5 to 9.5 per cent over the same period. Despite these improvements however, the resource envelope has remained relatively very small (see Figure 1.12). Similarly to the initial phase of transition, most of the budget has been devoted to current expenditure, with defence and security as a major spending item. This comes at the expense of priority sectors, leading which (given its critical role in poverty reduction) is agriculture. A measly 1 per cent of GDP on average was devoted to agriculture between 1998 and 2006 (see Figure 1.13), compounding the adverse effect of flagging aid flows towards the sector. The prioritization of defence and security spending has also come at the expense of capital expenditures, these ending up relatively marginalized and at the mercy of donor support.

FIGURE 1.12
Resource Envelope Remains Small
(Total Revenue as Percentage of GDP)

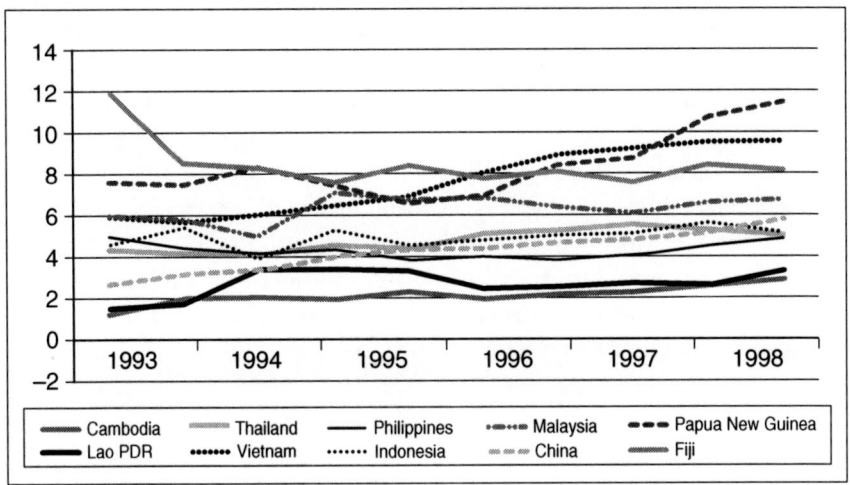

Source: ADB (2010).

FIGURE 1.13
Public Spending on Agriculture Has Lagged Behind
(Public Expenditure as Percentage of GDP)

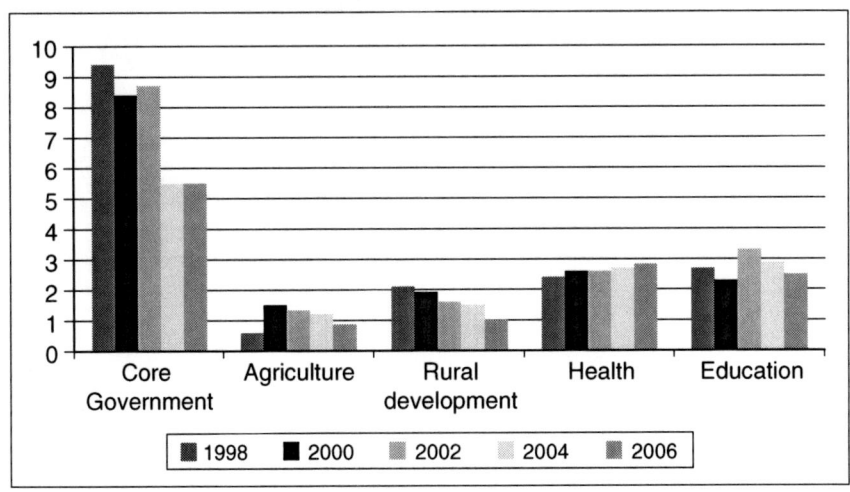

Source: World Bank (2009).

High but Poorly Diversified Trade and Investment

After the brief interlude caused by the coup and the Asian financial crisis, liberalization regained momentum such that Cambodia has become one of the most open economies in developing Asia. The country's trade openness index quickly outpaced those of its neighbours, jumping from 0.38 in 1998 to 0.69 in 2007 (see Figure 1.14). Meanwhile, its Chinn-Ito financial openness index showed positive signs by 2004 (see Figure 1.15), reflecting the significant loosening of legal restrictions on capital account transactions by the time the country joined the World Trade Organization (WTO) in the same year. The continuity in economic openness also coincided with the continuity in the growth structure that started in the initial phase of transition. This implies a lack of progression in diversification and sophistication.

FIGURE 1.14
Trade Openness Rapidly Caught Up with Neighbouring Countries
(Trade Openness Index of Selected Developing East Asian Countries)

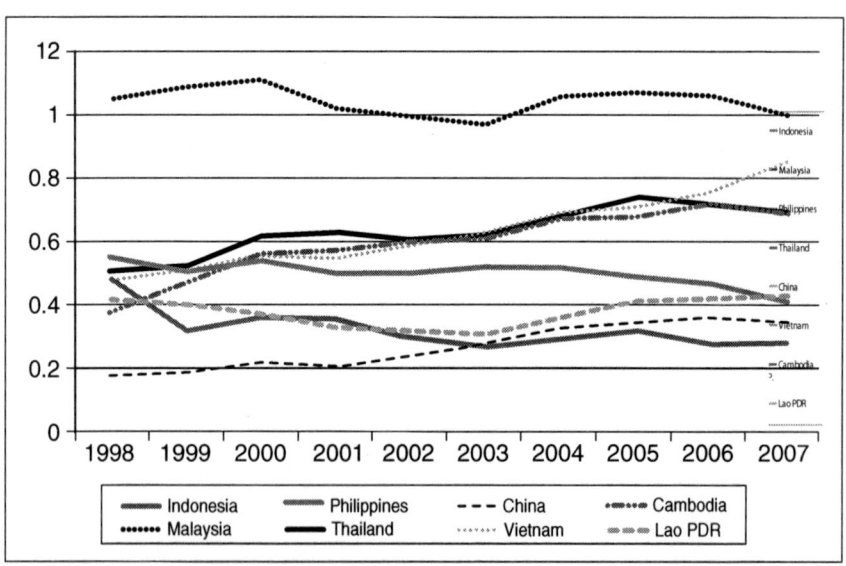

Note: The index is calculated by dividing the sum of exports and imports by two and then by GDP. A higher index means greater trade openness.
Source: Calculations based on data from World Bank WDI (2010a).

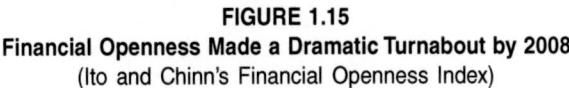

FIGURE 1.15
Financial Openness Made a Dramatic Turnabout by 2008
(Ito and Chinn's Financial Openness Index)

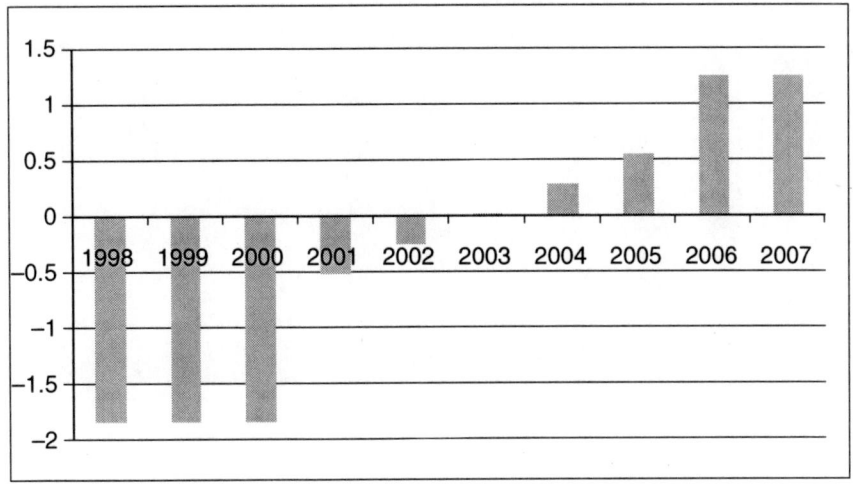

Source: Ito & Chinn (2010).

The export dominance of garments was clear by the turn of the century. The share of textile and textile articles in total annual export value swelled from half in 1998 to about three-quarters on average in the period 1999–2007. The remaining share was largely accounted for by the country's traditional and formerly dominant natural resource-based exports. There were few other manufacturing exports (see Figure 1.16). Private capital flows continued to be dominated by foreign direct investment (FDI), with the lack of equity and bond markets restricting the entry of portfolio investment. Net FDI inflows rose from about 8 per cent of GDP in 1998 to 10 per cent in 2007, overtaking the corresponding ratios for other developing Asian countries (see Figure 1.17). The sectoral composition of FDI, however, showed the same bias towards the garments, tourism and construction industries and thus the urban areas where the activities of these sectors have been concentrated.

Propped up by the trends in trade and investment flows, garments, tourism and construction have emerged as the clear growth drivers in the second phase of Cambodia's post-conflict transition. Agriculture represents the fourth growth driver, though flagging aid and public

FIGURE 1.16
Export Dominance of Garments Has Been Established
(Percentage of Total Export Values)

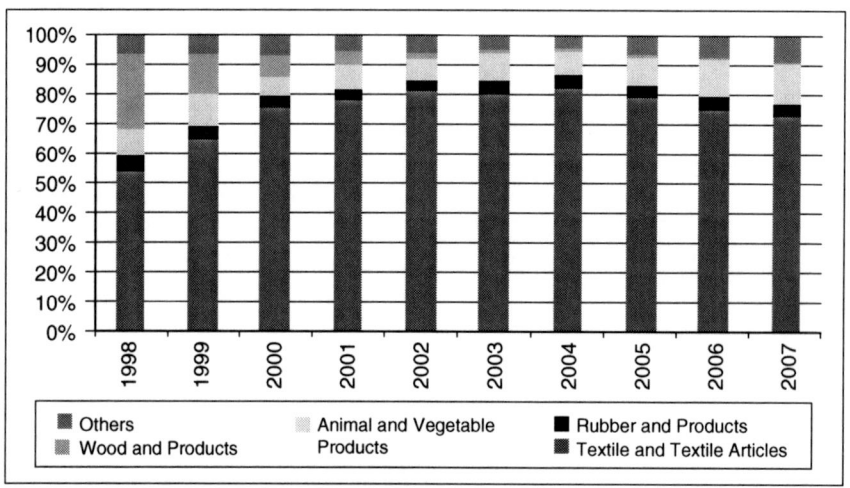

Source: Calculations based on data from NBC (2010).

FIGURE 1.17
Net FDI Considerably Increased
(Net FDI Inflows as Percentage of GDP)

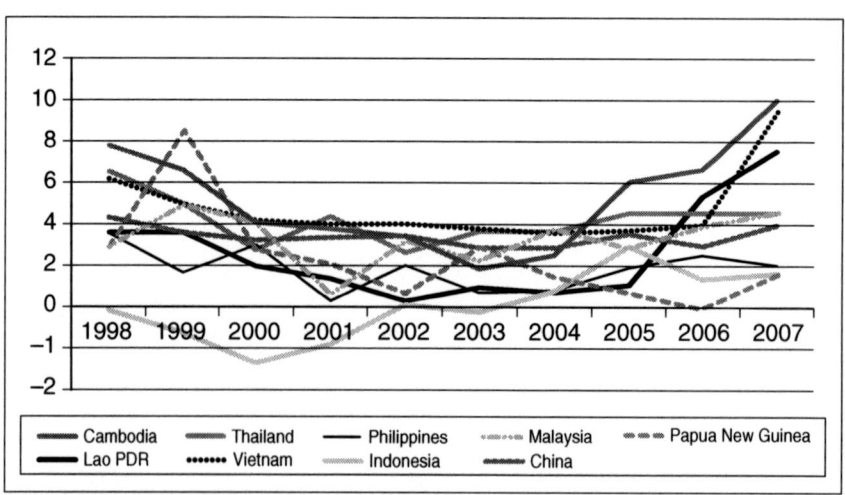

Source: World Bank WDI (2010*b*).

FIGURE 1.18
Garments, Tourism, Construction and Agriculture Emerged as the
Country's Key Growth Drivers
(Sectoral Growth, Per Cent)

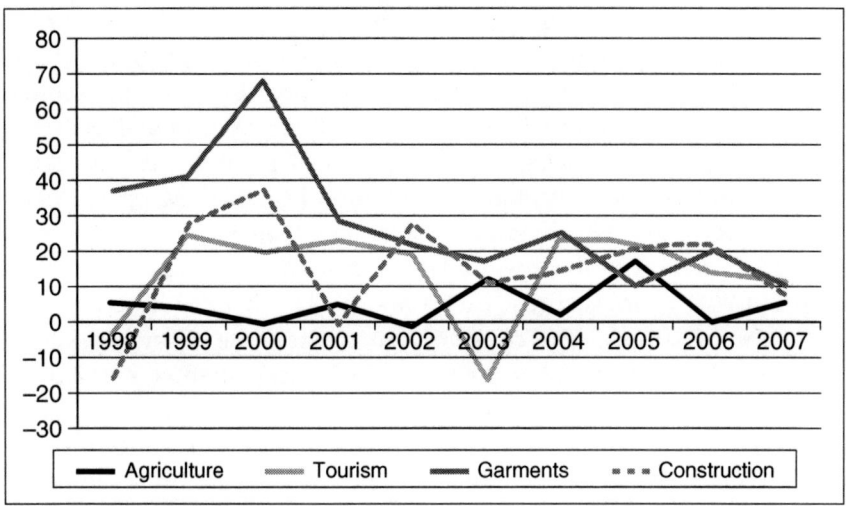

Source: World Bank WDI Online.

spending together with low private investment in the sector have caused it to markedly lag behind the others. Industry's real GDP contribution more than doubled between 1998 and 2007 due to the double-digit growth of garments and construction. Tourism similarly expanded at double-digit rates on average and this helped further boost the service sector's output contribution. Agriculture grew by 4.5 per cent on average between 1998 and 2007 (see Figure 1.18).

1.3.3 Food Shock Transmission

Converging demand, supply and policy developments caused the food crisis or the so-called near "perfect storm" (Heady and Fan 2008). Extraordinary price escalations have been seen in the past but what set the 2007–08 food shock apart was that it entailed a simultaneous increase in nearly all major commodity prices and possibly caused a long trend of above average food price levels. The short-term causes of the shock included competition from bio fuel production, higher input (particularly oil) prices and dollar depreciation while its long-term cause was the declining trend in agricultural spending and aid.[34]

The country and micro-level impact of this exogenous shock was influenced by a number of factors, namely the extent of price transmission, food import, composition of the consumption basket, income and expenditure patterns, and supply response and policy interventions (see Figure 1.19). Domestic prices in Cambodia soared even though the transmission of international price spikes into them was incomplete. Monthly domestic inflation leaped to roughly 36 per cent in May 2008 after averaging not more than 8 per cent in 2007. Monthly food inflation swelled year-on-year to 52 per cent (see Figure 1.20). Food security in Cambodia has been defined as the adequacy of supply and consumption of rice, the country's staple food (So. S 2009b). In May 2008, domestic rice inflation reached an alarming 106 per cent. The transmission of international rice price spikes to domestic prices was incomplete but high, so much so that the government's policy interventions (e.g., rice export ban, price subsidies) were still not enough to classify the country as food secure insofar as the staple food was concerned.[35] The stability of the riel against the

FIGURE 1.19
Food Shock: Determinants of Impact

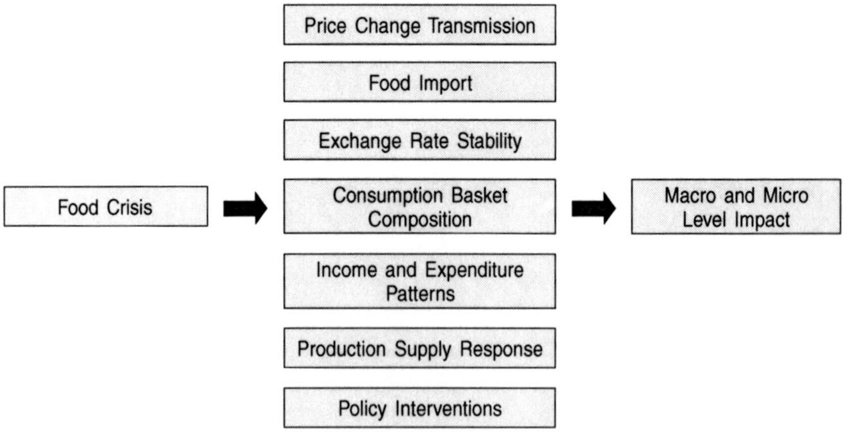

FIGURE 1.20
Food Shock Caused Unprecedented Escalation in Domestic Prices;
Global Economic Shock Caused Deflation
(Inflation y-o-y, Per Cent)

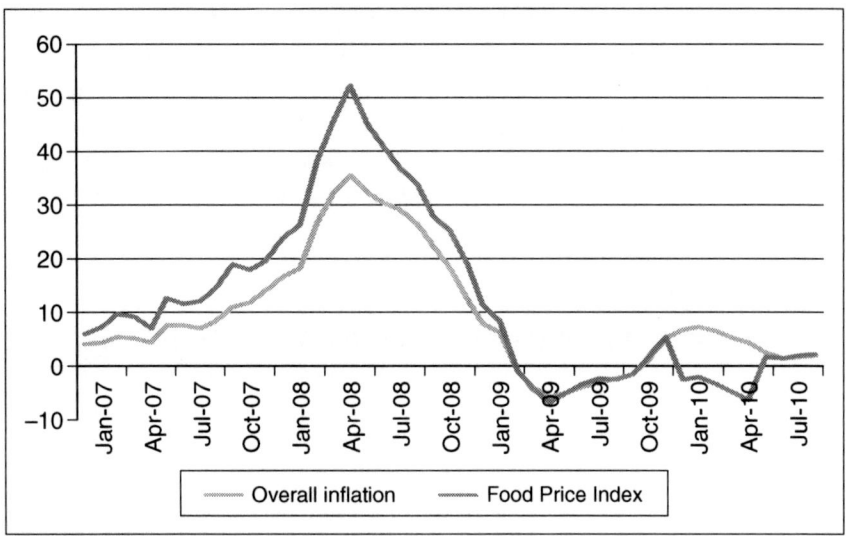

Source: NIS (2008, 2009).

U.S. dollar helped contain the rice price spikes. Food consumption, which takes a higher share of poorer groups' total consumption, was found to have fallen over the period of the crisis. A survey by the Cambodia Development Resource Institute (CDRI) found that just over 50 per cent of the sample households experienced declines in both the quality and quantity of food consumed (CDRI 2008). Cambodia is a net exporter of rice; regardless, the micro-level impact must have been differentiated depending on the household experience and intensity of food deficit or surplus. In the case of rice, the majority of rural households are net food sellers but they often have little surplus. A lag in production adjustments was expected. This restrained the gain and increased the cost of higher food prices (Jalilian et al. unpublished).

The agricultural supply response to the price escalation was held back by long-standing impediments (e.g. low mechanization, poor rural infrastructure) in turn reinforced by the long-term cause of the food shock itself, namely low agricultural investment and aid. Public spending on agriculture in Cambodia had been stuck at a mere 1 per cent of GDP. Despite the determination of poverty eradication as the government's topmost priority,[36] the budgets of the public agencies responsible for agriculture and rural development had stagnated (NGO Forum 2008). Considerable increments in agricultural spending had been sacrificed in favour of the civil service and defence wage bill. Along with agricultural spending, expenditures on social protection had been sidelined. This restricted the government's response to the crisis, which was already hampered by the fragmented social protection system. In 2007–08, the actual civil service and defence wage bill reached 24 per cent of annual spending on average, while expenditure on agriculture was about 2 per cent and on social assistance, 7 per cent.[37] Regular food aid and emergency food assistance programmes significantly depended on donors and NGOs for funding and execution. Meanwhile, the bias shown by private investment towards the other growth sectors — garments, tourism and construction — has been at the expense of private investment in agriculture.

While still trying to mend the damage caused by the food crisis, Cambodia was hit by the global financial and economic crisis. The food and economic shocks obviously constituted a "double blow to the poor" (Jalilian et al. 2009; von Braun 2008). On the upside, the downturn caused commodity prices to cool off after reaching record peaks. Overall price deflation was seen in Cambodia by the second quarter of 2009 (see Figure 1.20). The costs of the economic meltdown, however, were higher. Price deflation was also not good for everyone. In Cambodia, it proved disastrous to farming households who had borrowed money and made investments in production expecting that high prices would continue, thus increasing profit margins.

True to its description as the worst and longest-running recession since World War II, the global economic crisis caused record drops in world output and trade volume. Global real GDP and trade volume had experienced virtually uninterrupted growth in the past decades before contracting by 1.9 and –11 per cent respectively in 2009 relative to 2008. Average GDP per capita in the world fell by 3 per cent over the same period (see Figure 1.21). The collapse of the sub-prime industry in the U.S. triggered the crisis but global structural imbalances were said to be its root cause.[38]

The spread of the financial and economic crisis from the developed to the developing world was mainly facilitated by two channels: trade and capital. The macroeconomic impact via trade and capital was in turn shaped by country-specific attributes: degree of openness, composition and sophistication, exchange rate stability, and policy interventions. Putting this into context, the impact of the global financial and economic crisis in Cambodia was shaped by its high degree of trade and financial openness, narrow export base and FDI-dominated investment portfolio, high aid dependence, dollarization and limited fiscal space. From here, the impact flows to the sectoral level and is further shaped by the sectoral composition and orientation of real sector growth and attributes of the monetary and financial

FIGURE 1.21
World Output and Trade Experienced Historic Declines
(Percentage Growth)

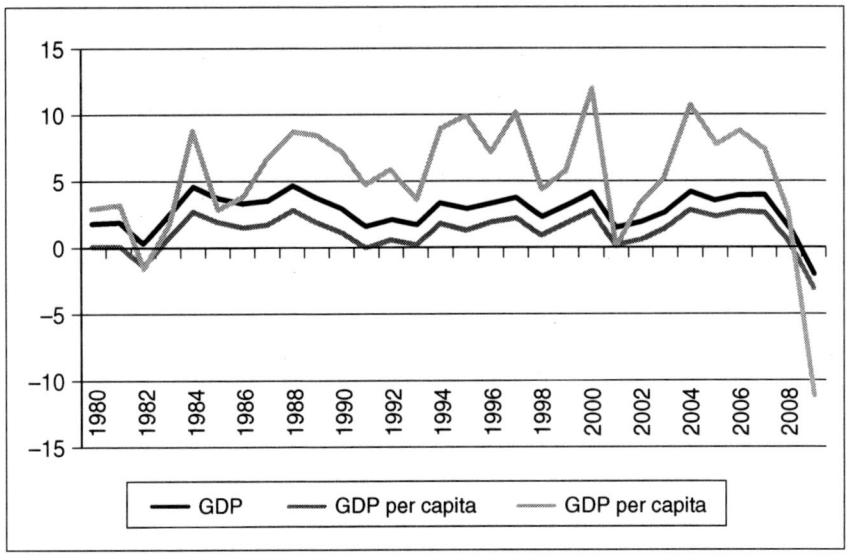

Source: World Bank WDI (2010b): IMF (2010).

system. Translating this in the case of Cambodia, the impact of the global economic downturn was shaped by its narrow and externally-dependent growth base. The garments, tourism and construction sectors that served as Cambodia's growth drivers in the second phase of its post-conflict transition have been poorly diversified. The impact was also shaped by the financial sector's dependence on foreign capital and exposure to the crisis-hit sectors. From here, the impact flows to the micro-level and is further shaped by available coping mechanisms and policy interventions. In the Cambodian context, this meant that the household impact of the shock was shaped by the limited range of coping strategies and social assistance, formal and informal, available to them. It is clear from these further delineations of the transmission of the global financial and economic shock into Cambodia that while the crisis was exogenously triggered, its impact was shaped by endogenous factors — the thesis underlying this chapter.

The following chapters examine the macro, sectoral and micro-level impacts of the global financial and economic slowdown based on the above thesis and conceptual framework. To reiterate, Chapter 2 looks into the broader effects of the shock while Chapters 3 and 4 probe into the micro-level effects; Chapter 5 considers the twin impact of food price increases and GFEC. Both qualitative and quantitative approaches are used to fulfil the ultimate objectives of relaying the Cambodian experience of the crisis and identifying the risks, opportunities and directions for reform towards a recovery that addresses some vulnerabilities of the post-conflict milieu. The road to recovery is touched upon in Chapter 6.

1.4 TOWARDS A STRONGER POST-CONFLICT MILIEU

The transmission of the triple crises into Cambodia was influenced by the country's post-conflict milieu. While the crises were exogenous in terms of origin and cause, their impacts were shaped by country-specific developments. The global financial and economic meltdown, the worst of the triple crises, battered Cambodia in a way that exposed vulnerabilities fostered in its post-conflict history now two decades long. Negative peace may have been restored, but there has been no significant progress towards the attainment of positive peace even in the late transition phase. Economic growth may have accelerated at enviable rates but the pervasive poverty and high inequality suggest serious debilities that also magnify the country's vulnerability to financial and economic shocks which erode the poorest groups' capacity to withstand crises. Aid dependence, triggered by the influx of aid during the initial transition phase, magnifies the risks facing the country as illustrated in 1997–98 when major donors pulled out and damaging revenue shortfalls were experienced as a result. It has translated into reliance on donors for capital and pro-poor spending and prioritization of defence and security in budgeting even though the threat of civil war has long since passed. Agriculture has been an unfortunate victim of this practice, as has social protection.

Complementary public investments in agriculture have been sorely lacking given the widely acknowledged role of the sector as a shock buffer. Higher food prices should have vastly improved the livelihood of poor farming households but, due to structural bottlenecks among others, agricultural supply response has been well below potential. The Asian financial crisis did not have a drastic impact in Cambodia, its economy being less integrated at that time. Since then however, facilitated by government policies, the country's trade and financial openness have markedly increased, surpassing even that of its neighbours in the region. This line of progress however did not coincide with greater diversification, resulting in the lack of broad-based development and lower resilience to shocks. Underpinned by the direction of trade and composition of capital inflows, post-conflict growth has come to rest on four sectors: garments, construction, tourism and agriculture. Unsurprisingly then, the trend of high growth was halted when the first three growth drivers contracted sharply as a result of the global financial and economic crisis. With the economy resting on a poorly diversified narrow growth base, output could have hardly been expected to emulate its previous remarkable expansion. The leading lesson from Cambodia's experience of the crisis is this: Cambodia was among the worst-hit by the global financial and economic crisis because of inherent weaknesses in its post-conflict milieu; hence, a more sustainable and crisis-resistant recovery rests on reforms to address such shortcomings.

Notes

1. This chapter follows the definition of civil war as an armed conflict between the state and a domestic rebel group which has resulted in at least 1,000 deaths (Gates and Strand 2004).
2. For instance, to supplement their wages, state cadres and their families engaged in private activities (Quinn 2008).
3. Following other communist states, the Hun Sen government initiated a spate of privatization.
4. Collier and Hoeffler (2002) divide the first post-conflict decade into three sub-periods: that in which the conflict ends or the peace onset period and the two succeeding periods.
5. These aspects included ceasefire monitoring, electoral administration, repatriation and resettlement of refugees and internally displaced persons, and humanitarian assistance.
6. FUNCINPEC stands for *Front Uni National pour un Cambodge Indépendant, Neutre, Pacifique et Coopératif*. In English, in translates to the "National United Front for an Independent, Neutral, Peaceful, and Cooperative Cambodia".
7. This party emerged from the Kampuchean People's Revolutionary Party.
8. Comparable 1960s data is not available; however, based on 1966 market prices, the average real GDP growth for the period 1961–65 was approximately 3.3 per cent (World Bank 1970).
9. The national poverty line.
10. See the pioneer research, Galtung (1964).
11. Another thesis centres on the role of greed as a cause of conflict; see Ahearne (2009) for more on the greed versus grievance dichotomy.
12. Galtung (1964).
13. For more on the paradoxes concerning post-conflict aid, see Collier (2000, 2006), USAID (2009), Schwartz and Halkyard (2006) and UNDESA (2007).
14. There was initially some debate about the role of UNTAC in triggering inflation. See UNTAC (1992), Curtis (1993) and Carnahan et al. (2005).
15. Dutch Disease refers to the "resource transfer", "spending" and "expenditure switching" effects of natural resource booms and massive capital inflows, including aid. These effects in turn cause the real exchange rate to appreciate and the tradable sector to lose competitiveness. See for instance Cordon and Neary (1984).
16. See de Zamaróczy and Sa (2002, Figure 1.15) for the real effective exchange rate trends.

17. Both the tradable and non-tradable sectors benefited from the use of aid for infrastructure and human capacity building and the mobilization of previously idle production factors. Two means by which aid could have resulted in some form of Dutch Disease in Cambodia pertain to its crowding-out effect on private investment and the internal brain drain that it caused. See Beresford et al. (2004) for further detail.
18. FCDs as per cent of broad money.
19. Calculation based on World Bank WDI online data.
20. Ibid.
21. A brief account of the origins of Cambodia's garment sector is also provided in Chapter 2.
22. For instance, the decline in rubber exports can be attributed to the aging of rubber trees (IMF 1998).
23. This had been vacant since 1990 when the U.S. refused to admit the Khmer Rouge to Cambodia's seat in the UN.
24. See Ravalilion (2001), Warr (2002), Cervantes-Godoy and Dewbre (2010), Fosu (2010).
25. See Berkmen et al. (2009), Tong and Wei (2009).
26. See World Bank (2009a).
27. The disputed border is rooted in the map authenticated by the International Court of Justice in the 1960s to determine the exact location of the Cambodian-Thai border. Upon declaration of the Preah Vihear Temple (near said border) as a World Heritage Site in 2008, Thailand claimed the land upon which the temple stands as its own and military fighting broke out between Thailand and Cambodia.
28. See for instance Barro (1991) and Alesina et al. (1992).
29. See Grindle (2005) for an account of these studies.
30. Based on data from CDC-CRDB (2008, 2010).
31. Global aid flows to agriculture have steadily declined in the past two decades (FAO and WFP 2009).
32. See World Bank (2008) for background to the PFMRP.
33. See Sok (2009) for progress updates on the PFMRP.
34. For related accounts, see Abbot et al. (2008), Timmer (2008), OECD and FAO (2008).
35. See Timmer (2008) and Dawe (2008) for more on the classification of countries based on transmission of international prices into domestic prices.
36. See for instance the National Strategic Development Plan (NSDP) 2006–10 and NSDP Update 2009–13.
37. Based on MoEF data.
38. See for instance Obstfeld and Rogoff (2009); Panouvic (2009).

References

Abbott, P., C. Hurt, and W. Tyner. *What's Driving Food Prices?* Oak Brook: Farm Foundation, 2008.

Ahearne, J. "Neoliberal Economic Policies and Post-Conflict Peace-building: A Help or Hindrance to Durable Peace?". *POLIS Journal*, vol. 2 (2009): 1–44.

Alesina, A., S. Ozler, N. Roubini, and P. Swagel. *Political Instability and Economic Growth*. NBER Working Paper W4173. Cambridge: National Bureau of Economic Research, 1992.

Asian Development Bank. *Key Indicators for Asia and the Pacific 2010: The Rise of Asia's Middle Class*. Manila: ADB, 2010.

Beresford, M., N. Ceema, S. Nguon, R. Rathin, and S. Sau. *The Macroeconomics of Poverty Reduction in Cambodia*. New York: UNDP, 2004.

Berkmen, P., G. Gelos, R. Rennhack, and J. Walsh. *The Global Financial Crisis: Explaining Cross-Country Differences in the Output Impact*. IMF Working Paper 09/280. Washington, D.C.: World Bank, 2009.

Cambodian Development Resource Institute. *Impact of High Food Prices in Cambodia*. Phnom Penh: CDRI, 2008.

Carnahan, M., S. Gilmore, and M. Rahman. "Economic Impact of Peacekeeping: Interim Report, Phase 1". New York: UN, 2005.

Cervantes-Godoy, D. and J. Dewbre. *Economic Importance of Agriculture for Poverty Reduction*. OECD Food, Agriculture and Fisheries Working Paper No. 23. Paris: OECD, 2010.

Collier, P. *Economic Causes of Civil Conflict and Their Implications for Policy*. Washington, D.C.: World Bank, 2000.

———. "Post-conflict Economic Recovery". Paper prepared for the International Peace Academy. New York, 2006.

Collier, P. and A. Hoeffler. *Aid, Policy and Growth in Post-Conflict Societies*. World Bank Policy Research Working Paper 2902. Washington, D.C.: World Bank, 2002.

Cordon, W. and J.P. Neary. "Booming Sector and Dutch Disease Economics: A Survey". *Oxford Economic Papers*, no. 36 (1984): 359–80.

Council for the Development of Cambodia — Cambodian Rehabilitation Development Board. *Cambodia Aid Effectiveness Report 2008*. Phnom Penh: CDC-CRDB, 2008.

———. *Cambodia Aid Effectiveness Report 2010*. Phnom Penh: CDC-CRDB, 2010.

Curtis, G. "Transition to What? Cambodia, UNTAC and the Peace Process". UNRISD Discussion Paper 48. Geneva: UN Research Institute for Social Development, 1993.

Dawe, D. "Can Indonesia still trust the world rice market?" *Bulletin of Indonesian Economic Studies*, 2008.

Food and Agriculture Organisation and World Food Programme. *The State of Food Insecurity in the World (Economic Crises — Impact and Lessons Learned)*. Rome: FAO, 2009.

Fosu, A.K. "Growth, Inequality and Poverty Reduction in Developing Countries: Recent Global Evidence". OECD background paper for the Global Development Outlook 2010. Paris: OECD, 2010.

Galtung, J. "An Editorial". *Journal of Peace Research*, vol. 1, no. 1 (1964): 1–4.

Gates, S. and H. Strand. "Modelling the Duration of Civil Wars: Measurement and Estimation Issues". Paper prepared for presentation at the 2004 Meeting of the Standing Group on International Relations, the Hague, 9–11 September 2004.

Grindle, Merilee. "Good Enough Governance Revisited". A report for DFID with reference to the Governance Target Strategy Paper, 2001 (February 2005).

Heady, D. and S. Fan. "Anatomy of a Crisis: The Causes and Consequences of Surging Food Prices". IFPRI Discussion Paper 00831. Washington, D.C.: IFPRI, 2008.

Hellman, J., G. Jones, and D. Kauffman. *Seize the State, Seize the Day: State Capture, Corruption and Influence in Transition Economies*. World Bank Policy Research Working Paper No. 2444. Washington, D.C.: World Bank, 2000.

Hellman, J. and D. Kauffmann. "Confronting the Challenge of State Capture in Transition Economies". *IMF Finance and Development*, vol. 38, no. 3 (2001).

Hughes, C. "Cambodia's Performance", undated. Available at <www. phnompenh.um.dk/NR/...40F3.../Cambodiasperformance.pdf> (accessed 26 October 2010).

International Monetary Fund (IMF). *Country Report No. 98/54*. Washington, D.C.: IMF, 1998.

———. *Country Report No. 99/33*. Washington, D.C.: IMF, 1999.

———. "Primary Commodity Price Database", 2010. Available at <http://www. imf.org/external/np/res/commod/index.asp> (accessed 1 February 2010).

Irvin, G. *Rebuilding Cambodia's Economy: UNTAC and Beyond*. Institute of Social Studies Working Paper No. 149. The Hague: Institute of Social Studies, 1993.

Jalilian, H., S. Chan, G. Reyes, Saing C.H., D. Pon, and D. Phann. *Global Financial Crisis Discussion Paper Series 3: Cambodia*. London: ODI, 2009.

Jalilian, H. and G. Reyes. *Global Financial Crisis Discussion Paper Series 43: Cambodia*. London: ODI, 2010.

Jalilian, H., G. Reyes and P. Lun. "Cambodia's Food Security in the Face of the Food and Economic Shocks". Unpublished, 2010*a*.

———. "Double Blow to the Poor: Cambodia's Food Security in the Face of the Food and Economic Shocks". CDRI Annual Development Review 2009–10. Phnom Penh: CDRI, 2010*b*.

Kauffmann, D., A. Kray, and M. Mastruzzi. *Governance Matters VIII: Aggregate and Individual Governance Indicators 1996–2008*. World Bank Working Research Paper No. 4978. Washington, D.C.: World Bank, 2009.

Kem, S. "Rapid Assessment of the Impacts of the Economic Crisis on Cambodian Households and Vulnerable Workers: Road to Recovery: Third Round". Phnom Penh: CDRI, 2009.

———. "Rapid Assessment of Impacts of Global Economic Crisis on Cambodian Household and Vulnerable Workers: Fourth Round". Phnom Penh: CDRI, 2010.

National Bank of Cambodia. *Annual Report 2009*. Phnom Penh: NBC, 2010.

National Institute of Statistics. *Statistical Yearbook of Cambodia 2008*. Phnom Penh: NIS, 2008.

———. *General Population Census of Cambodia 2008*. Phnom Penh: NIS, 2009.

NGO Forum. "2009 National Budget Should Favour Farmers". *Budget Brief*, no. 1. Phnom Penh: NGO Forum, 2008.

Nkusu, M. *Aid and the Dutch Disease in Low Income Countries: Informed Diagnoses for Prudent Prognoses*. IMF Working Paper 04-49. Washington, D.C.: IMF, 2004.

Obstfeld, M. and K. Rogoff. "Global Imbalances and the Financial Crisis: Products of Common Causes (Second Conference Draft)". Paper prepared for the Federal Reserve Bank of San Francisco Asia Economic Policy Conference, Santa Barbara, CA, 18–20 October 2009.

OECD and FAO. *Agricultural Outlook 2008–2018*. Paris: OECD and FAO, 2008.

Panouvic, I. "Causes and Consequences of the Global Crisis: Recognizing and Understanding Systemic Risk". Paper presented at the "Korea and the World Economy, VIII" conference at the Hong Kong Baptist University in Hong Kong, 9–10 July 2009.

Quinn, P. "Human Security and Development: The Case of Cambodia". Doctoral dissertation. Canberra: The Australian National University, 2008.

Radelet, S. and J. Sachs. *The Onset of the Financial Crisis*. NBER Working Paper No. 6680. Cambridge: National Bureau of Economic Research, 1998.

Ravallion, M. "Growth, Inequality & Poverty: Looking Beyond Averages". World Development 29, no. 11 (2001): 1803–15.

Rose, A.K. and M.M. Spiegel. *Cross-Country Causes and Consequences of the 2008 Crisis: International Linkages and American Exposure.* NBER Working Paper No. 15358. Cambridge: National Bureau of Economic Research, 2009.

Royal Government of Cambodia. "National Strategic Development Plan 2006–10". Available at <http://www.cdc-crdb.gov.kh/cdc/aid_management/nsdp.pdf> (accessed 26 October 2010).

———. "National Strategic Development Plan 2009–13". Available at <http://www.mop.gov.kh/Home/NSDP/NSDPUPDATE20092013/tabid/206/Default.aspx> (accessed 26 October 2010).

Schwartz, J. and P. Halkyard. "Post-conflict Infrastructure: Trends in Aid and Investment Flows". Public Policy for the Private Sector Note No. 305. Washington, D.C.: World Bank, 2006.

So S. "Rapid Assessment of Impacts of Global Economic Crisis on Cambodian Household and Vulnerable Workers' Income, Consumption and Coping Strategies: Second Round". Phnom Penh: CDRI, 2009*a*.

———. *Informal Risk Management/Safety Net Practices: Experiences of Poor Vulnerable Workers and Households.* Phnom Penh: CDRI, 2009*b*.

Sok S. "Public Financial Management Reform Programme (Progress after Third Annual Review)". Presentation during the PFM Technical Working Group Meeting, Phnom Penh, 6 April 2009.

Springer, S. *The Neoliberal Order in Cambodia: Political Violence, Democracy, and the Contestation of Public Space.* CCSEAS Working Papers. Toronto: York University, 2005.

Theng V. and Kem S. "Rapid Assessment of the Impact of the Economic Crisis on Cambodian Households: Focus Group Discussions with Vulnerable Workers and Households: First Round". Phnom Penh: CDRI, 2009.

Timmer. "Causes of High Food Prices". *Asian Development Outlook 2008 Update.* Manila: ADB, 2008.

Tong, H. and S.J. Wei. *The Composition Matters: Capital Inflows and Liquidity Crunch during a Global Economic Crisis.* IMF Working Papers, Vol. 56. Washington, D.C.: IMF, 2009.

Tong K., D. Khieng, M. Hem, D. Phann, and D. Pon. "Vulnerable Workers Survey in Phnom Penh, Kandal, Kampong Speu, Siem Reap and Battambang". Phnom Penh: CDRI, 2009*a*.

Tong K. and D. Pon. "Vulnerable Workers Survey in Phnom Penh, Kandal, Kampong Speu, Siem Reap and Battambang: Second Round". Phnom Penh: CDRI, 2009*a*.

———. "Vulnerable Workers Survey in Phnom Penh, Kandal, Kampong Speu, Siem Reap and Battambang: Third Round". Phnom Penh: CDRI, 2009*b*.

————. "Vulnerable Workers Survey in Phnom Penh, Kandal, Kampong Speu, Siem Reap and Battambang: Fourth Round". Phnom Penh: CDRI, 2010.

Tong K., C.H. Saing, S. Hem, D. Phann, and D. Pon. *Trends in Living Standards of 90 Rural Households in Poverty Dynamics Study Villages*. Phnom Penh: CDRI, 2009b.

UNDESA. "Governance Strategies for Post Conflict Reconstruction, Sustainable Peace and Development". UN DESA Discussion Paper — GPAB/REGOPA Cluster. New York: UN DESA, 2007.

UNTAC. <http://www.un.org/en/peacekeeping/missions/past/untacbackgr2.html>, 1992.

USAID. *A Guide to Economic Growth in Post-Conflict Countries*. Washington, D.C.: USAID, 2009.

von Braun, J. *Food and Financial Crises: Implications for Agriculture and the Poor*. Washington, D.C.: IFPRI, 2008.

Warr, Peter G. "Poverty Incidence and Sectoral Growth: Evidence from Southeast Asia". WIDER Discussion Paper No. 2002/20. Helsinki: UNU-WIDER, 2002.

World Bank. *Report of Economic Mission to Cambodia (Volume III-Statistical Appendix)*. Washington, D.C.: World Bank, 1970.

————. *Agenda for Rehabilitation and Reconstruction*. Washington, D.C.: World Bank, 1992.

————. *Cambodia: From Recovery to Sustained Development*. Washington, D.C.: World Bank, 1996.

————. *Cambodia: Progress in Recovery and Reform*. Washington, D.C.: World Bank, 1997.

————. *Cambodia Poverty Assessment*. Washington, D.C.: World Bank, 1999.

————. "Building the Foundations for Public Financial Management Reform, FM Solutions No. 3". Washington, D.C.: World Bank, 2008.

————. *The Global Economic Crisis: Assessing Vulnerability with a Poverty Lens*. Washington, D.C.: World Bank, 2009a.

————. *Sustaining Rapid Growth in a Challenging Environment: Cambodia Country Economic Memorandum*. Washington, D.C.: World Bank, 2009b.

————. *Poverty Profile and Trend in Cambodia: Findings from the 2007 Cambodia Socio-Economic Survey*. Washington, D.C.: World Bank, 2009c.

————. "How We Classify Countries". Available at <http://data.worldbank.org/about/country-classifications> (accessed 21 October 2010).

World Bank WDI Online. Available at <http://databank.worldbank.org/ddp/home.do?Step=2&id=4> (accessed 31 October 2010).

Zamaróczy, M. and S. Sa. "Macroeconomic Adjustment in a Highly Dollarised Economy: The Case of Cambodia". IMF Working Paper No. 02-92. Washington, D.C.: World Bank, 2002.

2

LOSING STEAM
Crisis Impact at the Macro and Sectoral Levels

Hossein Jalilian and Glenda Reyes

2.1 THE DRASTIC TURNABOUT

The global financial and economic meltdown is by far the worst shock that has struck post-conflict Cambodia. Against the backdrop of the most stable political scene in the country in almost three decades, the Asian financial crisis hit Cambodia in 1997–98 followed by the food and energy shocks ten years later. These shocks caused damage but not enough to elicit a turnabout in the country's macroeconomic growth and progress in poverty reduction. In contrast, the global financial and economic downturn, which became evident in Cambodia by 2008–09, put a stop to the country's nearly two-decade long positive growth and poverty reduction.

This chapter discusses the macroeconomic and sectoral impacts of the global crisis based on the crisis transmission framework described in the first chapter, that the impact of the shock was shaped by country-specific circumstances. The economic turmoil that erupted in the developed world spilled over to developing countries chiefly through its impact on trade and capital flows. The degree of a country's exposure to the external shock was hence influenced by its trade and financial openness and composition.

Following a brief account of the global recession's impact on aggregate output in Section 2, Section 3 tackles the overall impact of the global recession on Cambodia's trade and capital inflows. Sectoral exposure to the crisis ultimately depends on the bias in such flows and the country's overall economic growth pattern. Cambodia's double-digit growth in the decade before the crisis relied on a narrow economic base. As examined in Chapter 1, four sectors — garments, tourism, construction and agriculture — were primarily responsible for the country's growing trade and investment inflow. The first three sectors ushered in the country's economic structural transformation. Section 4 recounts how the growth sectors fared in the face of the external shock. It is interesting to note that the contractions in at least three of the growth drivers can be partly ascribed to the effects of other covariant crises.[1] This aspect of the sectoral downturn is also examined in Section 4. The global economic recession sprung out of the implosion in developed financial systems whose root cause lies in the sub-prime market. Because of its limited exposure to toxic sub-prime products, Cambodia was saved from the first-round effects of the financial crisis. However, its monetary and financial sector were eventually hit as collapse in the paper economy swept the real sector and liquidity and credit dried up. Section 5 discusses this adverse turn of events. Ultimately, the depth and spread of the recession depended on the fiscal stimulus and other policy responses that had been administered. Section 6 recounts the government of Cambodia's remedial actions to stem the downturn within the confines of its limited fiscal resources.

2.2 GROWTH GONE SOUR

Initial expectations gathered that Cambodia, along with other countries in developing East Asia, would emerge unscathed by the global financial and economic crisis. Not only was the country's financial sector still modestly integrated into the international markets, its defences against externally induced shocks were also fortified, this being one of the lessons learned from the Asian financial crisis. Nonetheless, the uncontrollable deepening of the global recession together with the adverse effects of other crises eventually put pay to such optimism.

Earlier growth forecasts by the Cambodian government and international institutions may have diverged but all suggested that the post-conflict Cambodian economy was in fact headed for an unprecedented slowdown. In the ten years before the crisis, Cambodia enjoyed a high-growth economy. It was among the ten fastest growing economies in the world, having registered an average annual GDP growth of 9.4 per cent. This growth spurt was suspended by the crisis. Economic fundamentals remained mainly strong until the growth sectors began to markedly contract in the third quarter of 2008. By year-end, real output growth had dipped below average, at 6.7 per cent (see Figure 2.1).

The economic slump was most severe in the first half of 2009. The government initially pegged its growth estimate at an optimistic rate of 6 per cent, expecting the economy to be buoyed by agriculture, the informal economy, donor assistance and the relaxed fiscal policy. It was,

FIGURE 2.1
The Crisis Put an End to Cambodia's High-growth Economy
(Cambodia's Real GDP Growth, Per Cent)

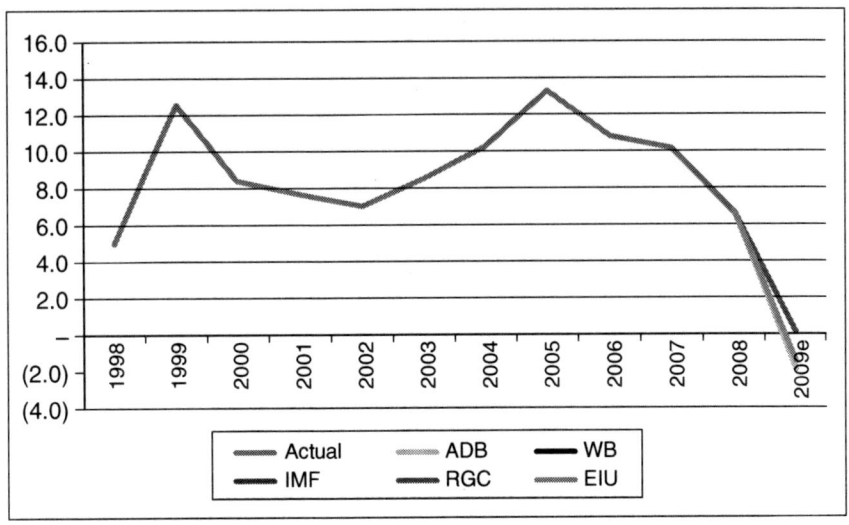

Source: NIS for 1998–2008; for 2009 and 2010 projections, MoEF, IMF (2010*b*), ADB (2010*a*), WorldBank (2010) and EIU (2010).

however, compelled to revise its growth projection as it became evident that these factors were not enough to overcome the upsets in the other three growth industries. International institutions, the World Bank, International Monetary Fund (IMF), Asian Development Bank (ADB), and the Economist Intelligence Unit (EIU), were pessimistic as soon as the gravity of the crisis became clearer. They all foresaw that Cambodia's output would shrink at the rate of not less than 1.5 per cent. At one point, the EIU projected a 3 per cent decline in the country's real GDP and, chiefly on the basis of the greater economic hardship, categorized the country as among the five countries most vulnerable to social and political unrest (EIU 2010).

The Cambodian economy seemed to have bottomed sometime in the second half of 2009. This was spurred primarily by the rebound in tourism, the stable growth of agriculture, and the effects of accommodative spending and monetary easing. The garment sector underperformed till the final quarter while construction continued to be dragged down by the real estate slump. By year-end, Cambodia's real output is estimated to have contracted by 2 per cent by the World Bank, IMF and ADB and 1.5 per cent by the EIU. The government drastically lowered its estimate but maintains that the economy escaped contraction, having managed a 0.1 per cent growth. Whichever figure is accurate, Cambodia apparently suffered one of the biggest declines in output in developing East Asia between 2007 and 2009 (see Figure 2.2). Unsurprisingly, the worst hit countries — Malaysia, Thailand, Cambodia and Mongolia — share the characteristic of being significantly reliant on export-oriented growth.

2.3 CONTRACTIONS IN TRADE AND CAPITAL INFLOWS

2.3.1 Trade

The Keynesian demand shock resulted in a record fall in world trade volumes. The extent of impact on trade at the national level was influenced by a country's trade openness and position in global value chains. The worst hit countries in developing East Asia were also the most open in terms of trade.[2] Their trade openness indices range between 0.64 and nearly 1 as depicted in Figure 2.3. On average, the total annual exports

FIGURE 2.2
**Cambodia Suffered One of the Biggest Output Contractions in
Developing East Asia**
(Percentage Change in Real GDP Growth 2007–09)

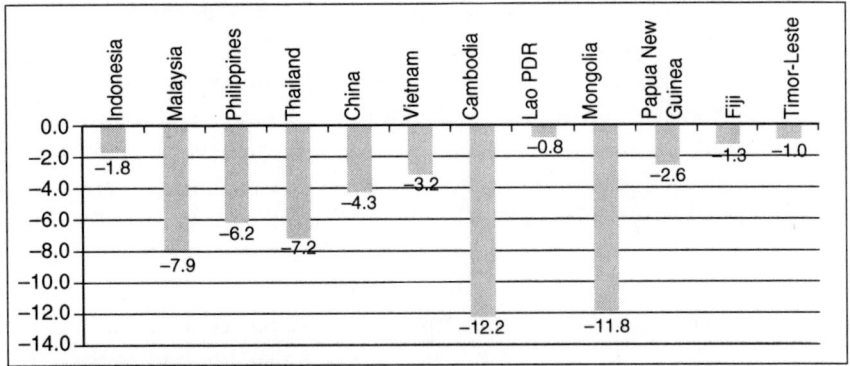

Source: World Bank (2010*b*); see also ADB (2010*b*) and IMF (2010*b*) though there are several
discrepancies in the growth figures.

FIGURE 2.3
Worst Hit Economics in Developing East Asia Were Highly Open
(Trade Openness Index of Select Developing East Asian Countries)

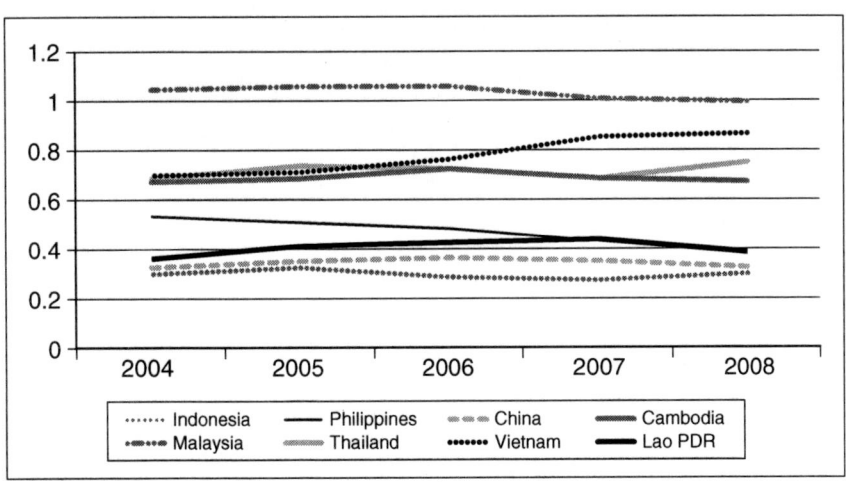

Note: The index is calculated by dividing the sum of exports and imports by two and then by GDP.
A higher index means greater trade openness.
Source: Calculations based on data from World Bank WDI online (2010); World Bank (2010*b*); ADB
(2010) for 2009 data on Cambodia and Malaysia.

of each country amount to about three quarters of their yearly GDP. The U.S., which happened to be the epicentre of the crisis, is one of their top three export markets.

Having emerged from a communist administration and decades-long civil war, Cambodia's trade levels were modest in the early years of its post-conflict development. As suggested in the first chapter, the year 1998 is a landmark in the country's economic history as the formal end of the civil war and political impasse finally made it possible to implement comprehensive economic reform. A chief factor explaining the restrained impact of the Asian financial crisis on Cambodia was its still modest level of trade openness and financial integration at that time. Between 1997 and 2007, the country's trade openness index leaped from 0.4 to 0.7 (see Figure 2.3). Its total annual exports as per cent of GDP rose from 34 to 65 per cent per year over the same period (see Figure 2.4). The U.S. had also come to replace the Soviet Union as the country's top export market. Exports to the U.S. from Cambodia increased from US$86 million to US$2.4 billion between 1997 and 2007.[3]

FIGURE 2.4
Worst Hit Economies in Developing East Asia Significantly Depend on Export-oriented Growth
(Exports as Per Cent of GDP)

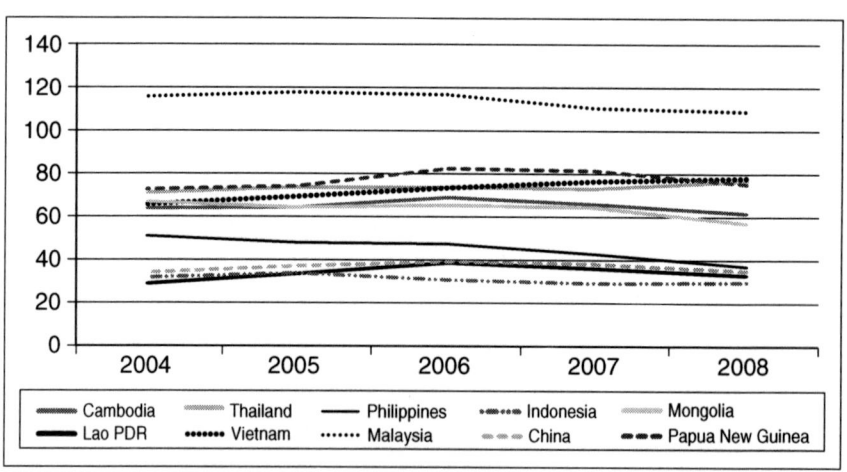

Source: World Bank WDI Online (2010); World Bank (2010*b*).

Cambodia is positioned at the low-end of the global export value chains. It was found to have had the lowest level of export sophistication among countries that maintained rapid growth before the crisis (World Bank 2009). As shown in Figure 2.5, about three-quarters of Cambodia's total exports are garments, around two-thirds of which are of the cut-make-trim (CMT) type and mostly exported to the U.S. The majority of the remaining exports are unprocessed agricultural products (see Figure 1.16 in Chapter 1). Rice exports are mainly in paddy form.

Led by the plunge in garment exports, Cambodia's total monthly export values declined year-on-year by an average of 9 per cent between November 2008 and November 2009. The export sector in particular experienced its worst slump in a long time in the first three quarters of 2009 (see Figure 2.5). The country's real effective exchange rate sharply appreciated in the middle of 2008 and remained at a high level through the first half of 2009.[4] This could have affected its export

FIGURE 2.5
Export and Import Growth Plunged
(Export and Import Values, y-o-y Percentage Change)

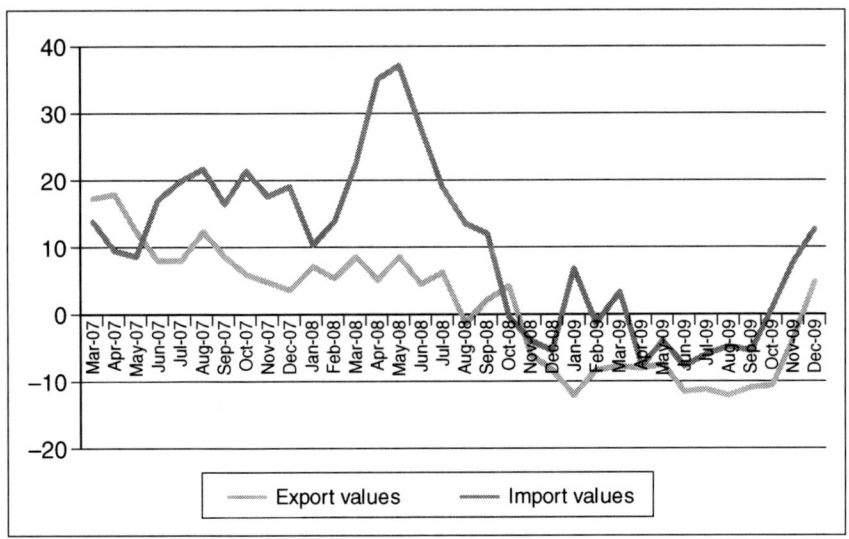

Source: Authors' calculations based on data from MoEF (2009).

competitiveness. Section 4 describes in detail the underperformance of the garment industry. Meanwhile, agricultural exports performed differently over the period of the crisis. Cassava and rubber exports fell owing to the significant cutbacks in external demand and export prices. Average rubber export prices in the international markets more than halved by May 2009 relative to their peak levels in 2008[5] while average cassava prices declined by about 30 per cent just six months after they peaked in March 2008 (FAO 2008). Rice export prices similarly tumbled; however, they remained above historical averages (FAO 2009). Higher price levels together with favourable weather conditions, government support and bumper crops boosted rice exports from Cambodia. On the demand side, the decline in prices and build-up in stocks increased imports of Cambodian rice. Figure 2.6 shows that between July 2008 and December 2009, official monthly milled rice exports from Cambodia soared year-on-year by an average of about 378 per cent in value and about 243 per cent in volume. However, paddy traded unofficially at the border constitutes a massive share of

FIGURE 2.6
Milled Rice Exports Surged as Price Decline Encouraged Stock Build-ups
(3mma, y-o-y Percentage Change)

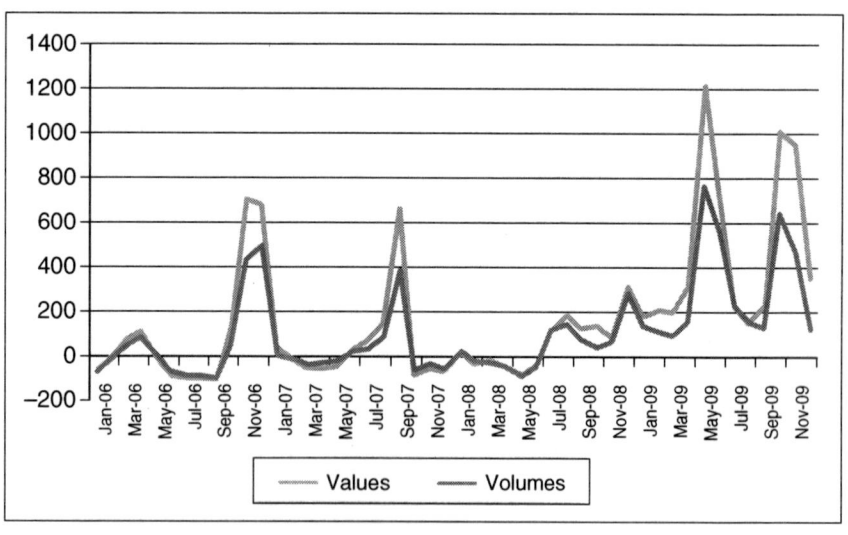

Source: Authors' calculations based on data from MoEF.

Cambodia's rice exports. Reportedly, about 400,000 tonnes of paddy rice are sold illegally at the country's borders with Thailand and Vietnam, resulting in a loss of about US$70 million a year in tax revenue. Another estimate places the share of official rice exports at a mere 15 per cent of the total per annum (An 2008). Furthermore, the country is exporting below-potential. On average, official export volumes of rice paddy account for a mere 1 per cent of total surplus paddy per annum (Tong 2010). Cambodia's paddy rice yields have lagged significantly behind its neighbours, Vietnam and Thailand, affecting the amount of exportable surplus.

Cambodia's imports likewise contracted during the recession, though at a much lesser degree compared to exports. Total import values per month went down by approximately 2 per cent on average between November 2008 and November 2009 (see Figure 2.5). This drop was caused primarily by deceleration in the country's three most dominant imports: fuel, transport equipment, and textile inputs. Oil price deflation and cutbacks in oil consumption were primarily responsible for the reduction in the value of petroleum and other related imports. The reduction reached 7 per cent in the first three quarters of 2009 relative to the same period in 2008. Although oil prices had deflated during the recession, they remained higher than pre-crisis levels. Such above-average prices on top of greater income uncertainty dampened the previously robust domestic appetite for transport equipment, cars and motorcycles in particular. Overall, the value of machinery and transport imports fell by a huge 26 per cent in the first three quarters of 2009 relative to the same period in the preceding year. As discussed in the next section, the growth of the domestic garment sector is impeded by the underdeveloped state of the upstream industry. Most of the textile and accessory needs of the sector are thus imported. As garment exports experienced their worst lull ever, the imports of textile inputs were also affected. The import value of textile and textile articles dropped by 16 per cent in the first three quarters of 2009 relative to the same period in 2008. Overall, the nominal exchange rate between the U.S. dollar and the riel remained stable over the crisis; however, the Cambodian economy is highly dollarized. The weakening of the greenback must thus have adversely affected the appetite for imports. The stability of the nominal exchange rate was due to aggressive market interventions by the National Bank of Cambodia (NBC). These interventions came at the cost of using up precious foreign exchange reserves and depriving the exchange rate from playing a more active role in making adjustments in the current account.

2.3.2 Capital Inflows

Cambodia's post-conflict evolution included its transformation into one of the most financially integrated economies in developing East Asia (ADB 2009). As suggested by the Chinn-Ito financial openness indices,[6] its investment climate has become one of the most liberal in the region. The Asian financial crisis only had a modest effect on the Cambodian economy because the country at that time had yet to embark on financial liberalization. Marked improvement in financial openness was seen in 2004–05 (see Figure 2.7). This coincided with Cambodia's membership of the WTO which in turn engendered a flurry of financial reform, particularly concerning the legal environment.[7] The Law on Investment

FIGURE 2.7
Cambodia's Financial Openness Made a Turnabout in 2008
(Financial Openness Index)

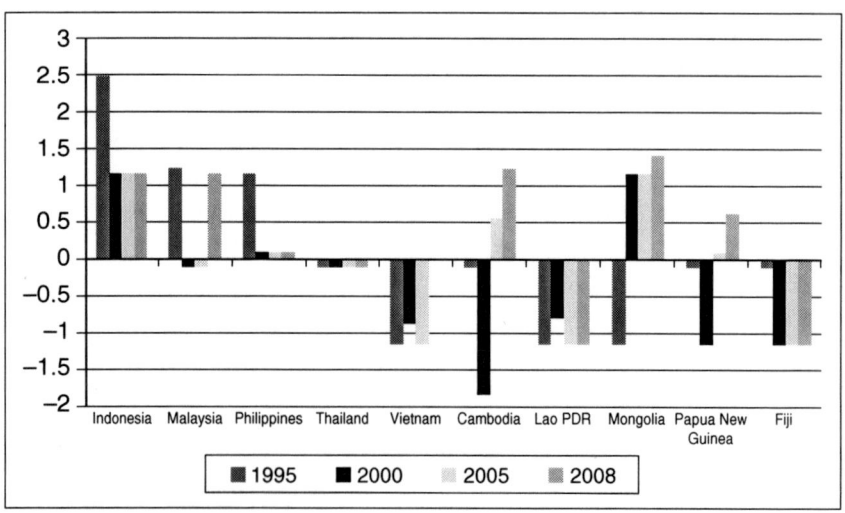

Source: Chin and Ito (2010).

was also amended in 2005, enhancing its status as one of the most investor-friendly in developing Asia.[8]

Financial market liberalization in Cambodia has been FDI-led. Much of the FDI has flowed into the three growth sectors. Despite extensive planning and publicity, an equity market is yet to be instated and the country is yet to participate in international bond markets. On the one hand, this has served the country well as it disabled the transmission of some of the worst effects of the financial and economic turmoil. Compared to other private transfers, FDI inflows (except for remittances) are found to be less volatile. Cambodia was spared from the spikes in borrowing costs and plunge in stock market prices that seriously hurt other developing Asian countries. On the other hand, the underdeveloped state of the capital market limited the budget financing options available to the government at a time when it needed liquidity the most. The extent and nature of financial openness inevitably shaped the impact of the global crisis on external transfers to Cambodia.

Foreign Direct Investment

Competing for FDI requires honing both country and firm level advantages. The government and private sector in Cambodia have long been working together on improving these two pull factors. Political stability, steady macroeconomic growth and policy liberalization made the country attractive to FDI inflows. At the firm level, labour costs have been comparatively cheap. Progress in trade facilitation and infrastructure building, particularly in the energy sector, has also brought down operational costs. FDI, as mentioned earlier, has been mainly attracted to Cambodia's three principal industries. The key pull of the garment sector had been its preferential access to major markets. That of tourism is Angkor Wat, the country's unique national asset, while that of construction was the real estate boom. However, securing a profitable and sustainable return on investments in the country has been endangered by other pressing issues, such as corruption, low labour productivity, and macroeconomic uncertainties.

The gains from financial market liberalization have been no less than those demonstrated by the influx of FDI into the country. Between 1995 and 2007, net FDI grew by 63 per cent per year on average or from

4 to 10 per cent of nominal GDP (see Figure 2.8). FDI inflows to the country have been mainly export-oriented and efficiency-seeking in nature.[9] They have been mainly responsible for the expansion of the growth sectors. However, high financial openness has a downside. Cambodia's highly liberalized investment regime together with the lack of diversification in its hosted FDI makes it especially vulnerable to market volatility and shock and any serious setback in the pull and push factors that attract FDI, as evidenced by what occurred during the recent global crisis. Net FDI nearly halved between 2007 and 2009, a far worse contraction than that during the Asian financial crisis. The credit crunch and bleak economic prospects put off or led to the withdrawal of investments. The three principal industries — garments, tourism and construction — found themselves in a serious slump due to both the shock and the near loss of their key appeal to FDI. The garment industry suffered from decline in external demand and loss of preferential treatment. Construction was disrupted by the drying up of liquidity and the real estate crash. Tourism temporarily lost momentum

FIGURE 2.8
The Contraction in FDI was Worse than the Decline during the
Asian Financial Crisis
(Net FDI)

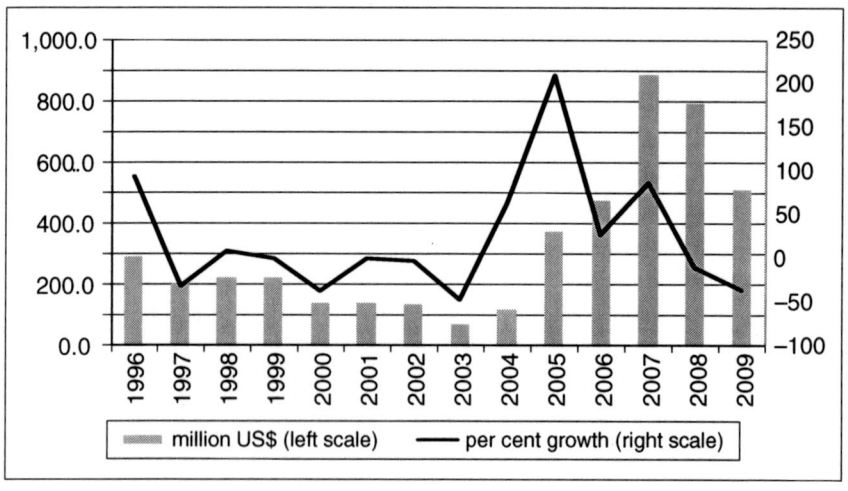

Source: NBC, World Bank WDI Online (2010).

due to the slowdown in tourist arrivals and, being poorly diversified, is largely dependent on Angkor Wat. Sectoral performance during the crisis is examined in detail in Section 4.

International Remittances

Remittances have shown greater resilience compared to other private transfers. They have also proven to be counter-cyclical, that is the tendency to increase in volume in times of adversity. These features of remittances make them highly valuable during crises. From the macroeconomic standpoint, they can significantly contribute to economic stabilization. At the micro-level, they can greatly help in smoothing household consumption.

International remittance inflows to Cambodia experienced a near uninterrupted growth averaging 17 per cent per year between 2000 and 2007. Over the same period, they almost tripled in value (from US$121 to US$353 million) and as proportion of GDP, surpassed the international remittance inflows to other developing Asian countries. The growth in the remittances flowing to Cambodia came to an abrupt halt in 2008 when such transfers suddenly contracted. At 8 per cent, the contraction was evidently lower than the decline in FDI, however. The total remittance amount also remained above pre-crisis levels and its share of GDP stayed at roughly 3 per cent (see Figure 2.9). This indicates the resilience of remittances. That there was contraction should not be readily considered as evidence against the observed counter-cyclical attribute of remittances. A lag was actually found in the response of remittance inflows to specific crisis episodes, such as the natural disasters in Bangladesh and the Dominican Republic and the Asian financial crisis (World Bank 2006). Indeed, international remittance inflows to Cambodia experienced a modest rebound by 2009.

Available data only account for remittances sent using formal means. Due to their clandestine nature, informal remittances and any change in their size are difficult to track. The majority of Cambodian emigrants are irregular foreign workers in Thailand. Malaysia is another popular destination for low-skilled Cambodian labourers as is South Korea, though only in more recent times. These three countries were hard-hit by the crisis, thwarting migrant job prospects in the process. The governments of Thailand and Malaysia went as far as temporarily refusing new

FIGURE 2.9
International Remittances Proved to be More Resilient than
Other Private Transfers
(International Remittance Inflows)

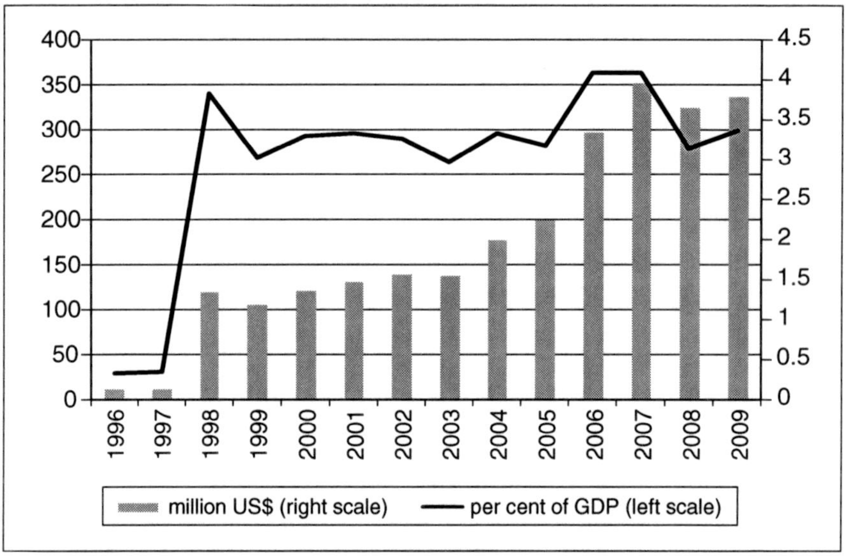

Source: Database for Ratha et al. (2010); World Bank WDI Online (2010).

migrants entry to their countries while implementing tough crackdowns on illegal migration. Although no mass return migration transpired, there were scattered accounts of returning migrants nonetheless. The unemployment or greater underemployment caused by the recession also reportedly forced migrants to consume or keep for themselves most or all of the savings that would have otherwise been sent to their families in Cambodia. All of these adverse developments must have driven the decline in both formal and informal international remittances.

Foreign Aid

Given that other major crises had led to painful reductions in and slow recovery of aid in the past, there was widespread fear that the global recession would have similar consequences. Development partners needed to explicitly affirm their promise to follow through their commitments

in order to assuage concern. Aid budgetary pressures made it difficult
to translate such affirmations into practice. In the end, the crisis forced
all or any of the following three responses from donors: cuts in aid,
re-allocation of aid across countries, and increased support for multilateral initiatives (te Velde and Massa 2009). Cambodia was spared
aid cuts at least up to 2009. To the contrary, aid flows to the country
carried on with its post-conflict growth. This came as a huge relief given
the high dependence of the country on aid. As broached in Chapter 1,
the government's capital expenditures and social interventions both of
which are critical in priming the economy and sheltering the vulnerable
during difficult periods, have been predominantly funded by donor
support. Actual disbursements amounted to US$956 million in 2008,
about 23 per cent higher than the previous year. A further increase of
3.5 per cent was seen in 2009, bringing the total aid disbursement to
US$989.5 million (see Figure 2.10).

FIGURE 2.10
Aid Flows to Cambodia Continued to Increase
(Actual Disbursements, US$ million)

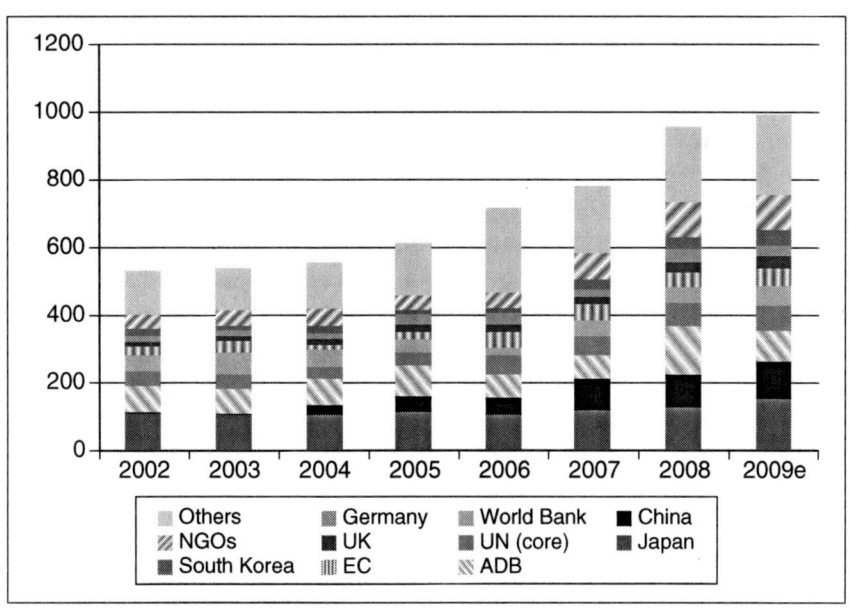

Source: CDC-CRDB (2007, 2008, 2009).

Aid predictability was commendable, with 93 per cent of the bilateral and multilateral aid pledged in 2008 actually disbursed. Japan kept its position as the country's leading bilateral donor; however, its share in total aid dwindled as aid flows from China in particular strengthened. From a measly 1 per cent in 2002, the share of Chinese aid in total donor support rose to about 12 per cent in 2009. Some European countries backed out of their earlier pledges or effectively lowered their aid either because they set their aid targets as per cent of their GNI which shrank as a result of the crisis or their currencies lost value. The global economic downturn also engendered serious aid re-programming in countries like the United Kingdom. Up to 2009 at least, Cambodia was spared the adverse implications of these developments. By 2011, however, a major change, in British aid to Cambodia for instance, is set to take place. This is touched upon in Chapter 6.

Total aid exceeded the total funding requirements of the country's NSDP for 2009. However, on a per sector basis, there were some under- and over-allocations. Aid disbursements for governance and administration considerably overshot the targeted allocation. Those for agriculture and rural development may have increased relative to 2008 but they fell considerably short of target. One of the strongest criticisms of the government's response to the crisis was its increased spending on civil service and military administration at the expense of priority projects that were deemed more helpful in stimulating the economy and cushioning the impact of the downturn on the poor. The prioritization of defence spending has been a consistent feature of the country's post-conflict milieu as discussed in the first chapter.

The government's supposedly priority projects can be categorized into three groups: economic growth boosters (mainly infrastructure and agriculture related projects); livelihood projects; and social safety net providers. Actual disbursements for these priority projects missed the target by 20 per cent overall. This aside, one welcome response to the crisis was the integration of two new programme areas — technical and vocational training and mitigation of vulnerability — into the NSDP Update 2009–2013. Over said period, the two areas were to be allocated funds of US$150 million and US$250 million, respectively (CDC-CRDB 2010).

In terms of aid modalities, bilateral aid programming continues to dominate even though many smaller donors have been increasingly channelling their aid through multilateral agencies (CDC-CRDB 2010). Budget support, which is ideal for increasing government ownership of aid delivery, remains very small. It accounted for only 2 per cent of the total aid disbursed in 2009. The choice of aid modality seems to be an issue that is little connected to the crisis. It rests more on the government and corporate interests of the donor country and the depth of trust between the Cambodian government and its donors.

2.3.3 Balance of Payments

For more than a decade, the overall external position had shown a surplus. The crisis put a stop to this trend. The still strong performance in the first three quarters of 2008 helped generate a surplus for 2008, though this surplus was already lower than in previous years. The current account deficit in 2008 widened significantly due to the faster decline in export growth relative to import growth. Net FDI had already dropped but the net foreign assets of commercial banks still managed an increase relative to 2007. In 2009, the overall balance finally registered an estimated deficit of US$23 million or about 2 per cent of GDP (IMF 2009). The significant deceleration in both export and import growth narrowed the current account deficit. The capital accounts position on the other hand was greatly weakened by the drop in net FDI, tourism receipts and other private transfers. It is estimated that gross official reserves amounted to just 3.5 months of imports in 2009 from 4 months of imports in 2008 due to the reversal in capital inflows.[10]

2.4 DOWN WENT THE GROWTH SECTORS

Cambodia's growth acceleration in the decade before the global crisis mainly rode on the back of four sectors: garments, construction, tourism and agriculture. As mentioned earlier, the Cambodian economy grew by 9.4 per cent per year on average between 1998 and 2007. About a quarter of this growth was contributed by the garment industry, 16 per cent by agriculture, 7 per cent by construction and 5 per cent by tourism. In sum, roughly half of the country's economic growth per year was due to these four industries. It was hardly surprising therefore that the contractions garments, construction and tourism translated easily into Cambodia's own economic downturn (see Figure 2.11).

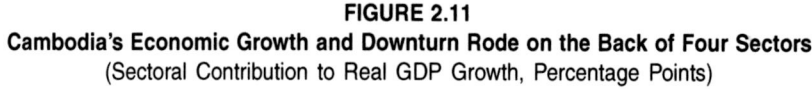

FIGURE 2.11
Cambodia's Economic Growth and Downturn Rode on the Back of Four Sectors
(Sectoral Contribution to Real GDP Growth, Percentage Points)

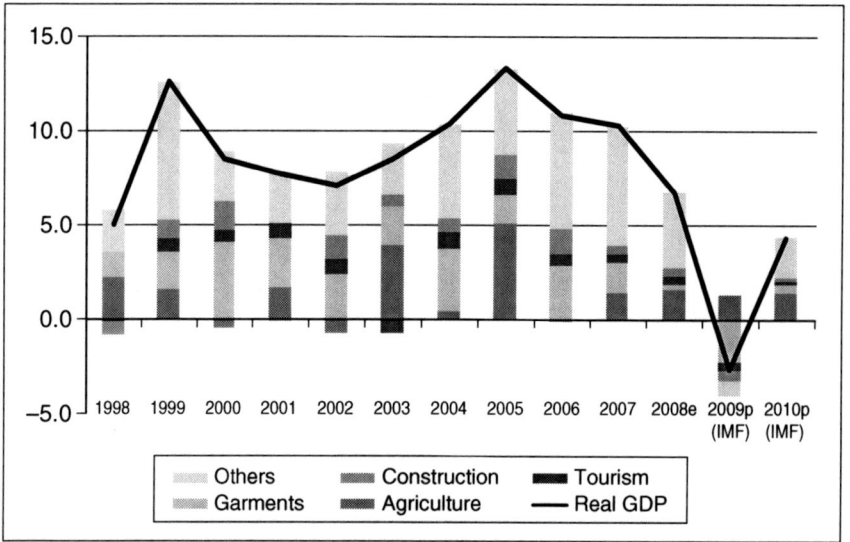

Source: Authors' calculations based on data from NIS (2009), IMF (2009).

The deceleration in trade and capital inflows can certainly be blamed for the lacklustre performance of these three growth drivers over the period of the crisis; however, as elucidated in the discussion below, other adverse developments were partly responsible as well.

2.4.1 Garments

Garments have been Cambodia's leading exports since the mid-1990s. Total garment export values rose from nearly nothing in the early post-conflict years to US$380 million in 1998 and then to almost US$3 billion in 2007. It may be that even at US$3 billion, the annual export value of garments from Cambodia is measly compared to the value of garments from huge exporting countries such as China. In terms of export share however, there is no other developing East Asian economy that relies on the garment industry as much as Cambodia does. The share of garments in Cambodia's total annual export values rose from half to three quarters between 1998 and 2007. Half of the country's annual output growth on average was contributed by the garment sector. This heavy dependence on one export product mainly underpinned the sharp decline in total exports during the crisis.

It is not only that the country's export base is limited, dominated as it is by garments. The garment sector itself is also poorly diversified. Roughly two thirds of annual garment exports are bound for the U.S. market and the majority of the remaining is shipped to the European Union (EU). As retail sales in the U.S. plummeted due to the shock, the demand for Cambodian garments was affected. Year-on-year declines in garment exports to the U.S. began in the third quarter of 2008 but the worst occurred throughout 2009. Data show that, on average, monthly U.S. imports of Cambodian-made garments dropped year-on-year by a huge 22 per cent in 2009 (see Figure 2.12). Imports of both knitted and non-knitted garments shrank significantly, though the latter more so. Also in 2009, monthly garment shipments to all markets from Cambodia

FIGURE 2.12
Cambodia's Garment Industry Suffered Severely from the U.S. Retail Slump
(Comparative Values of Garment Exports to the U.S., y-o-y Percentage Change)

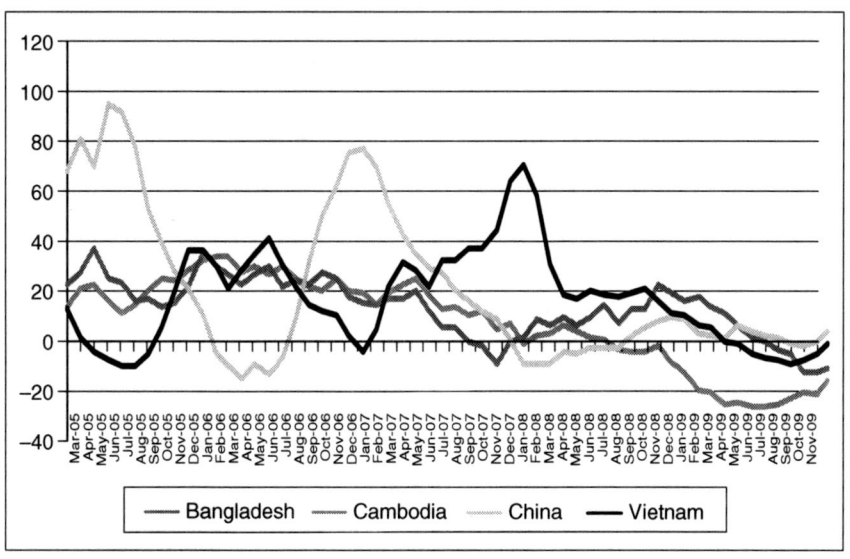

Source: Authors' calculations based on data from USITC.

dropped year-on-year and on average by 17 per cent in terms of value and 12 per cent in terms of volume (see Figure 2.13).

The global recession was certainly a factor that weakened the demand for Cambodian garments. A survey of the performance of other garment manufacturers in the region suggests, however, that there could have been other factors at work. In 2009, monthly U.S. garment imports from China increased year-on-year by 2 per cent on average, those from Bangladesh increased also by 2 per cent while those from Vietnam declined by a mere 2 per cent (see Figure 2.12).

Another plausible factor that explains the exceptional drop in garment exports from Cambodia is loss of competitiveness based on preferential access. The history of garment industry in the country started with the adoption of the Multi-fibre Arrangement (MFA) in the 1970s. By effectively imposing quota limits on the then established garment manufacturers, the MFA created a spillover that benefited latecomers in the garment business, including Cambodia. Manufacturers and buyers alike shifted their business to the emerging garment industries in these countries in order to overcome restrictions. In 1995, the MFA was replaced by

FIGURE 2.13
Garment Exports Plunged as the Crisis Worsened
(Total Monthly Clothing Exports, 3ma y-o-y Percentage Change)

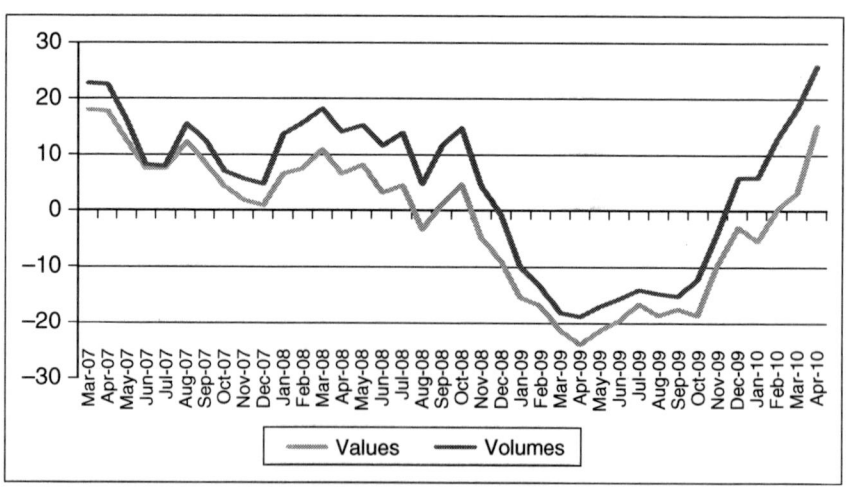

Source: Authors' calculations based on data from MoEF (various).

the Agreement on Textiles and Clothing (ATC) which required the elimination of all quota restrictions in ten years' time.

The escalation of U.S. imports from Cambodia put the country's garment industry in the limelight. Critiques of how the industry's competitiveness was based on worker exploitation forced the enactment of the Trade Agreement on Textiles and Apparel (TATA) between Cambodia and the U.S. in 1999. The TATA assigned quota bonuses to Cambodia depending on its garment industry's compliance with international and national labour standards. Cambodia was able to obtain the maximum quota in time.

The ATC and the TATA expired in 2004. There was much speculation that Cambodia's garment sector would crumble under open competition but this failed to materialize. While the growth of its garment exports did slow down, no contractions occurred. Small garment manufacturing countries like Cambodia were shielded from competition from China due to the safeguards imposed by the U.S. and the EU. These safeguards were only temporary however and expired in 2008. Hence, Cambodia's garment industry was simultaneously exposed to a double shock — the recession and loss of preferential access. Cambodia still benefits from the quota and duty-free access under the EU's Everything But Arms (EBA) initiative. However, the domestic garment sector's inability to meet the strict Rules of Origin (ROR) prevents it from fully exploiting such access. This inability springs mainly from the relative absence of the necessary domestic backward linkages in the country. The garment sector's competitiveness is undermined by the lack of domestic textile and accessory industries.

Weaker exports as a result of the sector's struggle to compete can be traced to other root causes. First, not only is the sector poorly diversified in terms of market but it is also poorly diversified in terms of output. The industry is dominated by CMT factories that operate under the instruction of parent companies overseas and subcontractors that take on CMT work. CMT is the simplest part of the garment value chain and thus has the lowest value added. The concentration on CMT disables the garment sector from buffering the decline in key clothing exports by increasing the manufacture of other garments.

The fact that the industry is roughly 90 per cent foreign-owned also helps clarify why it was most severely hit by the crisis. Local capital accounts for a mere 10 per cent of the industry's capital, whereas

60 per cent is accounted for by Chinese (mainland China, Hong Kong and Taiwan) investment. Responding to the crisis, multinational companies underwent cost restructuring and made divestments which in turn resulted in relocation of production, downsizing of firms and temporary closures (UNCTAD 2009). In Cambodia, the number of operating garment factories stood at 241 in November 2009 from a peak of 313 in October 2008. The factories that escaped permanent closure were only running at 60–70 per cent capacity (ILO-BFC 2010). The garment sector's workforce accounts for only 3 per cent of total employment, yet the factory shutdowns had serious implications for garment factory workers and their dependants. Between October 2008 and November 2009, 21 per cent of the total garment workforce or close to 75,000 workers were laid off (ILO-BFC 2010).

It was noted earlier that labour standard compliance was a condition to Cambodia being awarded quota bonuses. Even now that the TATA is defunct, the grant of export licence to garment factories is still contingent on their abidance of international and domestic labour standards as determined by Better Factories Cambodia (BFC).[11] There are divergent views as to whether such requirement hinders or helps the garment industry. On the one hand, the reputation of the industry as a global model of good governance is a positive source of product differentiation. It gives it edge in the ethical market. On the other hand, compliance can be costly. With the crisis and the post-quota environment having intensified price wars, corporate governance has been considered by buyers as a necessary but not sufficient condition to clinch orders. Further, BFC assessments do not necessarily capture the entire and real situation on the ground. It is not only that BFC does not inspect all the factories and subcontractors but also that corruption, worker intimidation and the nature of some labour violations make it difficult to uncover all malpractice. A significant number of garment worker unions and factory owners partly blamed these and the output loss from union action for their underperformance during the crisis. The number of industry-wide strikes reportedly doubled in the first half of 2009 relative to the same period in 2008, most of which transpired in the garment sector (O'Toole and Green 2009).

Two other major root causes of the garment sector's lagging competitiveness are corruption and high energy costs. The Second Investment Climate Survey in Cambodia found that the incidence as well as value of informal payments in Cambodia increased significantly between 2004 and 2008. It is speculated that garment firms doled out more of such payments. Meanwhile, the cost of electricity in Cambodia is much higher relative to the cost in other garment manufacturing countries. More than 80 per cent of garment factories have been reportedly using generators to meet more than half of their power needs. About 5 to 7 per cent of unit prices represent electricity costs, a high share given that the garment industry is not electricity-intensive (World Bank and IFC 2009; World Bank 2009).

2.4.2 Tourism

Between 1998 and 2007, Cambodia's tourism sector enjoyed an 11 per cent growth per year on average. It contributed about 5 per cent of the country's annual output growth. This positive trend was temporarily discontinued in 2008 when international visitor arrivals visibly slowed down. Year-on-year growth of such arrivals dropped to single digits by the second quarter of 2008 and turned negative by the final quarter of the same year (see Figure 2.14). The contractions in the sector were however

FIGURE 2.14
Tourism Visibly Slowed Down
(International Visitor Arrivals, y-o-y Percentage Change)

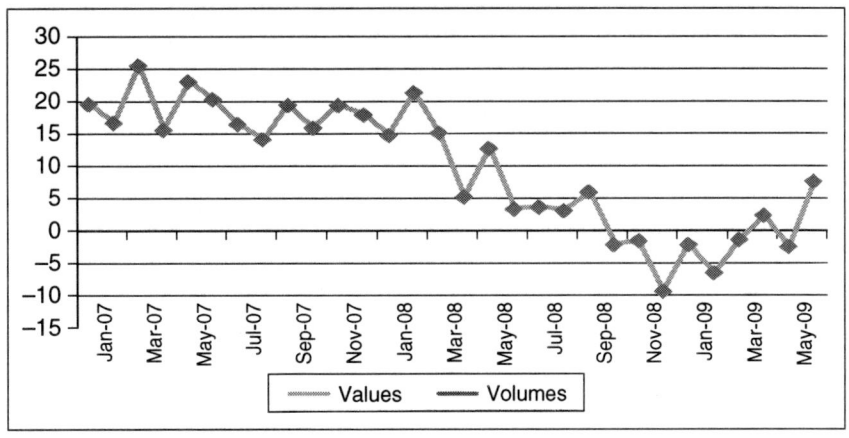

Source: MoT (2009); MoEF (various).

modest compared to what the garment and construction industries endured. Total international visitor arrivals still grew from about 2 million in 2007 to 2.12 million in 2008, a lower but still positive 5 per cent growth. Revenues from tourism also increased, though at a comparatively much lower rate. They amounted to roughly US$1.6 billion in 2008, a 5 per cent increase from the preceding year. The tourism sector was also the first among Cambodia's principal industries to recover (discussed further in Chapter 6). By the end of 2009, the number of foreign visitors totalled 2.16 million, again reflecting a much lower but still positive 2 per cent growth relative to 2008. Tourism receipts, however, dropped by 2 per cent to US$1.56 billion. The average length of visits also fell from 6.65 to 6.45 days (MoT 2010).

What caused the slowdown can be traced to both crisis and non-crisis related factors. Data show that the most severe decline in tourism was in Cambodia's major traditional markets, South Korea and Japan. The global recession had sent the economies of these countries into a tailspin.[12] A visible consequence of this was a decline in tourist outflows. In Cambodia, the number of South Korean visitors went down by 19 per cent between 2007 and 2008 while that of Japanese visitors barely increased. In January to May 2009 relative to the same period in 2008, arrivals from South Korea declined by 34 per cent and those from Japan by 14 per cent. Tourism from the U.S. and Western European countries virtually stagnated in 2009. Other adverse developments that must have compounded the impact of the recession on tourism were the internal political crisis in Thailand, the border stand-off between Thailand and Cambodia, and the H1N1 pandemic. The protracted political conflict in Thailand dealt a blow to tourism in the country. This automatically had a negative spillover to tourism in Cambodia given that many of the country's tourists come via Thailand. Meanwhile, the border skirmish between the two countries likely scared off tourist flows between them in general and those to the Preah Vihear temple, which is located near the disputed boundary, in particular. The military conflict re-emerged in July 2008; interestingly, tourism traffic bound for Preah Vihear fell by 22 per cent in the second half of 2008 relative to the same period in 2007.[13] As regards the H1N1 scare, the world has already reached the post-pandemic stage though some hot spots remain (WHO 2010). The death toll from the virus remains very small in Cambodia; however, the spread of the infection has not let up.

As of June 2010, there were seven casualties and 591 cases of H1N1 infection (Xinhua 2010).

What propped the tourism industry and enabled it to manage low but still positive growth in terms of total international visitors were the increases in regional and domestic tourism. Data show that the number of Lao and Vietnamese tourists shot up by about 150 and 40 per cent respectively in January to May 2009 relative to the same period in 2008. Visa fee waivers applicable to visitors from Laos and Vietnam can be deemed successful in light of this. Consistent with the boost in sub-regional tourism, foreigner arrivals by land and water registered an increase for two consecutive years (32 per cent in 2008 relative to 2007 and 23 per cent in 2009 relative to 2008). Meanwhile, arrivals by air experienced back-to-back declines (–4 per cent in 2008 relative to 2007 and –10 per cent in 2009 relative to 2008). The total spending of tourists from neighbouring countries cannot match the total spending of visitors from Cambodia's traditional and more developed markets. This can explain why even though the number of visitor arrivals still grew in 2009, tourism receipts dropped.

As in the case of the garment sector, there seems to be more behind the lull in Cambodia's tourism industry. The sector is similarly poorly diversified and lagging behind the competition among countries striving to become visitor economies. It relies mainly on cultural tourism, particularly on visitors to the Angkor Wat temples. In the 2009 travel and tourism competitiveness ranking, Cambodia ranked 118th out of 133 countries while its neighbours, Thailand and Vietnam, ranked 39th and 89th respectively. Cambodia proved most inferior in relation to infrastructure and the business environment (WEF 2009). It can thus be argued that the country's tourism sector would likely have hit a rough patch sooner or later with or without the global downturn.

2.4.3 Construction

The delay in the construction of the much-awaited skyscrapers in Phnom Penh demonstrates the downturn in Cambodia's construction industry. The sector finally began losing steam after overheating till about the middle of 2008. Its growth tumbled to roughly 6 per cent in 2008 relative to 2007, much lower than the pre-crisis average growth of about 15 per cent. By 2009, the sector could have contracted by as much as 8 per cent. Prior to the downturn, construction accounted for about 7 per cent of annual output growth on average. With the downturn, it contributed to the worst output contraction ever seen in the history of Cambodia's post-conflict economy (see Figure 2.11). Among the country's crisis-hit growth sectors, construction has taken the longest time to bounce back. The year-on-year growth of construction equipment imports turned negative by the third quarter of 2008 and was yet to become positive as of March 2010 (see Figure 2.15). There was still no robust sign of renewed investor confidence by the first quarter of 2010. The value of construction investment approvals was reportedly down by nearly 83 per cent in said period compared to the same period in 2009 (Soeun 2010).

The slump in the construction industry can be blamed on both the global economic recession and the domestic real estate bust. The economic boom years before the crisis resulted in over-optimism about

FIGURE 2.15
Construction Suffered a Severe Blow from the Crisis and the Real Estate Bust
(Import Volumes, 3mma y-o-y Percentage Change)

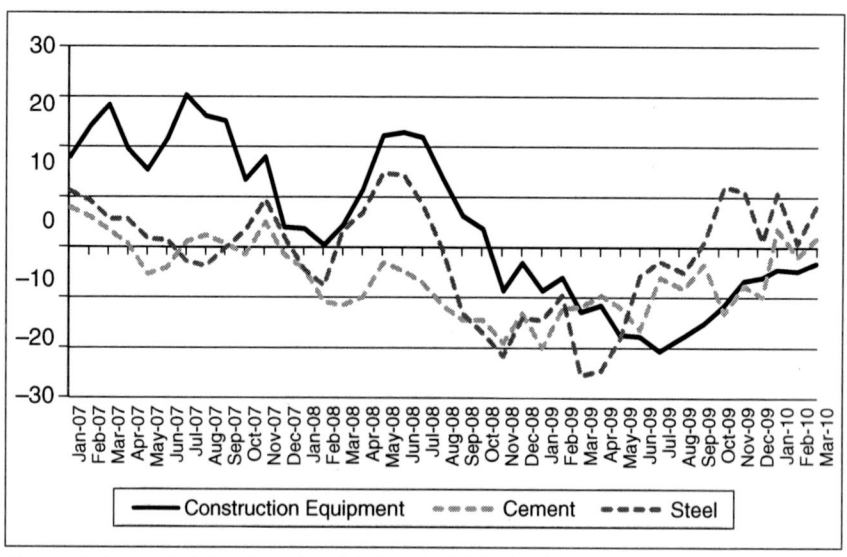

Source: Authors' calculations based on data from MoEF (various).

the performance of the property sector and inflated wealth expectations. While increases in per capita income and property value primarily in urban areas may have led to genuine demand for and supply of real estate, too much speculation eventually infiltrated the property market. This created the bubble. Property prices reportedly soared by 50 to 80 per cent in 2007 and by 50 to 100 per cent by the middle of 2008 *vis-à-vis* the prices in previous years (Jalilian and Reyes 2010). The banking industry helped inflate the bubble by making generous real estate loans but perhaps to a lesser extent than expected. Many property transactions in Cambodia are cash-based and real estate turned out to have a modest share in the commercial banks' loan portfolios.

It is speculated that the bubble would not have continued much longer. Even without the crisis, it would have burst eventually. What the recession did was to accelerate its onset and deepen the crash. On the supply side, it choked credit, drying up liquidity and dimming business prospects which in turn stymied investment. On the demand side, it decreased wealth and lowered income expectations which in turn diminished both the interest and the ability to accumulate and maintain assets. Commercial bank credit to the real estate sector experienced consecutive decreases from 7.6 per cent of total bank loans in August 2008 to 6.4 per cent in August 2009 (see Figure 2.17).

2.5 STRAIN ON THE MONETARY AND FINANCIAL SECTOR

Monetary conditions in Cambodia clearly tightened due to the liquidity and credit squeeze engendered by the financial and economic shock. On average, monthly broad money growth plunged year-on-year from 55 per cent in the first half of 2008 to a mere 3 per cent in the first half of 2009. The worst was seen in February 2009 when broad money actually contracted by 1 per cent (see Figure 2.16). The situation only turned around by the second half of 2009 as explained in Chapter 6.

Diagnoses concerning Cambodia's banking system early on in the recessionary period concluded that the sector was in a robust position. This was based on the sector's adequate capital cushions, small size of non-performing loans (NPL) and lack of direct exposure to the sub-prime market collapse. Banks dominate Cambodia's financial system and

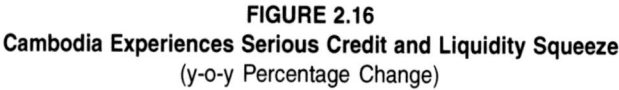

FIGURE 2.16
Cambodia Experiences Serious Credit and Liquidity Squeeze
(y-o-y Percentage Change)

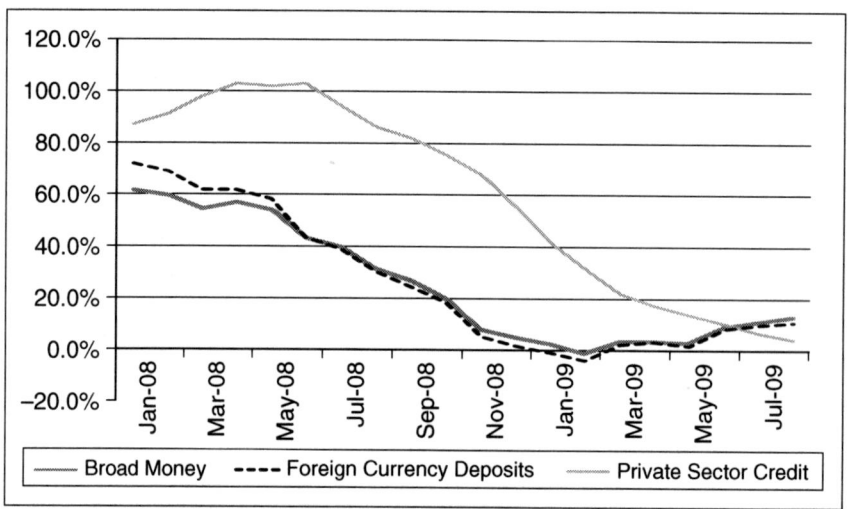

Source: Authors' calculations based on data from NBC (2010).

they have grown in number, reflecting confidence in the profitability of doing business in the country. By June 2009, there were 32 banks in total, including 27 commercial banks, one of which is state-owned, and six specialized banks.

The feedback effect of the financial turmoil on the real economy and the associated liquidity squeeze eventually put a strain on the banks' balance sheets, however. The real estate bust significantly compounded the risks to the banking sector. Liquidity became a serious concern as foreign currency deposits (FCDs), which comprise roughly 97 per cent of total bank deposits, declined continually throughout 2008 and finally contracted in early 2009. The year-on-year growth of FCDs had plummeted to –4 per cent by February 2009 from 72 per cent in January 2008 (see Figure 2.16). Emergency funds from overseas parent companies, reportedly, had to be injected, especially in view of major foreign currency withdrawals. Interest rates particularly on dollar accounts were raised to attract more deposits. With the easing in inflation, the NBC moved to decrease the reserve requirement from 16 to 12 per cent. It also put up an overdraft facility to help banks struggling with short-term liquidity shortages.

Credit also became sparser; the feedback loop between credit and the economy meant that scarcer credit stymied economic activity which in turn made credit more difficult to come by. During the credit boom, high year-on-year private sector credit growth breached the 100 per cent mark in the second quarter of 2008. Thereafter, it continuously dropped, tumbling finally to 4 per cent in August 2009 (se Figure 2.16). Real estate and related lending understandably tightened. Stricter lending policy resulted in a consistent drop in real estate loans. As already mentioned, as per cent of total bank lending, such loans dropped from 7.6 per cent in August 2008 to 6.4 per cent in August 2009 (see Figure 2.17). This was despite the removal of the 15 per cent cap on real estate lending by the NBC. Meanwhile, the NPL ratio increased from 3.7 per cent at the end of 2008 to 5.9 per cent in August 2009. This is considered a low level, however, especially considering how rapidly credit expanded prior to the crisis. Furthermore, the increase was partly

FIGURE 2.17
Real Estate Lending Tightened
(Share in Total Bank Loans, Per Cent)

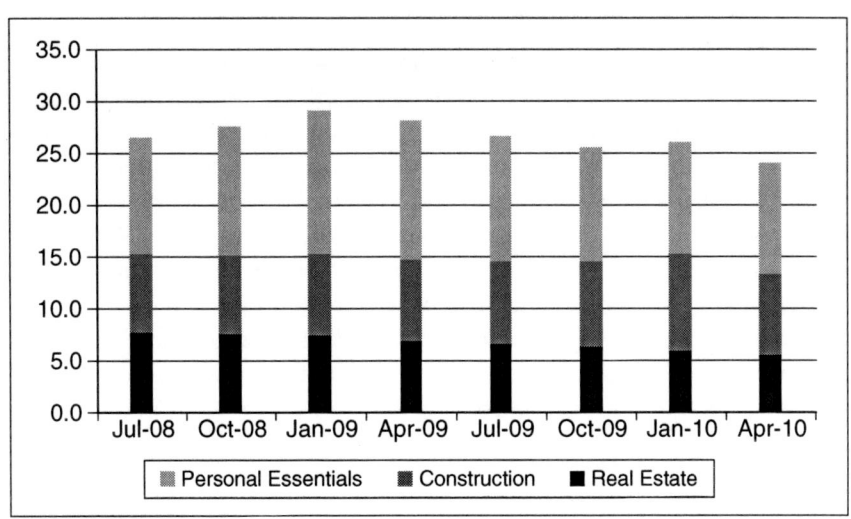

Source: NBC (2010).

due to the toughened NBC regulation on asset classification. Stricter provisioning requirements were also partly behind the decline in returns on earnings and assets.

Several disturbing issues have left some quarters not fully convinced about the vigour of the banking sector. For one, liquidity has been concentrated in big banks, implying that small banks may not have been out of danger. Also, while ample liquidity has been successfully restored, credit has remained scarce; so much so that liquidity overhang has then become the problem. Another key issue pertains to the NPL ratio. Its size could be significantly larger than official figures have indicated. Personal and construction loan proceeds may have been funnelled to or closely aligned with real estate activities. With some banks reporting no NPL, full compliance with the stricter asset reclassification regulation is also said to have been suspect. These issues are revisited in Chapter 6 as part of the update on Cambodia's recovery from the crisis.

2.6 THE GOOD IN THE BAD

Cambodia's experience of the crisis is a sad one for the evident reason that it involved a drastic reversal in the remarkable achievements of the past. Output, formerly one of the fastest to grow in the entire world, was choked so tightly that it suffered one of the biggest contractions in the region. This extent of deterioration was influenced by the nature of growth. Trade and capital flows, whose post-conflict surges served as the force that propelled the economy's take-off, significantly decelerated owing to push as well as pull factors that stymied consumer and industrial demand and dimmed the prospects for the three growth sectors — garments, construction and tourism. The burgeoning in trade and investment was biased towards these three industries. The boom in industrial exports was largely due to the boom in garment exports; unsurprisingly therefore, the considerable slowdown in external garment demand and thus imports buffeted Cambodia's garment industry. The slide in demand was facilitated by the sector's inferior competitiveness and exacerbated by the post-quota environment. This inferiority has been a product of enduring constraints at the firm and macro levels. The boom in services on the other hand was largely due to the boom in tourism. The global recession explained the slowdown in tourist arrivals but so did the industry's lower competitiveness.

The sector is poorly diversified in terms of tourist attractions and services and lagging in infrastructure and enforcement of standards. Construction benefited from the growth of the property sector which in turn benefited from the expansion of garments and tourism and other forms of commercial and residential demand. The bust in the property sector, which was accelerated and deepened by the crisis, was a serious blow to construction. Capital inflows were dominated by the FDI that flowed to the three principal industries. The loss in appeal of these industries significantly dried up FDI.

On the upside, international remittances and aid proved more resilient. The banking sector, which was initially unruffled by the crisis, eventually felt the strain owing to the weaker flow of foreign capital. Liquidity and credit squeeze ensued. The Cambodian experience of the crisis may have been depressing but it came replete with some valuable lessons. The realization of the post-conflict economy's inherent vulnerabilities along with the stronger will and commitment engendered by the struggle has resulted in the perfect window of opportunity for reform. This opportunity must be capitalized on to ensure that something positive and worthwhile comes of the downturn.

Notes

1. A covariant shock is felt across all households while an idiosyncratic shock is particular to a certain household. See for instance Farrington et al. (2004). The concepts of covariant and idiosyncratic shocks are central to the discussion of the micro-level situation during the global crisis in Chapters 4 and 5.
2. With the exception of Vietnam and Papua New Guinea, Vietnam's fiscal stimulus package, the biggest in the region, and the increase in investments by state-owned enterprises helped the country fare better than its neighbours in the face of the crisis. In the case of Papua New Guinea, its savings from its mineral revenues helped it better weather the storm. U.S. is not one of its top export markets as well (World Bank 2010b; ADB 2010b).
3. Based on data from ADB (2010a).
4. See Figure 4 in IMF (2009).
5. See for instance rubber prices quoted by the Malaysia Rubber Board.
6. The Chinn-Ito financial openness index measures the intensity of legal restrictions on cross-border capital account transactions (Chinn and Ito 2008).

7. In fulfillment of its WTO commitments, the Cambodian government passed the following critical laws: Law on Commercial Enterprises; Law on Negotiable Instruments; Law on Commercial Arbitration; Law on Government Bonds; Law on Secured Transactions; Law on Customs; Law on Concessions; Law on Insolvency; and Law on Financial Leasing (Sciaroni 2009).

8. The Law on Investment upholds equal treatment of nationals and foreigners, allows 100 per cent foreign ownership in most sectors, offers a generous package of tax incentives to qualified investment projects, explicitly denounces nationalization, and permits repatriation of invested capital (Jalilian and Reyes 2010).

9. See Dunning and Lundan (2008) for the four types of activity of multinational enterprises, i.e. natural resource seekers, market seekers, efficiency seekers and strategic asset or capability seekers.

10. See Jalilian and Reyes (2010) and IMF (2009).

11. The BFC is an ILO-managed programme aimed at monitoring and reporting working conditions in garment factories in Cambodia. See its official website <http://www.betterfactories.org/ILO/default.aspx?z=1&c=1>, for more.

12. In 2009, Japan's real GDP shrank by 5 per cent while that of South Korea hardly grew at all (IMF 2010*b*).

13. Based on data from MoEF (various years).

References

An, S. "Informal Rice Export: Cambodia Economy Loses Millions". *Economics Today*, 1–15 March 2008.

Asian Development Bank. *Asia Economic Outlook Update*. Manila: ADB, 2009.

———. *Asian Development Outlook: Macroeconomic Management Beyond the Crisis*. Manila: ADB, 2010*a*.

———. *Key Indicators for Asia and the Pacific 2010: The Rise of Asia's Middle Class*. Manila: ADB, 2010*b*.

Better Factories Cambodia. Available at <http://www.betterfactories.org/ILO/default.aspx?z=1&c=1> (accessed 27 October 2010).

Chinn, M.D. and H. Ito. "A New Measure of Financial Openness". *Journal of Comparative Policy Analysis*, vol. 10, issue 3 (2008): 309–22.

———. "Dataset for the Chinn-Ito Financial Openness Index". Available at <http://web.pdx.edu/~ito/Chinn-Ito_website.htm> (accessed 7 September 2010).

Chun S. "Rubber Prices Rise on Back of More Demand". *Phnom Penh Post*, 9 October 2009.

Council for the Development of Cambodia-Cambodian Rehabilitation Board. *Cambodia Aid Effectiveness Report 2007*. Phnom Penh: CDC-CRDB, 2007.

————. *Cambodia Aid Effectiveness Report 2008.* Phnom Penh: CDC-CRDB, 2008.

————. *Cambodia Aid Effectiveness Report 2010.* Phnom Penh: CDC-CRDB, 2010.

Department for International Development Official Website. Available at <http://www.dfid.gov.uk/Where-we-work/Asia-East--Pacific/Cambodia/> (accessed 10 September 2010).

Dunning, J.H. and S.M. Lundan. *Multinational Enterprises and the Global Economy.* Edward Elgar, 2008.

EIU. "Cambodia: Country Outlook". Available at <http://viewswire.eiu.com index.asp?layout=VWArticleVW3&article_id=307233215&country_id= 260000026&page_title=Latest+analysis&rf=0> (accessed 2 September 2010).

FAO. *Food Outlook: Global Market Analysis (November).* Rome: FAO, 2008.

————. *Food Outlook: Global Market Analysis (June).* Rome: FAO, 2009.

ILO-BFC. *Cambodia's Garment Industry Struggles in the Face of the Global Economic Downturn.* Phnom Penh: ILO-BFC, 2010.

IMF. *Country Report No. 09/325 (Cambodia: 2009 Article IV Consultation — Staff Report, Staff Supplement, and Public Information Notice on the Executive Board Discussion).* Washington, D.C.: IMF, 2009.

————. *World Economic Outlook April: Rebalancing Growth.* Washington, D.C.: IMF, 2010*a*.

————. *World Economic Outlook Update July: Restoring Confidence without Harming Recovery.* Washington, D.C.: IMF, 2010*b*.

Jalilian, H., S. Chan, D. Pon, D.S. Phann, G. Reyes, and C.H. Saing. *Global Financial Crisis Discussion Paper Series 3: Cambodia.* London: ODI, 2009.

Jalilian, H. and G. Reyes. *Global Financial Crisis Discussion Paper Series 43: Cambodia.* London: ODI, 2010.

Jalilian, H., G. Reyes, and P. Lun. "Double Blow to the Poor: Cambodia's Food Security in the Face of the Food and Economic Shocks". Unpublished, 2010.

————. "Double Blow to the Poor: Cambodia's Food Security in the Face of the Food and Economic Shocks". *CDRI Annual Development Review* 2009–2010. Phnom Penh: CDRI, 2010.

Malaysia Rubber Board. "Natural Rubber Prices and Charts (Monthly and Yearly Averages)". Available at <http://www3.lgm.gov.my/mre/YearlyAvg.aspx> (accessed 27 October 2010).

May, K. "Vietnam Aims to Lease Land for Rice Crops". *Phnom Penh Post,* 26 February 2009.

Ministry of Economics and Finance (MoEF). "Recent Macroeconomic Performance". Available at <http://www.mef.gov.kh/> (accessed 4 January 2010).

————. *Economic and Monetary Statistics Issues.* Phnom Penh: MoEF, various years.

————. *Monthly Bulletin of Statistics.* Phnom Penh: MoEF, various years.

Ministry of Tourism. *Tourism Statistical Report.* Phnom Penh: MoT, 2009.

————. *Tourism Statistical Report*. Phnom Penh: MoT, 2010.

National Bank of Cambodia. *Annual Report 2009*. Phnom Penh: NBC, 2010.

National Institute of Statistics. *Statistical Yearbook of Cambodia 2008*. Phnom Penh: NIS, 2008.

O'Toole, J. and N. Green. "Outlook for the Garment Sector Mixed". *Phnom Penh Post*, 27 August 2009.

Ratha, D., S. Mohapatra, and A. Silwal. *Migration and Development Brief 12: Outlook for Remittance Flows 2010–2011*. Washington, D.C.: World Bank, 2010.

Sciaroni, B. "Trends in Commercial Law and the Practicalities of Doing Business in Cambodia". Presentation for the Dutch Trade Mission to Cambodia, Raffles Hotel Le Royal, 25 November 2009.

Soeun, S. "Project Approvals Down 83 PerCent". *Phnom Penh Post*, 30 April 2010.

te Velde, D.W. and I. Massa. *Donor Responses to the Global Financial Crisis: A Stock Take*. London: ODI, 2009.

Tong K. "Agriculture as the Key Source of Growth: A Focus on Paddy Rice Production". Presentation during the 2010 Cambodia Outlook Conference, Phnom Penh Hotel, 10 March 2010.

UNCTAD. *World Investment Report: Transnational Corporations, Agricultural Production and Development*. Geneva: UNCTAD, 2009.

WHO. "Influenza Update". Available at <http://www.who.int/csr/disease/influenza/2010_09_10_GIP_surveillance/en/index.html> (accessed 15 September 2010).

World Bank. *Global Economic Prospects: Economic Implications of Remittances and Migration*. Washington, D.C.: World Bank, 2006.

————. *Sustaining Rapid Growth in a Challenging Environment (Cambodia Country Economic Memorandum*. Washington, D.C.: World Bank, 2009.

————. *East Asia and the Pacific Update 2010: Emerging Stronger from the Crisis*. Washington, D.C.: World Bank, 2010a.

————. *East Asia and the Pacific Update 2010 Volume 2: Robust Recovery, Rising Risks*. Washington, D.C.: World Bank, 2010b.

World Bank and IFC. "Cambodia: A Better Investment Climate to Sustain Growth (Second Investment Climate Assessment)". Washington, D.C.: World Bank and IFC, 2009.

World Bank WDI Online. Available at <http://databank.worldbank.org/ddp/home.do?Step=2&id=4> (accessed 31 October 2010).

World Economic Forum on East Asia. Seoul, Republic of Korea, 18–19 June 2009.

Xinhua. "Cambodia Reported A/H1N1Case Reaches 591". Available at <http://news.xinhuanet.com/english2010/health/2010-06/28/c_13373810.htm> (accessed 15 September 2010).

3

THE HUMAN FACE OF THE CRISIS
Key Findings of Vulnerable Worker and Rural Household Surveys

Tong Kimsun, Saing Chan Hang, and Hem Socheth[1]

3.1 DOUBLE BLOW FOR THE CAMBODIAN POOR

The past years have been challenging times for the poor. The price escalations resulting from the food and energy crises threatened food security and barely translated to profit for the many farming households constrained by higher input prices, lack of market access and land insecurity. While those adversely affected were still coming to terms with the negative effects of the food and energy shocks, the global financial and economic crisis struck. Prices may have gone down due to the recession but, as argued in the first chapter, the costs of the downturn were higher. In developing East Asia, as many as 9 million more people could have fallen into poverty in 2009 and 14 million more in 2010. Cambodia is one of the countries in the region expected to have experienced an absolute increase in poverty. Partially reversing earlier successes in poverty reduction, the crises of the recent years could have increased the country's 2007 poverty headcount of 30 per cent by 1–4 percentage points (World Bank 2009b, 2010).

This chapter examines the micro-level impact of the global financial and economic crisis by employing quantitative techniques. In particular, it uses the results of CDRI's vulnerable worker surveys (VWS) and rural household surveys (RHS). In doing so, it hopes to substantiate the poverty impact of the crisis based on the thesis that it was shaped by endogenous factors. Perhaps more importantly, this chapter also relates the actual hardship experienced by the poor and the vulnerable due to the shock. The severity of the blow of the crisis can only be appreciated by understanding how the contractions at the aggregate level translated to and were driven by developments at the micro-level. Section 2 describes the origins and components of the VWS before discussing its key findings. Section 3 on the other hand describes the origins and components of the RHS before also discussing its chief findings. Section 4 concludes.

3.2 THE VULNERABLE WORKER SURVEYS

3.2.1 Survey Description

The Vulnerable Worker Survey is a flagship survey of CDRI. It is a survey of a purposive sample of vulnerable Cambodian workers which is conducted at three monthly intervals, specifically in February, May, August and November. The survey was conceived in 1998, when the impact of the Asian Financial Crisis and an internal political deadlock was still fresh in Cambodia. Its underlying aim was to gauge the welfare change during and after the regional financial shock. The original sample comprised 80 respondents in total — 20 workers from each of the following four occupational groups: cyclo drivers, porters, small vegetable traders and scavengers (see Figure 3.1). All the workers were based in Phnom Penh.

The utility of the survey was enough justification to expand its scope (see Figure 3.1) while maintaining its original objective of measuring welfare changes. In 2000, the sample size was increased to 480, with the addition of 120 garment workers and 40 respondents from each of the following occupational groups: motor taxi drivers, unskilled construction workers, skilled construction workers, restaurant and hotel

FIGURE 3.1
The VWS Has Evolved with the Economic Environment
(Occupational Profile of Survey Sample, Number of Respondents Per Worker Group)

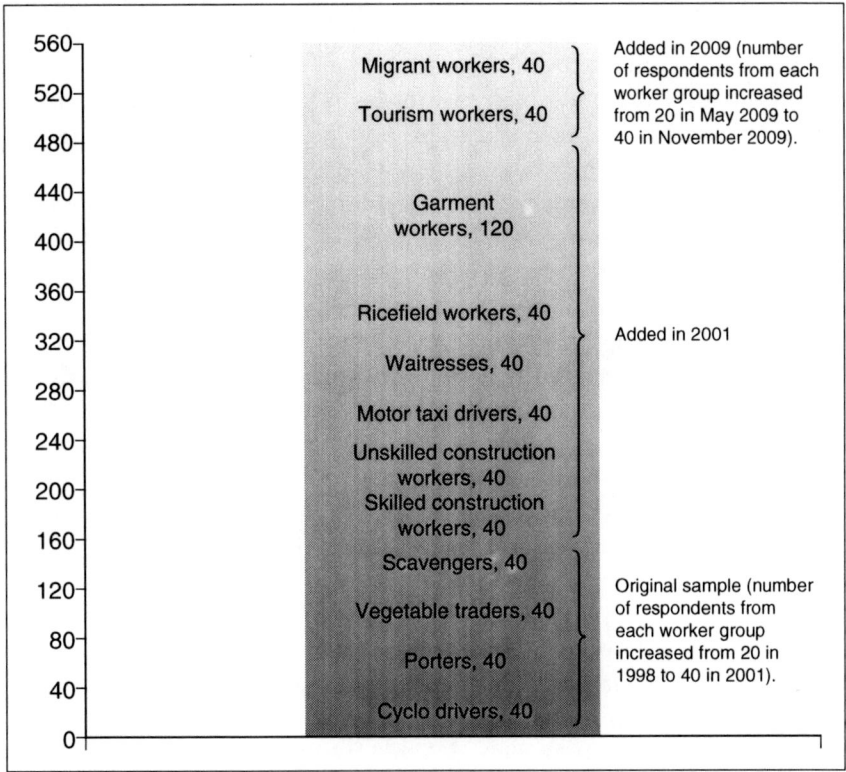

Source: Survey data.

workers, garment workers and rice field workers. The new participants were purposively selected from Kandal and Kampong Speu provinces.

In 2009, the survey was again upgraded. For the second time around, its key mission was directed at measuring the welfare change during and after an economic shock. Workers from two more groups — tourism workers from Siem Reap and migrant workers from Battambang — were added to the sample. Each group was initially represented by 20 respondents, bringing the total sample size to 520. Starting with the November 2009 survey, an additional 20 workers from each of the two groups were interviewed, bringing the total sample size to 560. The surveys for the years 2007 to 2010 are the main focus of this chapter. Comparisons of the data findings are intended to expose any exceptional change in the economic plight of vulnerable workers. The choice of purposive sampling was an effective solution to the time and resource constraints facing the researchers. On the downside however, it comes with a sampling bias and makes it problematic to extrapolate the findings to a broader population. For the purposes of this chapter, another serious problem is the unavailability of survey data for February, May and August 2008.[2] As hinted in Chapter 2, the impact of the crisis became visible in Cambodia by the second and third quarters of 2008. The lack of basic data for this period renders this assessment incomplete. The inability to interview the same individuals for the surveys and the eventual additions in the number of respondents for some worker groups to some extent undermine the soundness of data comparisons. The occurrence of other covariant as well as idiosyncratic shocks[3] also prevents the attribution of the findings solely to the global financial and economic crisis.

The two traditional indicators of poverty, income and consumption, were the specific variables of interest to the survey. Monetary measures of poverty and overall well-being have of course been ardently criticized in the literature. However, the debate focuses more on the weight that they deserve in poverty measurement rather than their roles as minimum and standard determinants of welfare.[4] The income and consumption data from the survey were originally in nominal terms. To get the real amounts, they were deflated by the official consumer price indices for the period of study.

3.2.2 Key Findings

As expounded in Chapter 2, three of Cambodia's growth drivers — garments, construction and tourism — endured the most pronounced contractions as a result of the global economic downturn. Agriculture, the other growth pillar, remained stable, buoyed by higher commodity prices (except for commodities such as cassava and rubber), increases in cultivation areas and productivity, and overall favourable weather conditions (though weather shocks and other natural disasters were experienced in some areas as discussed in Chapter 4). The first category of findings pertains to the welfare changes that affected workers in the four growth sectors. These sectors are not only Cambodia's main growth drivers, they also share the characteristic of being procyclical and or seasonal in nature. In light of this, the welfare changes are best expressed in year-on-year terms. Ideally, the six worker groups represented in the sample — garment workers, skilled and unskilled construction workers, rice field workers, tourism workers and, because they mostly do on-farm work in neighbouring countries, migrant workers — should have been included in this assessment. But the lack of 2008 data for tourism and migrant workers due to their later inclusion in the sample precludes assessment of year-on-year changes in income and consumption. Simple quarterly per cent changes are presented instead but these findings do not take the cyclical and seasonal trends affecting tourism and agriculture into account. The lack of 2008 data, except for November, for all worker groups is a major drawback as the effects of the shocks became evident in the second and third quarters of this year.

The second category of findings concerns the situation of the rest of the worker groups, namely cyclo drivers, porters, vegetable traders, scavengers, motor taxi drivers and restaurant and hotel workers. The workers in this group are mostly self-employed and based in the informal economy. Assessing the simple quarterly per cent changes in their income and consumption is deemed sufficient on the basis that their earnings and the informal economy as a whole are non-cyclical or even anti-cyclical to the extent that they serve as cyclical buffers.[5] The informal economy's role as cyclical buffer, or absorber of displaced workers from the formal sector, has two opposing impacts on earnings. Earnings can benefit from output growth but can also suffer from greater labour supply and competition.

Although much of this chapter focuses on the crisis and immediate post-crisis periods, it also looks at trends from 2004 to gauge atypical changes.

Growth Sector Workers

Income

Survey results show that all four worker groups — garment workers, skilled and skilled construction workers, and rice field workers

— experienced contractions in earnings during the crisis. As depicted in Figure 3.2, the contractions occurred particularly in November 2009 as against November 2008 for construction workers; this appears to be in line with the sector-wide trends which saw the steepest declines in import volumes of construction equipment and steel over the same period (see Figure 2.16, Chapter 2). The average real daily income of unskilled construction workers declined year-on-year by 10.5 per cent in November 2009 after experiencing back-to-back year-on-year increases in income of 43.5 per cent in November 2007 and 16 per cent in November 2008. The average daily earnings of skilled construction workers experienced the same consecutive increases of 7 and 16 per cent in the same months before dipping year-on-year by 1 per cent in November 2009. Data show that the declines in construction equipment imports narrowed around the second quarter of 2009. Survey findings are aligned with this to some extent, indicating year-on-year increases in the average earnings per day of unskilled (26 per cent) and skilled (1 per cent) construction workers in February 2010. The results of the focus group discussions (FGD) discussed in Chapter 4 suggest that unskilled construction workers were worse off than their skilled counterparts during the downturn. The results of the Vulnerable Worker Survey echo this.

In the case of garment workers, the recorded income changes appear to be somewhat disconnected with the sector-wide trends. The survey data show that their average daily income increased year-on-year by 14 per cent in November 2009. However, the slump in the garment industry was at its worst between the third quarter of 2008 and the second quarter of 2009 and was still experiencing negative growth based on the performance of its total clothing exports, particularly those to the U.S. which account for about two-thirds of total exports (see Figures 2.13, 2.14: Chapter 2). The FGD findings confirmed the adverse impact of the downturn on the garment workers' earnings. In February 2010, their average real daily income registered an increase of 12 per cent. Due to the incongruence of the earlier income changes with wider trends, it cannot be confidently posited that this rebound in income was due to the recovery of the garment sector.

The survey results on the earnings of rice field workers are illuminating. They seem to reflect the price trends. Figure 3.2 shows

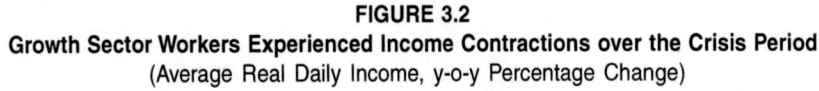

FIGURE 3.2
Growth Sector Workers Experienced Income Contractions over the Crisis Period
(Average Real Daily Income, y-o-y Percentage Change)

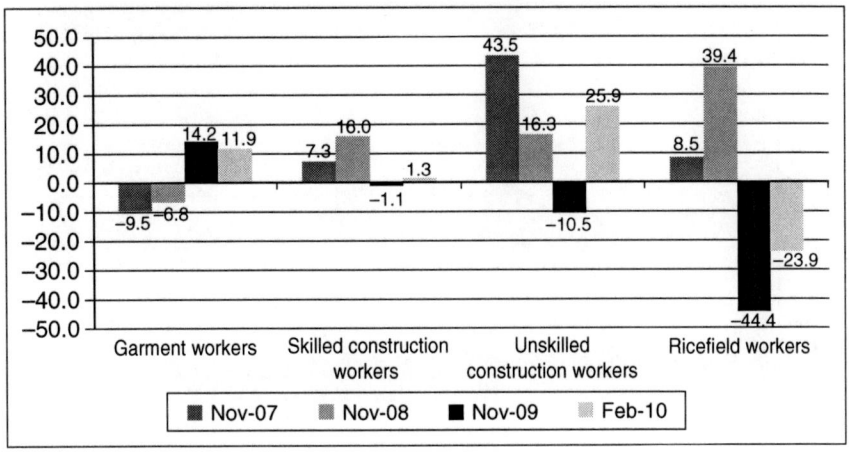

Source: Survey data.

that their average real daily income soared year-on-year by 39 per cent
in November 2008. In line with global trends, food prices in Cambodia
started escalating in the final quarter of 2007 and reached their peaks
in the second quarter of 2008 (see Figure 1.20: Chapter 1). Overall
inflation averaged 24 per cent and rice inflation in particular averaged
60 per cent between November 2007 and July 2008. Because increases in
most agricultural inputs cannot be made immediately, especially given
that price spikes also affect farm inputs, there is an expected time lag
in the response of agricultural production to price signals as mentioned
in Chapter 2. Overall, therefore, the income increase indicated by the
survey data can be considered a confirmation of the positive response
of agricultural output, though with some time lag, to price incentives.
Even without a supply response, however, the higher food prices
alone should have been enough to boost rice field workers' incomes.
This is supported by the findings of another CDRI study (CDRI
2008).[6] Because most agricultural production in Cambodia is small-
scale (on less than 1 hectare of land), any increase in earnings must
have been significantly limited. By November 2009, the average daily
income of rice field workers had plummeted by 44 per cent relative
to November 2008, during which period overall inflation also plunged

FIGURE 3.3
Most Income Contractions Were Not Exceptional Based on Historical Movements
(Average Real Daily Income, y-o-y Percentage Change)

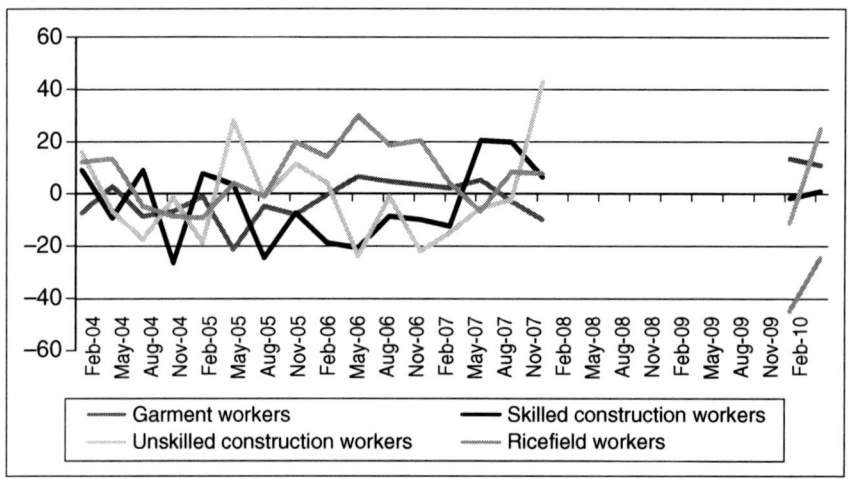

Source: Survey data.

to 1.6 per cent per month on average, with episodes of deflation. Once again, these concurrent trends seem to demonstrate the positive relationship between agricultural production and price incentives.

A quick look at the income movements since 2004 (see Figure 2.3) suggests that income fluctuations are quite common for garment, construction and agricultural sector workers. This is an attestation to the cyclical and seasonal nature of these industries. The income trends since 2004 also suggest that there is nothing exceptional about the changes observed between November 2008 and February 2010. This is at least true for the garment and construction workers. The monthly income contraction that they had to cope with in November 2008 and or November 2009 is below or close to the average monthly contraction that they experienced from February 2004 to November 2007 (7 per cent in the case of garment workers; 15 per cent for skilled construction workers and 10 per cent for unskilled construction workers). In contrast, the 44 per cent dip in rice field workers' earnings in November 2009 appears to be exceptionally steep in relation to past movements. The biggest monthly income contraction between February 2004 and August 2007 was only 9 per cent.

The lack of survey data strictly limits a more meaningful assessment of any welfare change concerning tourism and migrant (mostly agricultural) workers, who are affected by the seasonal nature of their sectors. The available data show that the average real daily earnings of tourism workers increased from about 11,000 to 25,000 riels between May and November 2009 before falling to 21,000 riels by February 2010. Those of migrant workers fell from about 6,800 to 5,800 riels between May and November 2009 before increasing by about 500 riels by February 2010. Data for the same months of the previous years is necessary in order to roughly assess whatever impact the downturn had.

Consumption

From the survey data, it is interesting to note not only the changes in consumption but also the extent to which such changes are aligned with changes in income. Perceptions of the relationship between income and consumption vary on both theoretical and empirical fronts. The Keynesian theory of consumption, permanent income hypothesis, life cycle model of consumption and habit persistence models are established consumption theories that, simply put, see consumption expenditure as stationary. They are significantly independent from income variability. Consumption smoothing occurs over a lifetime in consideration of lifetime income. These notions have not gone unchallenged, however. Studies have found that consumption can closely follow income especially in the face of serious liquidity constraints and consequent build-up of precautionary savings for future insurance. Consumption smoothing occurs in the near horizon in consideration of income in the near horizon.[7]

Survey results indicate that the changes in the consumption of unskilled and skilled construction workers closely followed the trend in their incomes. Year-on-year declines in their average daily consumption (11 and 11.5 per cent respectively) in November 2009 coincided with the declines in their average daily income in the same month. Both declines were preceded by back-to-back improvements.

The rebound in their earnings also coincided with a rebound in consumption by February 2010 (11 per cent and a smaller contraction of 4 per cent, respectively). As far as the construction workers are concerned therefore, it can be tentatively argued that consumption captured the income variability. The FGD results discussed in Chapter 4 reveal that the unskilled construction workers especially had to make significant sacrifices in terms of both the quantity and the quality of their food and non-food consumption as a result of their increased hardship over the period of the crisis.

Similarly to the trend of their income, the changes in the consumption of garment workers were somewhat disconnected from sector-wide trends. The survey data show that their average consumption per day rose year-on-year by about 5 per cent in November 2009 (see Figure 3.4). The consumption trend also did not follow the income trend. The average daily income of garment workers fell by 9.5 while their average daily consumption increased by 24 per cent in November 2007 and stagnated in November 2008. The FGD results found that the garment workers made sacrifices not so much in the quantity of their food intake but the quality. This consumption behaviour may or may not explain the lack of notable contractions in their consumption according to the VWS results.

The consumption changes of the rice field workers were somewhat at odds with the income changes that affected them. As discussed

FIGURE 3.4
Consumption Changes Were Not All Aligned with Income Changes
(Average Real Daily Consumption, y-o-y Percentage Change)

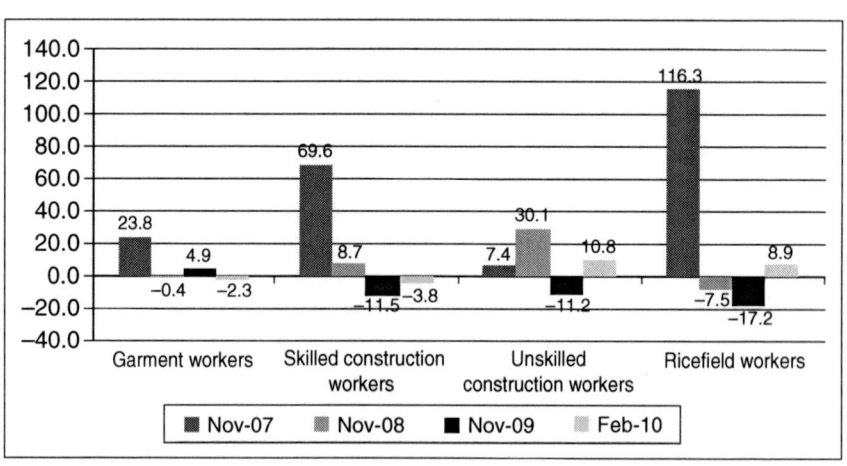

Source: Survey data.

earlier, these income changes seemed to have captured the effects of the extreme price movements. According to the survey results, the average daily consumption of the rice field workers dropped year-on-year by 7.5 per cent in November 2008 and a huge 17 per cent in November 2009. Two plausible explanations for this are that the surveyed rice field workers were net food buyers and they could have built up their precautionary savings for consumption smoothing purposes. As net food buyers, the workers might still have needed to consume less despite the boost in their earnings. The variability of their output prices could have also forced them to increase their precautionary savings at the expense of consumption. The FGD results, however, found that the savings of most vulnerable workers were used up during the crisis.

Looking at the consumption trends since 2004 (see Figure 3.5), there seems to be nothing exceptional about the changes observed during or immediately after the shock. This is indeed the case for the garment, construction and rice field workers. The average monthly income contractions that they suffered in November 2008 and or November 2009 are below or close to the average monthly income contractions that they endured between February 2004 and November 2007 (9 per cent for garment workers, 14 per cent for skilled construction workers,

FIGURE 3.5

Consumption Changes Were Not Exceptional based on Historical Movements

(y-o-y Percentage Change)

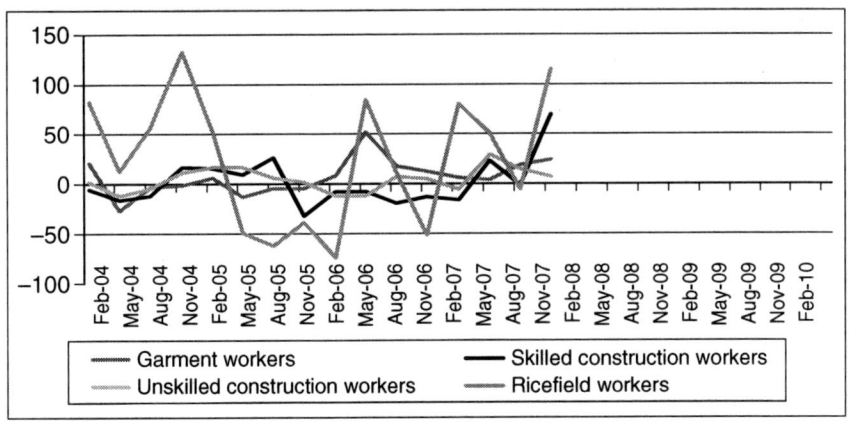

Source: Survey data.

9 per cent for unskilled construction workers, and 48 per cent for rice field workers). The survey data show that the average real daily consumption of tourism workers rose from about 6,500 to 8,000 riels between May and November 2009 before dropping to 5,600 riels by February 2010, whereas that of migrant workers continuously increased from 1,700 to 2,600 riels between May and February 2010. Once again, data for the same months of the previous years is required, even to roughly estimate whatever impact the downturn had.

Other Workers

Income

No single dominant trend characterizes the income changes relating to the other surveyed vulnerable worker groups, namely cyclo drivers, porters, vegetable traders, scavengers, motor taxi drivers and waitresses. All worker groups suffered from at least one contraction in average real daily income in 2009 (see Figure 3.6). For the cyclo drivers, the quarterly contractions occurred at the high rate of 32 per cent in

FIGURE 3.6
All Other Worker Groups Experienced at least One Income Contraction in 2009
(Average Real Daily Income, Quarterly* Percentage Change)

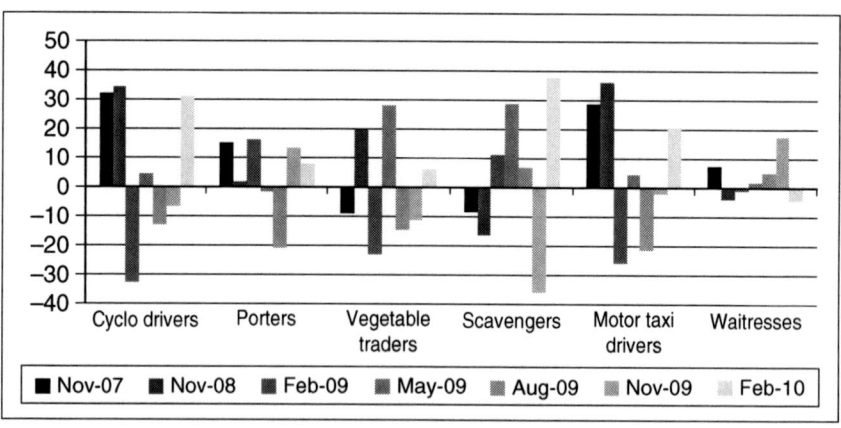

Note: * Except for the data for November 2008 which is year-on-year.
Source: Survey data.

February, 13 per cent in August and 7 per cent in November. The quarterly contractions in the average daily income of motor taxi drivers were similarly considerable, at 26 per cent in February and 21 per cent in August. The porters experienced consecutive quarterly income declines of 1.5 per cent in May and 21 per cent in August. The average daily incomes of the vegetable traders went down by 23 per cent in February, 15 per cent in August and 11 per cent in November. Those of the scavengers contracted twice, the steepest being 36 per cent in November. The waitresses experienced the smallest income reduction of a mere 1 per cent in February. All worker groups, with the exception of waitresses, saw a notable recovery in their daily incomes by February 2010. The road transport groups, cyclo and motor taxi drivers, gained the biggest increases, at 31 and 21 per cent respectively.

When set against the income trends since 2004 (see Figure 3.7), there is, however, nothing remarkable about the abovementioned income declines and improvements in general. Income fluctuations were commonly experienced across all the worker groups. The average quarterly contractions between November 2008 and November 2009

FIGURE 3.7
Income Changes Affecting Other Worker Groups Were Also Not Exceptional based on Historical Movements
(Average Real Daily Income, Quarterly* Percentage Change)

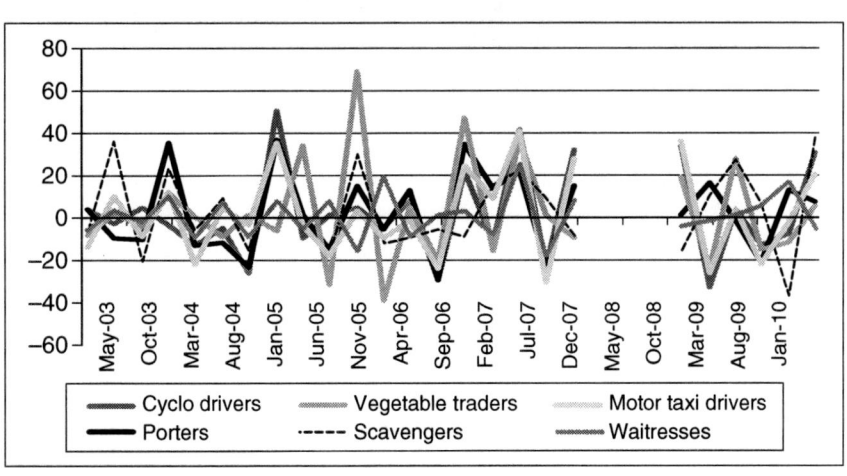

Note: * Except for the data for November 2008 which is year-on-year.
Source: Survey data.

were either within or just modestly higher than the average quarterly contractions between February 2003 and November 2007. Much bigger declines in real daily income have been seen in the past. The income trends relating to the scavengers were the only exception. The average quarterly contraction in their income during the crisis reached 26 per cent, much higher than the average quarterly contraction between February 2003 and November 2007 of 10 per cent.

Earlier, it was mentioned that the informal economy has been considered anti-cyclical, meaning that it expands during downturns as it absorbs displaced workers from the formal sector. The increased economic activity can positively benefit earnings but the greater labour supply and competition can also harm them. No conclusion can be drawn in relation to this matter given the varying trends discussed above.

Consumption

Similarly to the analysis of changes in income, no single dominant trend can be traced in the changes in the consumption expenditures of the other workers. However, all the occupational groups also experienced at least one contraction in consumption in 2009 (see Figure 3.8). The months of February and August proved particularly difficult. Cyclo drivers saw their average real daily consumption contract three times at the rate of 19 per cent in February, 20 per cent in August and 5 per cent in November, while motor taxi drivers saw their average real daily consumption contract twice, by 8 per cent in February and 24 per cent in August. The average real daily income of porters dropped by 1 per cent in February and 23.5 per cent in August, and that of vegetable traders fell by 39 per cent in August. The waitresses experienced the worst declines in average real daily consumption among all the worker groups, at the rates of 34 per cent in February, another 34 per cent in August and a huge 50 per cent in November. The consumption decrease in November was also huge for scavengers at 46 per cent.

The income and consumption of the cyclo and motor taxi drivers moved in the same direction in general. Those of the other workers were, by and large, disconnected with each other. This disconnection was particularly pronounced in the case of the waitresses.

Unlike the case of income, the consumption changes experienced during the crisis turned out to be exceptional when compared to earlier

FIGURE 3.8
Consumption of Other Workers Also Experienced at least
One Contraction in 2009
(Average Real Daily Consumption, Quarterly* Percentage Change)

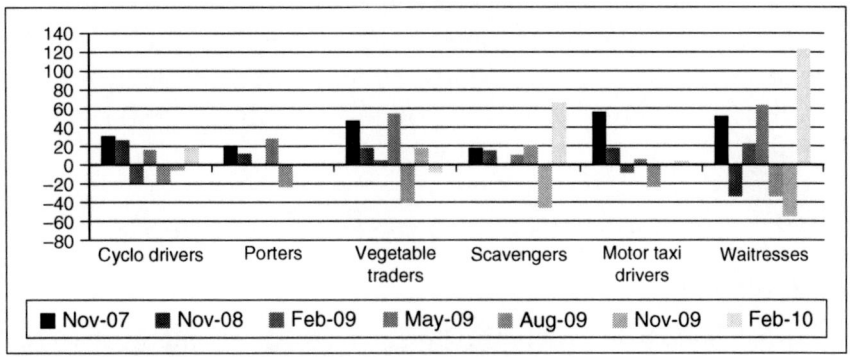

Note: * Except for the data for November 2008 which is year-on-year.
Source: Survey data.

FIGURE 3.9
Quarterly Changes in Average Real Daily Consumption of Other Workers
(Per Cent)

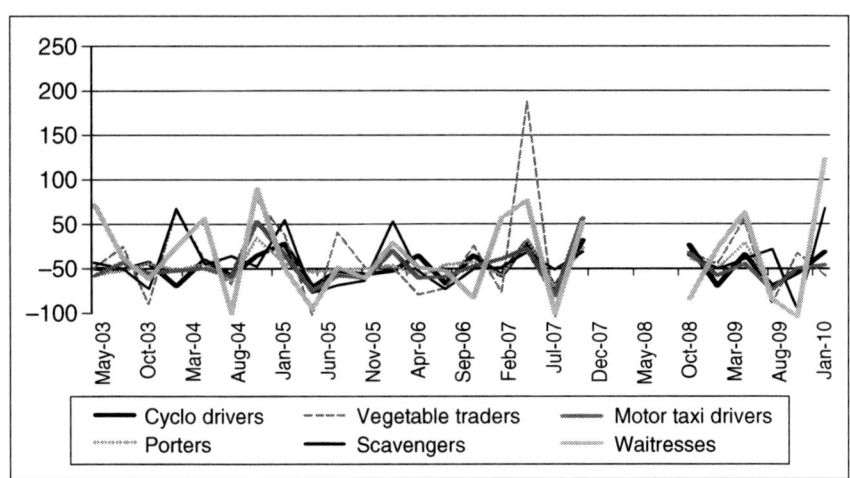

Note: * Except for the data for November 2008 which is year-on-year.
Source: Survey data.

movements (see Figure 3.9). The average quarterly contractions in the consumption of the worker groups between November 2008 and November 2009 were all higher than the average contractions these groups experienced between February 2003 and November 2007. The difference in the averages was particularly considerable for scavengers (–30 percentage points) and waitresses (–12 percentage points). The gaps were as follows for the other worker groups: –4 percentage points for both the cyclo and motor taxi drivers, –5 percentage points for porters and –3 percentage points for vegetable traders.

3.3 THE RURAL HOUSEHOLD SURVEY

3.3.1 Survey Description

The rural household survey (RHS) conducted by CDRI with World Bank assistance in May 2009 is another crisis assessment tool. The key aim of the panel survey was to quantify the household-level impact of the crisis. The sample consisted of households purposively selected from the same nine rural villages featured in CDRI's Poverty Dynamics Study (PDS):[8] Andoung Trach and Krasang in Battambang province; Khsach Chi Ros and Dang Kdar in Kampong Thom; Prek Kmeng in Kandal; Ba Baong in Prey Veng; Kanhchor in Kratie; Trapeang Prei in Kampong Speu and Kampong Tnaot in Kampot. Five poor and five middle income households were chosen from each of the nine villages, bringing the total sample size to 90. The economic status of the households in the sample villages was determined by ranking their per capita food consumption and splitting the results into three groups (poor, middle, and rich). On average, the respondent households comprised six members with 3.4 years of schooling and had 1.7 hectares of farmland. The survey adopted the same questionnaire used in a March 2008 survey, making some revisions to reflect the purpose of the survey. The results of the March 2008 survey also serve as the benchmark data. This minimizes the influence of seasonal variation on the survey results.[9]

The survey sought to assess the impact of the crisis on household welfare as represented by the following indicators: per capita household real daily income, per capita household real daily consumption,[10] asset ownership and indebtedness. It also sought to probe into the crisis coping mechanisms used by households. The survey data on income and consumption, originally in nominal terms, were deflated by the consumer price index to get the corresponding real amounts.[11] Real consumption, both food and non-food, was converted to its individual adult equivalent. This was obtained by dividing total real consumption expenditure by household size, giving children under 14 years of age a weight of 0.5. To gauge any change in poverty status, as defined by change in per capita consumption, a quintile transition matrix was constructed (see Table 3.1). The five quintiles represented the following poverty statuses: "always poor" (shaded), "better off" (dotted), "worse off" (vertical strip) and "never poor" (horizontal strip).

The RHS suffers from the same weaknesses that affect the VWS, the FGDs and semi-structured interviews (SSIs), as discussed in the next chapter. The choice of purposive sampling as well as the small sample size makes the representativeness of the survey findings problematic. Additionally, the occurrence of other covariant crises as well as idiosyncratic shocks at the time of the economic downturn means that the contractions uncovered by the survey cannot be exclusively attributed to the impact of the economic crisis; 35 per cent to 45 per cent of the respondent households were reportedly hit by idiosyncratic shocks, particularly between March 2008 and May 2009.

TABLE 3.1
Poverty Quintile Transition Matrix

	Poverty Status in May 2009				
Poverty Status in March 2008	Bottom	2nd	3rd	4th	Top
Bottom	Always poor			Better off	
2nd					
3rd					
4th	Worse off				Never poor
top					

Source: Adapted from Tong et al. (2009a–c).

3.3.2 Key Findings

Income and Consumption

The change in per capita household income was evident. This was true in terms of both the level and sources of income. As shown in Table 3.2, the per capita household real income dropped considerably by 31 per cent on average between March 2008 and May 2009. This finding was statistically significant at the 1 per cent level. What clearly elicited the drop was the cutback in off-farm and other sources of income. Mean per capita income inflows from each of these two sources nearly halved between the two survey periods. Off-farm income from small businesses, trade and migrant work, both internally and in Thailand, dwindled though it was boosted by migrant income from countries other than Thailand. Income inflows from other sources such as foreign donations, NGOs, charity and land sales also slowed, offset to some extent by surges in land and house rental payments and gifts from political parties.

Not all of these findings are attuned with the FGD and SSI results discussed in Chapter 4. For instance, the FGDs and SSIs found that, with the exception of migrant work, off-farm income sources played an important role in cushioning the blow of the crisis. They also highlighted the significant shortage of public safety nets and traditional informal social assistance during the crisis. One common inference from the results of the RHS, the FGDs and the SSIs, however, is that common property resources assume critical importance in the event of a shock. Table 3.2 shows that per capita household income from exploiting the commons soared by about 27 per cent on average between March 2008 and May 2009, and that from on-farm sources rose by roughly 4 per cent. Another common inference that can be made is that the crisis did not cause mass return migration. Migration flows in fact did not abate as a result of shock. According to the survey data, the mean per capita consumption expenditure declined less than the mean total consumption expenditure between March 2008 and May 2009. This implies a reduction in the average household size which in turn implies that some household members must have migrated between the two survey periods. The mean per capita expenditure decreased specifically by 31 per cent. A plot of the kernel densities of the per

TABLE 3.2
Per Capita Income Dropped Considerably, Mainly due to the Decline in Off-farm and Other Income
(Per Capita Household Real Daily Income by Source, '0000 Riels at March 2008 Prices)

	March 2008			May 2009			% Change (Mean)	t-Statistic
	N	Mean	Median	N	Mean	Median		
On-farm	55	5.03	3.48	54	5.22	5.22	3.76	(−0.170)
Off-farm	63	4.76	3.05	43	2.39	2.39	−49.66	(2.907)*
Common property resources	85	2.19	1.16	69	2.77	2.77	26.90	(−0.945)
Others	43	7.12	2	45	3.73	3.73	−47.62	−1.393
Total	90	11.86	8.27	90	8.26	8.26	−31.14	(2.428)*

Notes: (1) Inflation is assumed to be 16 per cent between the two survey periods.
(2) Official exchange rates: 4131.6 riels to US$1 (May 2009); 3994.6 riels to US$1 (March 2008).
*Statistically significant at 1 per cent level.

Source: Adapted from Tong et al. (2009a–c).

capita consumption data shows that more households spent less on consumption in May 2009 relative to March 2008 (see Figure 3.10). The coincident declines in per capita income and consumption may be taken as confirmation of the thesis that the two variables closely follow each other in the face of liquidity shocks.

Both food and non-food consumption suffered, though the latter more so. Per capita food intake shrank by 31 per cent, while per capita non-food consumption declined by 10 per cent on average between March 2008 and May 2009. The intake of staples, including rice, fish, meat, vegetables and fruit, was affected. Because other food expenditures did not vary, it can be inferred that staple foods must have been substituted for lower quality and cheaper food items. This echoes the FGD and SSI findings that the quantity but more so the quality of food consumed deteriorated over the period of the crisis. In the case of non-food expenses, spending on such items as gasoline, communication equipment, clothes, footwear and accessories was tightened. As in the latter case, there must have been a switch to inferior goods to make the most of smaller budgets.

FIGURE 3.10
More Households Spent Less on Consumption

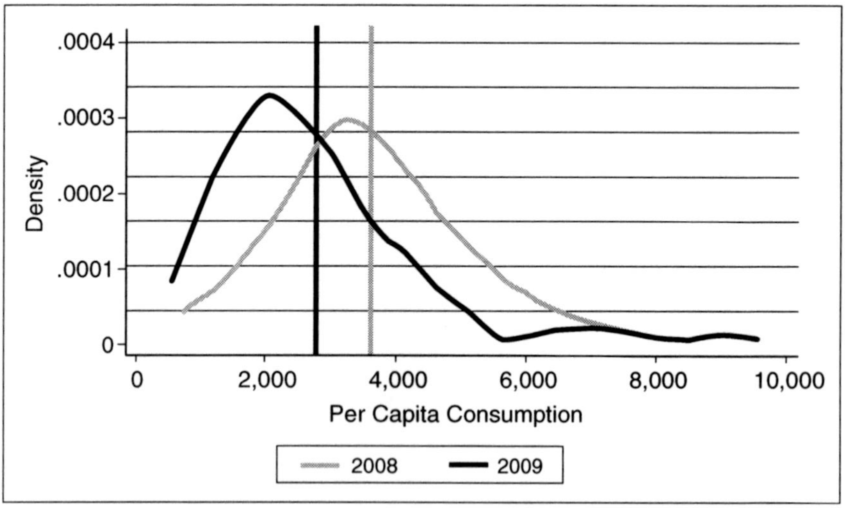

Source: Adapted from Tong et al. (2009a–c).

Poverty, it turns out, worsened for some but diminished for others. Table 3.3, which is the transition matrix on poverty status as defined by per capita consumption, shows that 26 out of the 90 surveyed households became worse off between March 2008 and May 2009. This worse off group saw their per capita consumption plunge by 57 per cent which affected both their food and non-food intake, though the decline in the latter was found to be statistically insignificant (see Table 3.4). Between the two survey periods, 26 out of the 96 households became better off. Unlike the rest, this better off group witnessed their per capita consumption rise by 32 per cent. This was underpinned by the boost in spending on non-food items of a huge 163 per cent. Within the group of the constantly poor, 13 households retained their previous poverty status, three moved down the poverty ladder and three moved up. This group's per capita consumption dwindled from about 40 to 30 per cent of that of the richest group between March 2008 and May 2009. Their food consumption went down by 38 per cent and non-food consumption by 30 per cent, though the latter decline was statistically insignificant. Within the "never poor" group, four retained their status, seven households got demoted and seven became richer. This group's per capita consumption decreased by 19 per cent, at the expense of their non-food but more so their food expenditures. In sum, overall poverty incidence might not have changed; however, attention must be paid to the depth of poverty and the condition of the near poor. Any slight change in these two groups' circumstances has catastrophic effects for those poor households involved.

Asset Ownership

The RHS also intended to gauge how the crisis might have impinged on asset-based welfare. Asset ownership has been considered a meaningful alternative to money-metric measures of poverty. The usefulness of assets as a preventative tool becomes evident during economic crises when they act as financial cushions to avert setbacks in poverty.[12] Table 3.5 shows that there was very limited ownership of non-land fixed assets among the surveyed households. A mere 4 out of

TABLE 3.3
Poverty Worsened for Some but Diminished for Others
(Poverty* Quintile Transition Matrix)

Poverty Status in March 2008	Poverty Status in May 2009					Total No. of HHs**
	Bottom	2nd	3rd	4th	Top	
Bottom	10	3	2	1	2	18
2nd	3	3	6	3	3	18
3rd	3	5		6	3	18
4th	1	6	3	1	7	18
Top	1	1	6	7	3	18
Total No. of HHs	18	18	18	18	18	90

Notes: *As represented by per capita real daily consumption.
**HH stands for households.
Source: Adapted from Tong et al. (2009a–c).

TABLE 3.4
All Clusters Experienced Declines in Food Intake
(Average Per Capita Real Daily Consumption by Poverty Status, Riels)

	March 2008			May 2009			Difference		
	Total	Food	Non-food	Total	Food	Non-food	Total	Food	Non-food
Always poor	2,152	1,619	533	1,378	1,006	372	774	−613	−161
							(5.59)*	(5.51)*	(−1.86)
Better off	2,799	2,065	734	3,694	1,760	1,934	895	−305	1,200
							(−2.53)***	(3.17)**	(−3.74)**
Worse off	4,438	2,487	1,951	1,927	1,282	644	−2,511	−1,205	−1,307
							(15.59)*	(11.06)*	(7.63)*
Never poor	5,121	2,575	2,546	4,170	2,016	2,153	−951	−558	−393
							(2.02)***	(2.99)**	(−0.99)

Notes: *statistically significant at 1 per cent level.
**statistically significant at 5 per cent level.
***statistically significant at 10 per cent level.
Source: Adapted from Tong et al. (2009a–c).

the 30 assets listed in the table were owned by at least 50 per cent of the households.

Among the means of transport, bicycles, boats, motorbikes and oxcarts were the most widely owned, with every owning household having about one of each. Between March 2008 and May 2009, 4 of the 30 owning households sold their motorcycles. No sale of other transport assets was reported. Among the communication devices, television was the most widely owned asset followed by telephones. There were fewer households with television and cassette player but more with radio and telephone by May 2009. Communication equipment in Cambodia has become much more affordable. This, together with increased competition in the telecommunications industry which has brought down call and messaging charges, has increased user rates. Only one of the owning households sold their phone. In the case of agricultural equipment, ploughs and harrows were owned by the greatest number of households. Only four to five households owned hand tractors while none had a more modern tractor. A look at livestock asset ownership shows that cows were the most widely owned after chickens. In March 2008, 44 respondent households had about three cows each and ten households had about three buffalo each. From these it can be inferred that animal power, as opposed to machine, dominated land preparation techniques. This supports the widely shared finding of low agricultural mechanization in Cambodia. Except for one, respondent households had not sold any agricultural equipment. The story, however, is markedly different with reference to their livestock assets. About 30 per cent of the cattle-owning households and 40 per cent of those with chickens had sold some of their livestock by May 2009. Also, six households sold their pigs and two sold their buffalo. Among the other fixed assets, a battery is the most widely owned (see Table 3.5).

As can be seen in Table 3.6, all the non-land assets except radio, boats and pigs experienced price deflation between the two survey periods. The average values of bicycles fell by 19 per cent, motorbikes by 39 per cent and oxcarts by 34 per cent. The value of televisions dropped by 27 per cent, while that of telephones plunged by 35 per cent and cassette players fell by 54 per cent on average. The average reduction in the value of hand tractors reached 20 per cent while that of fishing

TABLE 3.5

Distress Asset Sale Was Not a Common Coping Strategy Given Limited Asset Ownership to Start with

(Household Ownership of Non-land Fixed Assets, '0000 Riels at March 2008 Prices)

Fixed Asset Type	March 2008			May 2009			No. of HHs that Sold Assets
	No. of Owning HHs	Mean No. of Assets	Mean Asset Value	No. of Owning HHs	Mean No. of Assets	Mean Asset Value	
Machinery and Equipment							
Transport Equipment							
Motorcycle	30	1.03	245.73	27	1.04	149.65	4
Bicycle	65	1.37	6.10	61	1.43	4.93	
Car	0	na	na	0	na	na	
Boat	34	1.26	52.81	34	1.26	61.00	
Oxcart	24	1.00	43.03	27	1.00	28.28	
Horse cart	1	1.00	50.00	1	1.00	12.93	
Remorque	1	1.00	60.00	1	1.00	34.48	1
Communication Equipment							
Radio	19	1.00	1.05	22	1.05	1.14	
Television	52	1.04	9.02	47	1.02	6.54	
Telephone or ICOM	22	1.05	17.39	31	1.16	11.27	
Cassette player	18	1.11	14.33	9	1.11	6.56	1
Agricultural Equipment							
Water pump	16	1.13	61.53	14	1.21	55.07	
Threshing machine	0	na	na	0	na	na	
Rice Mill	4	1.00	144.75	2	1.00	74.79	
Plough and harrow	30	1.43	7.50	30	1.50	5.78	
Modern tractor	0	na	na	0		na	
Hand tractor	4	1.25	456.59	5	1.00	365.09	1
Fishing tools	6	62.23	41.17	5	1.00	7.38	

Others

Generator	3	1.00	98.33	2	1.00	69.97	14
Battery	64	1.17	7.96	62	1.19	4.16	2
Sewing machine	5	1.20	28.93	4	1.25	18.75	6
Sawing machine	3	1.00	83.33	1	1.00	51.72	
Cultivated Assets							
Livestock							
Cow	44	3.05	357.99	43	2.91	184.12	
Buffalo	10	2.70	354.85	11	2.36	202.19	
Pig	17	2.00	65.40	9	3.22	118.77	
Horse	1	1.00	150.00	1	1.00	86.21	
Chickens	58	3.93	5.39	54	5.39	4.84	25
Ducks	8	4.63	6.88	9	4.00	3.93	2
Farmed fish	0	na	na	0	na	na	
Others	0	na	na	0	na	na	

Source: Adapted from Tong et al. (2009a–c).

tools reached 82 per cent. Among the livestock assets, the biggest price declines affected cows (–49 per cent) and buffalo (–43 per cent). The asset price deflation must have been by and large connected to the bleak expectations about the future returns on assets, hence, the low demand for them. The worse-off households bore the most severe reduction in fixed asset values. On average, their machinery and equipment lost 50 per cent while their livestock lost about 70 per cent of their values between March 2008 and May 2009. The always poor group experienced smaller price reductions (see Table 3.6), though the ramifications of this deflation may be worse for them given their more limited asset ownership but at the same time greater need for assets as financial buffers during crises.

From the data gathered, it can be inferred that distress sales of fixed assets was not a popular crisis coping mechanism. An evident reason for this is that rural households typically have few durable assets of much value to begin with. This is a strong confirmation of the same findings from the FGDs and SSIs. Asset disposals over the period of the crisis mostly involved draught animals. They were probably not as lucrative as when sold at other times because of the asset price declines caused by low demand and pessimistic valuation of future asset returns. The always poor and worse-off groups must have reeled from significant deterioration in their asset-based welfare.

The incidence of landlessness and land insecurity in Cambodia, while it decreased, remains high. According to the results of the Cambodia Socio–Economic Survey (CSES), the per cent of households owning or

TABLE 3.6
Non-land Assets Experienced Serious Price Deflation
(Average Values of Non-land Fixed Assets by Poverty Status, Percentage Change)

	Total	Machinery and Equipment	Cultivated Assets
Always poor	–26.78	–13.32	–30.23
Better off	–29.59	–26.38	–35.24
Worse off	–62.57	–49.65	–72.63
Never poor	–22.39	–27.88	–9.75
Total	–38.38	–30.64	–45.37

Source: Adapted from Tong et al. (2009a–c).

operating agricultural land increased from 83 to 89 per cent between 2004 and 2009. Roughly two-thirds of these households, however, do not have legal titles on their lands (World Bank 2009a). The prevalence of landlessness in the country was somewhat corroborated by the findings of the RHS. About 30 per cent of the surveyed households did not own[13] land for cultivation but only three out of the 90 households had no residential land. The mean area of residential land was small, so was the area of agricultural land owned, supporting the finding that most farming households in Cambodia are small-holders. The total size of agricultural plots declined by 17 per cent and the number of plots fell by 26 per cent between March 2008 and May 2009 (see Table 3.7). The bigger reduction in the number of plots may be taken to mean that some households might have sold their smaller plots of land.

The four poverty status groups had more or less an equal share of households with no agricultural land. Both the total size and number of plots owned increases as one goes up the poverty ladder. The never poor households bore the biggest drop in both cases. On average, the number of plots they owned went down from 1.8 to 2.7 while the size of their agricultural landholdings shrank from being about 2.2 times to about 1.5 times bigger than the landholdings of the always poor households. The number of plots owned by the worse-off

TABLE 3.7
Land Ownership* Shrank as Size of Landholdings Decreased

	March 2008	May 2009	% Change	t Statistic
Residential Land				
No. of owning HHs	87	87	0	
Average no. of plots per HH	1.06	1.07	0.94	−0.28
Average size of HH holdings (ha)	0.13	0.12	−7.69	0.56
Agricultural Land				
No. of HHs	65	65	0	
Average no. of plots per HH	2.66	1.98	−25.56	−2.24**
Average size of HH holdings (ha)	1.74	1.44	−17.24	−1.26

Notes: *Ownership may not be tantamount to legal ownership.
   **statistically significant at 5 per cent level.
Source: Adapted from Tong et al. (2009a–c).

TABLE 3.8

The Never Poor Cluster of Land Owners Experienced the Biggest Decline in Land Size and Number of Plots

	March 2008			May 2009		
	No. of HH	Average No. of Plots per HH	Average Size of Holdings per HH (ha)	No. of HH	Average No. of Plots per HH	Average Size of Holdings per HH (ha)
Always poor	13	1.54	1.05 (0.12)	13	1.69	1.10
Better off	20	2.55	1.6 (−0.41)	20	2.05	1.45
Worse off	19	3.21	1.91 (−0.79)	19	2.28	1.47
Never poor	13	3.15	2.39 (−1.18)	13	1.79	1.69

Source: Adapted from Tong et al. (2009a–c).

group also declined from 3.2 to 2.3 while the size of their landholdings became smaller by 0.4 hectares (see Table 3.8). As mentioned in Chapter 2, the bursting of the real estate bubble in mid-2008 featured a sharp deceleration in property demand and prices. True to this phenomenon, the RHS found that there were fewer land transactions by May 2009. In the same month, only 4 per cent of the respondent households, compared to 21 per cent in March 2008, reported selling agricultural land. Their lands did not lose much value over the same period, however.

Credit

One of the most disconcerting findings of the FGDs and SSIs is that many households were pushed further into the debt trap as a consequence of the crisis and other concurrent shocks. The dwindling of remittances, exhaustion of savings and lack of assets to sell drove households to seek credit which the crisis made more difficult and expensive to access. The RHS results do not echo the finding of increased debt burden. Between March 2008 and May 2009, the number of indebted respondent households was found to have fallen from 57 to 46 or from about two thirds to one-half of the total. The average loan size decreased by about 18 per cent, though this change was found to not be statistically significant. The survey results confirmed the increase in borrowing costs. The average rate of loan interest rose from 3.48 to 4.69 per cent between the two survey periods. The difference was statistically insignificant (see Table 3.9).

The informal credit market is known to be popular in rural Cambodia, so are the microfinance institutions (MFI) which have a wider presence in rural areas than the commercial banks. The survey findings confirm this. About half of the indebted households sourced their loans from their social contacts and private moneylenders. Fourteen of them borrowed from existing MFIs and sixteen borrowed from ACLEDA, an MFI until 2003. One finding that stood out was how loans from private moneylenders sharply contracted and became much more expensive. The loans availed from them shrank in size by more than 60 per cent and cost 3.25 percentage points more by May 2009 relative to March 2008. ACLEDA had few borrowers but the loans secured from it

TABLE 3.9
Debt Burden Did Not Necessarily Increase Though Borrowing Costs Did
(Loans by Source)

	Number		Average size ('0000 riels)			Average interest rate per month (%)		
	Mar 2008	May 2009	Mar 2008	May 2009	t Statistic	Mar 2008	May 2009	t Statistic
Relative/friend	14	12	44.33	59.42	−0.66	0.54	1.18	−0.7
Moneylender	13	13	144.13	51.15	2.09**	7.52	10.77	−1.18
MFI	14	12	72.50	73.00	−0.02	3.08	3.07	0.13
ACLEDA	16	9	146.88	177.78	−0.76	3.13	2.77	2.19**
Total	57	46	102.79	83.78	1.02	3.48	4.69	−1.35

Notes: (1) Excluding one case where the source is unidentified.
(2) Official exchange rates: 4131.6 riels to US$1 (May 2009); 3994.6 riels to US$1 (March 2008).
**Statistically significant at 5 per cent level.

Source: Adapted from Tong et al. (2009a–c).

TABLE 3.10
Social Networks and MFIs Were the Most Common Sources of Credit
(Number of Loans by Source and Poverty Status)

	Always Poor	Better Off	Worse Off	Never Poor	Total
Relative/friend	4	9	8	5	26
Moneylender	3	5	10	2	20
MFI	5	7	8	6	26
ACLEDA	4	6	9	5	24
Total	16	27	35	18	96

Source: Adapted from Tong et al. (2009*a–c*).

increased in size by 21 per cent and cost 0.36 percentage points less over the same period. Given the covariant nature of shocks, it is surmised that loans from personal contacts could have dried up. Indeed, fewer households reported having borrowed money from relatives and friends. While the loans secured were bigger in amount, they also cost roughly double than in March 2008. The worse off group took out the biggest number of loans, followed by the better off group (see Figure 3.10). There are two plausible explanations for this. One relates to the timing of borrowing: the worse off households were yet to see the effect of their loan utilization while the better off households had already experienced the benefits. The other explanation is that the debt proceeds were not sufficient enough to counter the welfare deterioration experienced by the households in the worse off group. The always poor group had the least number of loans. This is cause for concern given that it likely implies the much more limited credit access of the poorest households.

As indicated in Table 3.11, more than half of the loans were used for productive purposes, particularly as investment in agricultural and business activities. Loans are better used in this manner as they are then likely to result in a stream of, rather than just one-time, benefits. This loan use was most widely observed among the better off households. Another disturbing finding from the FGDs and SSIs is how, during the crisis, some households needed to borrow money just to satisfy their most basic needs, particularly food. This was seconded by the survey results. Eleven of the total loans contracted between March 2008 and May 2009 were used to purchase food; 15 were used to get medical care for ailing family members (see Table 3.11).

TABLE 3.11
About Half of the Loans Were Used for Productive Purposes
(Loan Use by Poverty Status)

	Always Poor	Better Off	Worse Off	Never Poor	Total
Consumption					
Food	3	2	3	3	11
Healthcare	5	3	5	2	15
Others	1	2	10	5	18
Production					
Agriculture	4	12	5	2	23
Business	3	8	12	6	29
Total	16	27	35	18	96

Source: Adapted from Tong et al. (2009*a–c*).

Coping Mechanisms

Coping mechanisms have been classified into *ex ante* and *ex post* strategies (Murdoch and Sharma 2002). *Ex ante* strategies are those that can strengthen immunity from the impact of a crisis while *ex post* strategies can mitigate losses when a crisis has already made its impact. *Ex post* strategies can be further classified into three types: adaptive strategies which mainly refer to adjustments in consumption; active strategies which pertain to adjustments in human, physical and financial assets (e.g. increasing labour force participation, distress sales, migration, and seeking credit); and social network strategies which involve seeking formal and informal social assistance (Fiszbein et al. 2003).

Table 3.12 shows that active strategies were the leading coping mechanisms. Nearly all the surveyed households employed these strategies by May 2009. The FGD and SSI results discussed in the next chapter together with this chapter's earlier discussions on asset ownership and indebtedness help substantiate the wide use of active coping strategies. Social network strategies, it turns out, were not that popular. This could be attributed to the lack of available formal assistance, uncovered by the FGDs and SSIs, and the fact that people in one's social networks could have likely reeled from the impact of shocks as well.

TABLE 3.12
Active Strategies Were the Most Widely Used
(Coping Strategies, Per Cent of Using Households)

	March 2008	May 2009
Adaptive strategies	3.13	5.56
Active strategies	81.25	94.40
Social network strategies	12.50	13.80

Source: Adapted from Tong et al. (2009*a–c*).

Poverty Incidence

The survey results strongly point to the worsening of poverty, as defined by per capita consumption, between March 2008 and May 2009. Figure 3.11 shows the 2008 and 2009 poverty incidence curves. These curves are basically the cumulative distribution functions of per capita real consumption, i.e. the proportion of population with per capita real consumption less than the amount found at the corresponding x-axis point. It can be gleaned from Figure 3.11 that for consumption

FIGURE 3.11
Changes in Poverty Incidence 2008–09

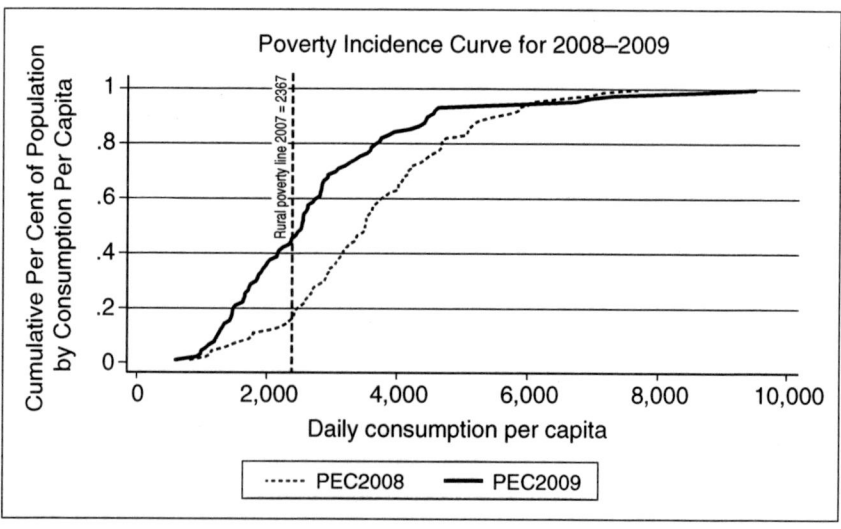

Source: Adapted from Tong et al. (2009*a–c*).

expenditure below about 6,000 riels, there were more households in poverty with such expenditure in May 2009 relative to March 2008. In sum, the poverty incidence in May 2009 was higher than the poverty incidence in March 2008 up to 6,000 riels. Set against the 2007 poverty line of 2,367 riels a day, the poverty rate increased from less than 20 to more than 40 per cent over the same period.

3.4 THE REALITY OF THE CRISIS TRANSMISSION

One consequence of the global crisis in Cambodia that was worse than the output contraction was the setback in poverty reduction. Cambodia may have been one of the countries that experienced an absolute increase in poverty. The results of the VWS and RHS, CDRI's flagship crisis assessment tools, generally suggest deterioration in the welfare of vulnerable workers and rural households as measured by income and consumption. All vulnerable workers experienced at least one contraction in income and consumption. Not all consumption changes, however, were aligned with the income changes, suggesting consumption smoothing. Set against earlier movements, the changes in income and consumption during the crisis were not exceptional. Fluctuations in the income and consumption of vulnerable workers have proved quite common in the past. Some previous declines were even worse than those experienced during the meltdown. Among the vulnerable worker groups, the unskilled construction workers appear to have been the most seriously affected. Rural households evidently suffered from deterioration in welfare. Due mainly to the decline in income from off-farm and other activities, average total per capita income dropped by a huge 31 per cent between March 2008 and May 2009. Poverty, as defined by per capita consumption, worsened for nearly 30 per cent of the surveyed households over the same period; for per capita consumption up to 6,000 riels, the poverty incidence increased. People had to reduce both food and non-food consumption. Poverty, as defined by asset ownership, seems to have also worsened but to a lesser extent than consumption. There may have been negligible change in the ownership of durable equipment but the changes in the ownership of livestock and land assets (number of plots and size) were significant. Further, both durable equipment and livestock assets experienced considerable price deflation. The number of loans may not have dropped but borrowing costs increased. On the upside, most loans were used for productive purposes the benefits of which would not have been observable in the short term. Active strategies were the most widely used coping mechanisms. While the results of the VWS and RHS are undermined by methodological weaknesses, they are enough to substantiate the reality of the crisis transmission into Cambodia at the micro level. The dramatic impact at the macro level does not justify policy-makers giving micro-level effects of the crisis secondary importance given that a sustainable recovery rests on ensuring that macroeconomic progress channels into the grassroots level at more or less an equal pace. Recovery from the crisis means not only the rebound of growth but also the acceleration of poverty reduction.

Notes

1. The authors would like to thank Pon Dorina, Phann Dalis and Hem Metta for their contribution and assistance in the preparation of this chapter.
2. Due to lack of funding, no surveys were conducted in said periods.
3. See footnote 1 of Chapter 1 for the definition of these concepts.
4. For a concise account of the debate, see for instance Maxwell (1999).
5. For details on the contention regarding the anti-cyclical nature of informal employment, see Maloney (1997), Galli and Kucera (2003), Charmes (1998), and Gërxhani (1999).
6. See also Jalilian, Reyes, and Lun (unpublished). CDRI (2008) presents relevant survey findings, one of which is that in spite of the 50 per cent increase in rice production costs, gross profit margins from selling rice increased by 38 per cent between 2007 and June 2008.
7. For more on these contentions, see Mody and Ohnsorge (2009), Caroll and Summers (1989), Campbell and N.G. Mankiw (1990), Palley (2005), and Miller (1996).
8. The PDS builds upon the Moving Out of Poverty Study conducted by CDRI in partnership with the World Bank in 2004–05. See Fitzgerald and So (2007) for the findings.
9. The dry season in Cambodia runs from November to May.
10. References to per capita income and per capita consumption are always in real and daily terms unless otherwise stated.
11. The inflation rate between March 2008 and May 2009 was estimated at 16 per cent..
12. See for instance Paxton (2001) and Sherraden (1991).

13. For purposes of simplifying the discussion, the term ownership and possession are used here liberally though without alluding to their legal validity.

References

Cambodian Development Resource Institute (CDRI). *Impact of High Food Prices in Cambodia*. Phnom Penh: CDRI, 2008.

Campbell, J. and N.G. Mankiw. "Permanent Income, Current Income and Consumption". *Journal of Business & Economic Statistics*, vol. 8, no. 3 (1990): 265–79.

Caroll, C. and L. Summers. *Consumption Growth Parallels Income Growth: Some New Evidence*. NBER Working Paper No. 3090. Cambridge: NBER, 1989.

Charmes, J. "Informal Sector, Poverty and Gender: A Review of Empirical Evidence". Background Paper for the World Bank's World Development Report 2001.

Fiszbein, A., P.I. Giovanoli, and I. Aduriz. "The Argentine Crisis and Its Impact on Household Welfare". *Cepal Review* 79 (April 2003).

Fitzgerald, I. and S. So. *Moving Out of Poverty Study: Trends in Community Well-Being and Household Mobility in Nine Cambodian Villages*. Phnom Penh: CDRI, 2007.

Galli, R. and D. Kucera. "Informal Employment in Latin America: Movements Over Business Cycles and the Effects of Worker Rights". International Institute for Labour Studies Discussion Paper 145/2003. Geneva: International Institute for Labour Studies, 2003.

Gërxhani, K. "The Informal Sector in Developed and Less Developed Countries". Tinbergen Institute Discussion Paper 1999-083/2. Amsterdam: Tinbergen Institute, 1999.

Jalilian, H., G. Reyes and P. Lun. "Cambodia's Food Security in the Face of the Food and Economic Shocks". Unpublished, 2010*a*.

Maloney, W. *Labour Market Structure in LDCs: Time Series Evidence on Competing Views*. World Bank Policy Research Working Paper No. 1940. Washington, D.C.: World Bank, 1997.

Maxwell, S. "The Meaning and Measurement of Poverty". Overseas Development Institute Poverty Briefing 3. London: Overseas Development Institute, February 1999.

Miller, T. "Explaining Keynes' Theory of Consumption and Assessing Its Strength and Weaknesses". Available at <http://www.economic-truth.co.uk/bsc/keynesconsumption.pdf> (accessed 28 October 2010).

Mody, A. and F. Ohnsorge. "After the Crisis: Lower Consumption Growth but Narrower Global Imbalances?". IMF Working Paper 10/11. Washington, D.C.: IMF, 2009.

Murdoch, J. and Manohar Sharma. "Strengthening Public Safety Nets from the Bottom Up". *Development Policy Review* 20, no. 5 (2002): 569–88.

Palley, T.I. "Social Attitudes, Labor Law, and Union Organizing: Toward A New Economics of Union Density". Working Papers wp93, Political Economy Research Institute, University of Massachusetts at Amherst, 2005.

Paxton, W. "The Asset Effect: An Overview". In *The Asset-Effect*, edited by J. Bynner and W. Paxton. London: Institute for Public Policy Research, 2001.

Sherraden, M. *Assets and the Poor: A New American Welfare Policy*. New York: Sharpe Incorporated, 1991.

Tong K., S. Khieng, M. Hem, D. Phann, and D. Pon. "Vulnerable Workers Survey in Phnom Penh, Kandal, Kampong Speu, Siem Reap and Battambang". Phnom Penh: CDRI, 2009*a*.

Tong K., C.H. Saing, S. Hem, D. Phann, M. Hem, and D. Pon. *Trends in Living Standards of 90 Rural Households in Poverty Dynamics Study Villages*. Phnom Penh: CDRI, 2009*a*.

———. "Vulnerable Workers Survey in Phnom Penh, Kandal, Kampong Speu, Siem Reap and Battambang: Second Round". Phnom Penh: CDRI, 2009*b*.

———. "Vulnerable Workers Survey in Phnom Penh, Kandal, Kampong Speu, Siem Reap and Battambang: Third Round". Phnom Penh: CDRI, 2009*c*.

———. "Vulnerable Workers Survey in Phnom Penh, Kandal, Kampong Speu, Siem Reap and Battambang: Fourth Round". Phnom Penh: CDRI, 2010.

World Bank. "Poverty Profile and Trends in Cambodia 2007: Findings from the Cambodia Socio-Economic Survey". Washington, D.C.: World Bank, 2009*a*.

———. "East Asia and Pacific Update — Transforming the Rebound into Recovery". Washington, D.C.: World Bank, 2009*b*.

———. "East Asia and the Pacific Update 2010: Emerging Stronger from the Crisis". Washington, D.C.: World Bank, 2010.

4

THE HUMAN FACE OF THE CRISIS
Key Findings of Focus Group Discussions with Vulnerable Workers and Households

Kem Sothorn, Theng Vuthy, and So Sovannarith[1]

4.1 COPING WITH THE GLOBAL CRISIS AND MORE

The human face of the global financial and economic meltdown vividly demonstrates the shock's catastrophic effects. The poor and the vulnerable are most at risk in the event of economic shock because, already living from hand to mouth, every penny counts to ensure their meagre income, minimum consumption, and the already fragile state of their overall human development. The range of coping mechanisms available to them is much more limited. Given that least developed countries such as Cambodia constantly suffer from insufficient funds, the availability and sustainability of social protection for the poor cannot always be guaranteed. The near-poor likewise are highly exposed to crises as they can easily fall under the poverty line given a loss of employment or greater underemployment. There is a lot to celebrate from the end of the global recession and movement towards economic recovery, albeit weak. However, the world cannot be comfortable as yet. It is not only that the threat of a double dip can become real anytime. It is also because even though the crisis has ended, some of its effects on the poor linger.

Cambodia's poverty headcount stood at 30 per cent in 2007. This could have increased by 1 to 4 percentage points due largely to the global crisis (World Bank 2009a). As outlined in Chapter 2, the poverty impact of the shock was the end result of the contraction in trade and capital inflows which in turn severely hurt Cambodia's garment, construction and tourism sectors. Although agricultural growth was not upset by the shock, the sudden deflation over the period of the crisis proved devastating especially for farmers who had made production investments against the expectation that the previous commodity price spikes would continue. The role of agriculture as crisis buffer was also undermined by its low absorptive capacity.

This chapter substantiates the estimated poverty increase in Cambodia during the crisis by overviewing the results of the FGDs and SSIs conducted by CDRI with vulnerable worker groups and rural households. It first provides a brief description of the aims and structure of the FGDs and SSIs before discussing each of their key findings. Two realizations from the discussions merit emphasis at the outset. First, the findings of the FGDs and SSIs cannot be exclusively attributed to the impact of the economic downturn. Such impact is hard to untangle from the effects of other past covariant shocks,[2] particularly the food and energy crises prior to the global recession. As emphasized in Chapter 2, some contractions felt in Cambodia over the period of the crisis were partially caused by the Thai-Cambodian political crisis, fiercer competition in the global garment business and the real estate bubble burst. There were also other micro-shocks such as weather abnormalities and pest infestations which resulted in crop failure, and idiosyncratic shocks such as family tragedies that occurred during the crisis period and contributed to the deterioration in household welfare. There were cases where it was not even the economic crisis but the coincident shocks that were reportedly the dominant reasons for the setback in well-being.[3] The results of the SSIs, for instance, showed family tragedy and illness as the most widely experienced shock. Divorce was another idiosyncratic shock often cited as a major cause of poverty, particularly for women and children. The second major realization is that ex post, as opposed to ex ante, coping mechanisms were the more pragmatic strategies for vulnerable workers and households. Chapter 3 introduced the concepts of ex ante and ex post coping strategies. The ex ante mechanisms mainly refer to employment and production strategies that seek to contain income variability while ex post strategies are those that are resorted to after income losses have been sustained (Morduch and Sharma 2002). Given the severe resource constraints that they were facing and the immediate monetary needs that were driving them to indulge in higher-risk higher-return livelihood activities, the vulnerable workers and households that participated in the FGDs and SSIs were only capable of adopting mainly ex-post, as opposed to ex-ante, coping strategies.

4.2 THE FOCUS GROUP DISCUSSIONS AND SEMI-STRUCTURED INTERVIEWS

4.2.1 Focus Group Discussions

There were four rounds of FGDs. The first three were conducted in May, August and November 2009. The final round took place in February 2010. Commissioned by the World Bank, the FGDs were a rapid assessment tool aimed to uncover: (1) the nature and scale of impact of the global crisis at the micro-level; (2) the coping strategies employed and the changes in them; and (3) the coverage and effectiveness of social safety nets.

FGD participants fell into two broad groups. The first represented vulnerable worker groups likewise targeted by CDRI's VWS while the second constituted households from the same provinces featured in CDRI's PDS (see Chapter 2). The first round of FGDs involved 64 participants while the subsequent three rounds had an average of 120 each. In total, 424 poor and vulnerable individuals took part in the four FGD rounds. This participation may be considered modest, thus putting into question the representativeness of the FGD findings. Ensuring the attendance of some participants in all the four rounds also proved tricky. Labour mobility made it difficult to keep track of all of them. This to some extent undermines the comparability of the FGD findings. Regardless, the results of the FGDs constitute a rich bank of empirical information about the household impact of the global crisis. Figure 4.1 shows that more than 90 per cent of the participants were aged between 15 and 64. This allowed a meaningful investigation of the labour market effects of the downturn. Approximately 60 per cent were female, allowing examination of any gender bias in the impact of the crisis.

Representatives of vulnerable worker groups comprised rice field workers, unskilled and skilled construction workers, garment factory workers, tuktuk drivers, cyclo drivers, waiters and waitresses, hotel and restaurant workers, small traders, and migrant workers. At the time of the FGDs, they were based in the capital Phnom Penh and major provinces of Siem Reap, Battambang, Kandal and Prey Veng. The workers had a mean number of only 4.7 years in school. About a quarter of them reported having had no education at all while 45 per cent had between 1 and 6 years of education. The rest reported having studied for 7 to 13 years (see Figure 4.1).

Participants were from rural households in Kandal, Kampot, Kampong Speu and Prey Veng provinces. Poverty in Cambodia is

FIGURE 4.1
FGD Participants Were Mostly of Working Age with Little Education
(Profile of FGD Participants)

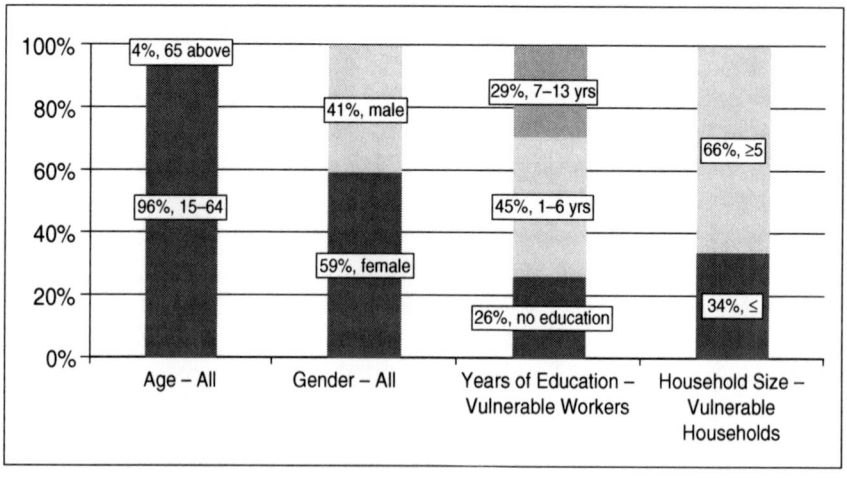

Source: Authors' calculations based on survey results.

concentrated in the rural areas, as mentioned in the earlier chapters. Based on the results of the CSES, the rural poverty rate stood at 34.7 per cent in 2007 while that for Phnom Penh was less than 1 per cent (World Bank 2009a). The provinces represent different geographical zones. Kampong Speu, which is situated in a mountainous area, is one of the poorest provinces in Cambodia with more than half of its population living below the poverty line in 2004. Prey Veng, located in the plains, had a poverty rate of 37 per cent in the same year. Kandal, which is on the plains flanking Phnom Penh, and Kampot, a coastal province, had much lower poverty rates in 2004 of 22 and 30 per cent respectively (World Bank 2007).[4]

4.2.2 Semi-structured Interviews

One round of semi-structured interviews (SSIs) with vulnerable workers, poor rural households and village chiefs was conducted in May 2009. The workers were based in the same locations and came from the same labour groups that took part in CDRI's Vulnerable Workers Survey. The interviewed rural households and village chiefs were from the same villages selected for CDRI's PDS. There were a total of 56 interviewees — 29 vulnerable workers, 18 households and 9 village chiefs. The workers represented the following labour groups: motor taxi drivers, small vegetable traders, porters, scavengers, unskilled construction workers, skilled construction workers, waiters/waitresses, restaurant and hotel workers, tuktuk drivers and rice field workers.[5] The households and village chiefs resided in the provinces of Battambang, Kampong Thom, Kratie, Prey Veng, Kampong Speu and Kampot.

The SSIs were also a rapid assessment tool like the FGDs but they had a narrower key research objective, namely to identify the informal safety nets that were adopted in response to the economic crisis. Informal support systems are ingrained in the Cambodian social fabric; the SSIs mainly aimed to uncover how and to what extent they were important during the economic turmoil. Additionally, the SSIs also attempted to get a sense of the general impact of the economic crisis. However, the end results of the SSIs, as those of the FGDs', cannot be attributed exclusively to the impact of the economic slump. Other covariant crises as well as idiosyncratic shocks were also cited as prominent grounds for resorting to informal social assistance during the period of the economic crisis.[6]

Furthermore, the small sample size makes generalizing the findings problematic. The results of the SSIs mostly appear in the sub-section on social safety nets.

4.3 KEY FINDINGS

The timing of the FGDs makes it possible to trace the changes in individual and household welfare as the Cambodian economy reacted to the different phases of the economic downturn and associated price trends. Chapter 2 explained that Cambodia's garment, tourism and construction sectors were hard hit by the external shock. Deflation occurred with the deepening of the crisis. As illustrated in Figure 4.2, the two FGD rounds in May and November 2009 occurred just as

FIGURE 4.2
The FGD Rounds Coincided with Different Phases of the Downturn
(Sectoral Performance and Inflation over the Period of the FGD Rounds,
y-o-y Percentage Change)

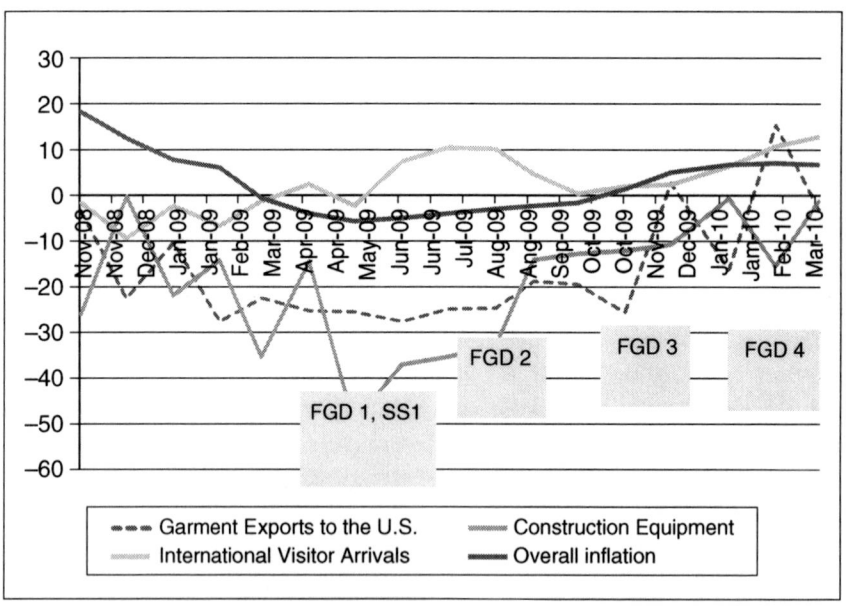

Source: Authors' calculations based on NBC (2010) and MoT (2009, 2010) data.

the garment and the construction industries seemed to have hit their lowest point while tourism was on the rebound and price levels were contained. The Cambodian economy appeared to have bottomed in the second half of 2009. The third and fourth FGD rounds took place when tourism and garments in particular were more clearly on the road to recovery. At the same time, however, prices began rising once again.

Despite the timeliness of the FGD rounds, the occurrence of micro or idiosyncratic shocks over the period of the crisis precludes the attribution of the FGD findings solely to the economic downturn. These more localized crises include family tragedies and diseases, though two recurring problems that stood out were weather abnormalities (e.g. longer dry season, above-average rainfall) and pest outbreaks. As mentioned in the introduction, the FGD findings may have also reflected the impact of the preceding food and energy shocks and the non-crisis related factors that helped bring about the downturn in the growth pillars (see Chapter 2).

With the above factors in mind, the key findings of the four FGD rounds are discussed in detail below. First, the changes in job availability and wage and earnings security of the affected workers and households are discussed. Then the coping mechanisms are identified. These strategies fall under six broad headings: labour market participation, consumption effect, migration and remittance, debt burden, utilization of common property resources, and social safety nets.

4.3.1 Employment and Income Effects

Impact on Job Availability and Security

Job search and retention became very difficult over the period of the crisis. The results of the first FGD in May 2009 round suggested a reduction in available jobs of 30 to 40 per cent. Those of the SSIs suggested a worse reduction of about 50 per cent.[7] The adverse employment impact of the global crisis was most pronounced for workers and households depending on the hard-hit garment and construction sectors, whereas construction jobs reportedly decreased by about 70 per cent. Jobs in the rural agricultural sector likewise became scarcer as lower commodity prices discouraged production and lessened demand for labourers. Cross-border migrant workers with on-farm jobs were no less unfortunate as the deflationary trend also dampened demand and production in neighbouring countries. Pest infestation,[8] unfavourable weather[9] and land sales during the property boom in 2007–08 caused further cuts in agricultural production and jobs. Job availability in other occupations was similarly problematic partly because of some non-crisis related factors. For instance, growing competition from the increasing number of tuktuk and motor taxi drivers consequently dimmed job prospects for cyclo drivers.

The labour market situation had become bleaker for most of the workers by the time of the second FGD round. As illustrated in Figure 4.2, tourist arrivals began to pick-up by August 2009. This reportedly enhanced the job prospects for tourism-dependent workers but not by a significant extent. Job search became an even greater struggle for unskilled construction workers even though to some extent it became easier for their skilled counterparts. Many dismissed garment workers turned to the construction sector for possible employment. This increased the supply of unskilled construction workers without any comparable increase in demand. Labour competition in unskilled construction work was also intensified by the migration of rural people during the off-farming season in the hope of landing a job in the construction industry.

The labour market situation had started to pick up for most workers by the third and fourth FGD rounds. With the economy yet to return to its pre-crisis vibrancy, however, job uncertainty remained a serious concern. The turnaround was most obvious for workers and households reliant on the garment and tourism industries. Laid-off garment workers were being re-hired by garment factories though their job security remained uncertain. This was ultimately because of fluctuations in the demand for Cambodian-made garments. Hotel and restaurant workers and small traders were also facing better job prospects due to the revival in international visitor arrivals. The chance of working full time for an entire month in the hotel and restaurant industry was greater. The employment situation for unskilled construction workers still had not changed, however. The FGD findings suggest that, among the vulnerable worker groups, the deterioration in the plight of the unskilled construction workers was the worst. More jobs opened up for their skilled counterparts but not for them. Two other worker groups for whom job prospects stayed gloomy were the cyclo drivers and migrant workers. Competition from tuktuk and motor taxi drivers continued to undermine the job security of cyclo drivers. Meanwhile, adverse weather conditions, particularly in bordering Thai provinces, cut the demand for migrant agricultural labour.

One notable finding from the FGDs is that off-farm employment and migration are important "job buffers" or sources of back-up employment. During the dry season or whenever demand for farm labour is lack lustre for whatever reason, agricultural workers engage in low-skilled off-farm work such as sea fishing, salt production, rice cake selling, shrimp and crab peeling and other manual jobs such as carrying rice sacks and soil. The FGD results suggest that these local off-farm job opportunities were not adversely affected by the down-turn. This is not supported by the VWS findings cited in Chapter 3. Meanwhile, internal and international migration has long been a popular alternative livelihood strategy for the poor everywhere. Increasing the poor's income security requires income source diversification. Migra-tion presents itself as one lucrative option. In Cambodia, many rural people migrate to the border areas for agricultural work or to urban areas for employment in the garment and construction sectors. Unfortunately, the global crisis severely impaired migration prospects. By no means, however, did this dry up migration flows, as discussed in more detail later.

Impact on Wage and Earnings

Mixed results came out of the FGDs in relation to wage trends. The daily wage rates appeared to have increased particularly for workers in the tourism sector, which as previously noted, had already started to recover by the time of the first FGD. With the rebound in tourist arrivals more apparent by the third FGD round, tuktuk drivers in Siem Reap saw their daily income rise by US$7 to US$8 between August and November 2009. A further increase of US$3 to US$5 was seen by March 2010. Tougher competition, however, often drove fares down to the minimum. Small traders also benefited from the revival in tourism though they also had to slash prices to stay competitive. Product and service diversification was another strategy used to enhance competitiveness.

In contrast, earnings of rural rice field workers at best stagnated over the period of the crisis. Around the peak of the downturn in Cambodia, their daily wage rates reportedly declined by a huge 30 to 50 per cent. As previously mentioned, adverse weather conditions and low commodity prices dampened demand for agricultural labour while the shift of laid-off workers from other sectors to agriculture expanded labour supply in that sector. With a greater number of workers fighting for a more limited number of jobs, rice field workers were compelled to accept lower wages. Lower agricultural prices alone trimmed profit margins. This was particularly true for cassava producers who, together with the rubber farmers, suffered from the biggest decline in demand and price during the economic recession. At one point, cassava sellers in Kanhchor village of Kratie province were being paid only a quarter of the old price for their goods (from 1,000 to 250 riels or US$0.2 to US$0.05 per kg between 2007 and around the third quarter of 2008).[10] Pest epidemic and livestock fatalities also hurt agricultural earnings. Rice field workers in Cambodia are hard pressed to undertake effective pest and animal disease control because of the high costs of inputs and lack of management know-how.

Construction workers and cyclo drivers were more or less in the same boat as the rice field workers. Even with the upturn and the associated improvement in job prospects, skilled construction workers had reportedly accepted daily wages that were about 30 per cent lower than the rates in 2008. The daily wages of some unskilled construction workers also reportedly fell from 20,000 riels (US$4.8) in May 2009 to less than 15,000 riels (US$3.6) in December 2009. A further decrease of 10 per cent was experienced by March 2010. The SSIs even uncovered incidences of construction workers being cheated of their wages by their foremen. Cyclo drivers reported lower or stagnant earnings. In the six months before the first FGD, they saw their daily earnings decline by about 30 per cent. Fiercer competition forced them to work longer hours in order to maintain their incomes. The SSI findings echoed the frustrations about the tougher competition. Waiters and waitresses in Phnom Penh generally did not experience any considerable decline in their daily wages but their incomes did suffer greatly due to the decline in tips and monthly financial perks. The restaurants where they worked were already offering discounted prices and running various promotions just to maintain their share of customers. One disconcerting finding is that competition, made even tougher by the crisis, seemed to have led to deterioration in working conditions. For restaurant workers, breaks were shortened or cancelled and leave benefits were curbed.

The unfavourable impact of the economic recession on earnings was most evident in the case of garment workers. As far as daily wage rates are concerned, some garment factories retained their base salary systems. Others switched to quota-based pay, an unwelcome development for their employees, given the fluctuations in the orders for Cambodian-made garments. Regardless of the developments affecting wage rates in the garment industry, however, reductions in working days, working hours and overtime work were enough to sharply bring down the income of garment workers. The turnaround in the performance of the garment industry did not necessarily lead to a reinstatement of their previous earnings. The third and fourth FGD rounds did not report any significant income change.

Across worker groups, the drop or stagnation in earnings resulted in smaller savings. In real terms, incomes and concomitant savings were further squeezed by the return of inflation. Consistent with overall price trends, participants in the August 2009 FGD round reported having to cope with prices higher than last May's, particularly those of meat and fish. These developments led to suspensions or reductions in remittance transfers. Incomes of rural migrant households consequently suffered to a significant degree, remittances typically being one critical source of such income.

4.3.2 Coping Strategies

Consumption Effect

Faced with tighter incomes and bleak labour market prospects, vulnerable workers and households had no choice but to cut back on their consumption. Reductions in both food and non-food consumption needed to be made at the time of the first and second FGD rounds. While decreases in terms of the quantity of food consumed were seen, the deterioration in terms of the quality of food consumed was more pronounced. The results of the SSIs confirmed this. Across worker groups, there was difficulty in sustaining the pre-crisis level of quality of food consumed. The rebound in food prices exacerbated this difficulty. The vulnerable workers and households were compelled to eat lower quality meat and fish or switch to eating less meat and fruits and more fish and vegetables. Meanwhile, cut backs in non-food consumption mainly came in the form of less spending on non-food items such as clothes, make-up, alcohol, cigarettes and recreation.

By the time of the third FGD round during which economic troubles eased the FGDs reported a general improvement in food intake. Pre-crisis levels of food consumption seemed to have been fully restored by the time of the fourth round. The quality of food consumed remained inferior, however. The vulnerable workers and households also continued to keep a tight rein on non-food consumption. This was especially true for the workers in urban areas who had to deal with rising house rents and utility costs. Among all the labour participants in the FGDs, the unskilled construction workers seemed to have experienced the worst impact of the crisis and other aggravating circumstances on consumption. Both their food and non-food consumption continued to suffer despite the economic upturn.

There are five other relevant findings from the FGDs worth noting. First, adult household members endured almost all the reductions in food consumption to spare the younger family members. Second, single workers had to make less sacrifices compared to those workers who were married and had children to support. This was observed in the case of the garment workers in particular. Third, food sharing or communal eating was a popular strategy to cope with the adverse consumption effects of the shocks and inflationary episodes. Workers, particularly in the construction and garment sectors, pooled their monies and cooked and ate together to save on food expenses. Fourth, internal remittances in the form of food were also made. Garment workers in the capital reportedly asked their parents to send them rice. Fifth, the consumption effect of adverse weather conditions and pest outbreaks, which in turn devastated rural agricultural production, was expected to endure. This problem was considered to be one of the longer-term challenges to rural household income generation.

Labour Market Participation

A leading strategy employed by vulnerable workers and households in order to cope with their embattled livelihoods and incomes was to make some tactical changes in their labour market participation. The most notable changes were the increase in the number of earners within the family, increase in the number of hours worked, juggling of several jobs, and shift in employment. Former non-participants in the labour market, particularly adult children and women, were compelled to join the throng of active job seekers in the hope that they could get work and contribute to household income generation. Older female children in particular tried to get work in the garment factories. One disconcerting finding from the FGDs is that there were cases where minors were forced to work. With reluctance, some parents reportedly had to withdraw their young children from school so they could do paid work. This was confirmed by the SSI findings. Children reportedly engaged in work such as salt production, one of the three occupations considered as the worst forms of child labour in Cambodia.[11] Children aged 13 to 18 also reportedly had to drop out of school for migrant employment in major urban areas, notably Phnom Penh, Sihanoukville and Koh Kong. They ended up working in domestic service (the young females specifically), food processing, agricultural plantation and the restaurant business.

Further, workers and rural household members felt compelled to increase their number of working hours in order to maintain or at least stay close to their pre-crisis income levels. Cyclo drivers, for instance, had to work an extra two or three hours each day to fight off the adverse effect of having had more competitors on the road. There were also many cases of individuals being engaged in more than one job in order to insure against any loss of one employment and or counter any decrease in working hours and earnings. Rural rice field workers and household members, for instance, depended on the off-farm and construction sectors to insure them against the setbacks in agriculture.

One other widely used coping mechanism uncovered by the FGDs was employment shift, which at times also entailed a shift in work location. This came in two forms, namely between formal sectors and from the formal to the informal sector. One example of the former involved the change in employment from being a rural farmer to being an unskilled construction worker in an urban area. The other type of employment shift gives cause for serious concern. In many cases, it involved the change in employment of laid-off or underemployed female garment employees to workers in the entertainment or waitressing industry where girls and women are highly exposed to sexual harassment and being coerced into prostitution.

The increases or drastic changes in vulnerable workers and rural employment had spill over effects on the responsibilities of other family members. Children below working age and the elderly in particular had to do a bigger share of household chores and other tasks such as childcare, gardening, tending to animals and foraging for food in common property resources. This enabled adult household members to devote more time to earning money.

Migration and Remittances

Several findings relating to migration and remittance trends stood out from the FGD results. First, no mass return migration, internal or international, took place. This affirms cross-country findings.[12] Some migrant workers were indeed reported to have returned and, once home, struggled to find employment. One of the SSI findings was that some garment and construction workers had headed back to their provinces and ended up working in agriculture. However, the more dominant trend seemed to have been that of migrant workers choosing to weather the crisis in their host countries or provinces and cities rather than go home. More of the workers who had lost their jobs opted to wait it out in their work areas till a job opportunity came along. Many migrant agricultural workers who were affected by the heavy rains and the consequent low demand for paid farm labourers in neighbouring Thailand chose to linger along the borders for any news on potential job vacancies.

Second, migration flows appeared to have not abated. Quite the opposite reportedly happened. This was contrary to popular expectations at the time. Rural-to-urban migration intensified but so did rural-to-rural migration, affirming the observations that many worker movements occur even between areas with no significant economic differentials.[13] Vulnerable workers and households were generally aware of the gloomy economic situation but they either considered the condition in their home provinces to be worse or were optimistic that they would get migrant employment one way or another. Ironically, in the six months before the first FGD round when the crisis was at its high point, outward migrants from Kampong Tnaot village in Kampot province reportedly increased by 30 to 40 per cent. Labour migration from Don Vong village in Kandal province for plantation work in Kampong Cham province, which was a rare occurrence in the past, intensified. The crop calendar also has significant influence on migration flows. The off-season has been generally associated with more emigration from agricultural areas while the on-season has generally seen more immigration and return migration. The crisis did not alter this trend. However, it did seem to limit, migrant visits during the off-season by increasing the direct and opportunity costs of travel.

Third, while migrant stocks and flows did not change drastically, remittance transfers did — according to the FGD and even the SSIs. The combined impact of greater job unavailability and insecurity, higher food and non-food prices, and lower earnings overall, squeezed savings and thus the amount that was left for remittance. Vulnerable rural households reported sharp declines in remittances from their migrant members, male or female, based in the urban areas. This was confirmed by the interviewed vulnerable workers. The SSI findings suggested a reduction in remittances of about 50 per cent and greater irregularity in the remittance schedule.[14] The slowdown in remittances appeared to have continued even as the economy began to recuperate. By the third FGD round, the cyclo drivers, skilled and unskilled construction workers and migrant workers still had nothing to remit. By the fourth FGD round, only a few garment workers could still afford to send between US$30 and US$60 per month to their expectant families.

Fourth, over the period of the crisis, "reverse remittances" or "rural-to-urban remittances", both in cash and in kind, were seen. Barely surviving, garment workers to be specific had called on their families or relatives in the provinces to send them money or rice.

Indebtedness

One trend was clear from the FGD and even the SSI results. The debt burden of vulnerable workers and rural households increased over the period of the crisis. Many of them fell into the debt trap or, for those already in serious debt before, became even more deeply entrenched. This finding is not supported by the VWS findings. The debt profile of the FGD participants indicates that loans were owed to formal, semi-formal and informal lenders. Commercial banks were not a popular source of credit; formal loans were nearly all secured from MFIs. In Trapeang Prei village alone, the number of microfinance borrowers reportedly went up by roughly 50 per cent in the six months preceding the first FGD round and SSI. Semi-formal and informal loans on the other hand were sourced from savings groups, unlicensed money-lenders, rice and cow banks, and personal contacts including co-family members, relatives, friends and neighbours. Savings groups that were initiated in several villages by NGOs proved helpful to distressed households over the period of the crisis. SSI interviewees reported having successfully borrowed money from savings groups at a monthly interest of 3 per cent.[15]

In brief, the economic downturn and coincident shocks increased the debt burden by forcing poorer workers and households to incur new loans which, given the tighter credit market, were more difficult to access and came at a higher cost. Debt proceeds were used to repay outstanding liabilities, finance migration of family members, pay for agricultural investments, house construction, repairs and other asset purchases, secure medical care, and cover traditional ceremonial expenses (e.g. weddings and funerals). Under normal circumstances, savings would have helped in covering such major expenses. Some participants mentioned that during the economic boom, they had little problem repaying loans out of the extra income they earned mostly from working off-farm or the remittances sent by co-family members. However, as previously explained, savings and remittances were virtually exhausted or drastically reduced over the crisis period. The direness of vulnerable people's financial situation was no less than that demonstrated by the fact that some borrowing was just to cover the most basic expenses, notably food. The VWS results confirm this. Some rice field workers even entered informal financing arrangements where they promised to repay their debt with a certain fraction of their wage or agricultural output. Alternatively, assets would be sold. Unfortunately, poor households typically have few or no assets to begin with as revealed by the VWS. Quite a number of interviewed households also reported losing whatever asset they had, typically land and house, to lenders, having failed to meet their payment obligations. FGD results suggest that the increased landlessness in Kampong Tnaot can be explained by collateral repossessions by lenders and distress sales by land owners in order to generate cash for loan repayment. Some FGD participants from Kampong Tnaot also mentioned making forced sales of their houses and or homestead lands so they could repay their debt. Some households in Don Vong village attempted to sell their draught animals for the same purpose[16] but were discouraged by the low bid prices. The debt burden reportedly had become unbearable for some individuals in that they were forced to "disappear" from their villages and permanently escape their debt collectors. Much to their frustration, the guarantors for these runaway borrowers then inherited the debt burden. Scores of loan defaults also bankrupted or nearly bankrupted savings groups and rice and cow banks.

As the crisis progressed, securing credit from MFIs seemed to have become less and less an option. Only a few participants reported having taken out loans from MFIs by the third FGD round. The migrant workers were on a par with the cyclo drivers who wanted to buy or upgrade their motorcycles. Lands were pledged as collateral. In place of formal credit, borrowing from informal lenders, particularly personal contacts, assumed greater importance as a coping strategy. Money lending at no interest was practised among co-workers. The size of loans that could be obtained from informal sources was often insufficient, however. The covariant nature of several shocks also debilitated the expected lenders and made them much more reluctant to lend money in a highly uncertain environment. The revival of the economy brought hope to indebted workers and households but not much. Many interviewed garment, hotel and restaurant workers were able to meet their regular payment obligations. Migrant households that started to receive remittances again were also able to find some debt relief. However, other workers, particularly cyclo drivers and unskilled construction workers who appeared to have experienced the worst of the crisis among all worker groups, continued to struggle to repay their debt. With great reluctance, more villagers from Don Vong, Andoung Trach and Kampong Tnaot had to sell their houses to raise the cash necessary to pay off their microfinance lenders. Some were also forced to sell their motorcycles and draught animals. For rice field workers, their chances of getting out of the debt trap were even slimmer due to the crop damage caused by harsh weather and pest outbreaks.

Exploitation of Common Property Resources

One other coping mechanism that proved popular all throughout the crisis was the exploitation of common property resources. FGD results indicate that this task primarily fell on young children and the elderly. As discussed earlier, the global crisis and coincident shocks forced adult household members to increase their labour force participation. This meant the rest of the family had to either become income-earners or help by any other means to support the family livelihood and mitigate nutritional risks. One of these means was foraging for food and other resources in the commons, including fish, crabs, snails, bamboo shoots, vegetables and wild leaves. The greater pressure on common property resources naturally raised concern about possible resource depletion. Kampong Tnaot, a coastal village, was reportedly already suffering from badly depleted fish stocks.

Social Safety Nets

Social safety nets refer to interventions that aim to alleviate the risks facing the poor and the vulnerable or, in other words, to insure the uninsured. They are distinct from other types of social protection in that they are non-contributory (Grosh et al. 2008). Given their objective, social safety nets assume critical importance in periods of crisis. Based on source of funding and provider, there are two types: the public or formal safety nets which are financed by national budget and international aid and provided by the government and non-government organizations; and the private or informal safety nets which are basically household and community transfers.[17]

One clear finding from the FGDs is that only minimal public safety nets reached the interviewed vulnerable workers and households during the economic downturn. Some infrastructure construction, medical service provision, health awareness campaigns, food-for-work schemes and school feeding programmes were undertaken by government and non-government bodies alike; however, these were routine activities, not crisis-responses. No intensification in their provision was observed. In Trapeang Prey village, food aid and livestock were distributed by World Vision and LICADHO[18] to poor households. Some assistance also reportedly came from the Cambodian Red Cross.[19] However, reflecting the overall nature of social safety net programmes in the country, these forms of support were limited in geographical scope and duration and seemingly unsustainable. They were mostly emergency relief for calamity victims (e.g. victims of natural disasters and fire).

In the absence of formal safety nets, people depended more on private support systems. Informal social assistance, as mentioned in the beginning, is ingrained in Cambodian social fabric. It is anchored on kinship, communal and patron-client relationships and considered a social, cultural and religious obligation. Alternatively, household shocks are viewed as having spill-over effects to the rest of the community; hence, they entail collective responses. For the vulnerable workers and households, the covariant nature of several shocks meant that the difficulties they experienced were also shared by many in their support networks. FGD participants confided sensing an increase in individualism among people over the period of the crisis. Many were strongly reluctant or simply had no means to help. Of the private transfers actually received, more were in kind and in the form of service rather than in cash. For instance, the social ties that vulnerable workers had built enabled them to become privy to information about job prospects and skill training opportunities among others. Construction workers, who took good care of their relationship with foremen, turned to them for much-needed assistance in their job search. Social networks proved extremely useful in coping with other micro shocks as well. For example, cyclo drivers, construction workers, porters and garment workers had helped their co-workers get medical attention and or banded together to protect themselves from crime and violence. Group travelling also became a popular strategy, especially among female garment workers and waitresses. The SSI informants reported an increase in the incidence of theft and robbery from late 2008. Another outstanding collective crisis response was job hunting and wage bargaining as a group. Rice field workers, for example, had reportedly been able to negotiate for full pay by selling their labour as a group. These workers' risk pooling strategies help perpetuate the culture of informal mutual insurance. Community members and associations had also helped households struck by family tragedy. Help came in the form of cash, rice and other food donations, labour and other in-kind support. For example, one participant from Ba Baong village reported receiving 400,000 riels from the community funeral association. Traditional support networks in Cambodia also include pagoda committees and other religious groups. Political parties in the country, being essentially rooted in patron-client relations, can also be considered a traditional source of social assistance. The FGDs found that all these specific institutions failed to provide significant social protection over the period of the crisis. Assistance from the pagodas was mostly limited to ill elders while those from political parties were essentially in the form of electoral sweeteners[20] and thus perceived as politically motivated and restricted to the electoral period.[21] Unions are relatively modern sources of informal social assistance in Cambodia. Unions in the garment industry have generally offered worker protection against labour rights violations and support in negotiations with employers. With the industry severely hit by the global crisis as described in Chapter 2, many factories shut their gates permanently or temporarily halted their operations or downsized their workforce. Unions proved highly useful as a support network, ensuring that these developments did not trample on the legal rights of workers. Their success rates varied, however.

4.4 INSURANCE IS ASSURANCE

In times of adversity the poor are at greater risk because of the narrower range of coping mechanisms available to them. It is estimated that poverty in Cambodia may have worsened during the crisis. The FGDs and SSIs, and CDRI's qualitative crisis assessment initiative sought to find evidence for such a claim and determine the coping strategies employed to deal with any adverse impact. One important revelation is that the global crisis alone cannot account for the welfare deterioration observed during the recession. Along with other covariant shocks such as the preceding food crisis and weather abnormalities, idiosyncratic shocks such as family tragedies were also central causes of increased hardship. Jobs became scarcer and difficult to retain during the crisis period. The adverse employment impact of the slump in the growth sectors was compounded by the problems of unfavourable weather, pest infestations, increased competition and lower food prices which discouraged agricultural production. Even with the pick-up in economic activity, job uncertainty remained high. For some worker groups, earnings had stagnated. Tougher competition basically forced price wars. The quantity, but more so the quality, of food consumption went down, giving rise to concern about the longer-term problem of food security. Labour market participation increased and tactical employment shifts were undertaken, leading to concerns about increased child labour and exposure to sexual exploitation. Mass return migration may not have transpired but stagnation in earnings resulted in stagnation in remittances, cutting off one vital source of rural household income and multiplying the effects of the relevant shocks. The debt burden intensified as demonstrated by the incurrence of more expensive loans in order to buy food. Dependence on common property resources increased, risking resource abuse and depletion. Formal social protection was barely present while informal assistance was less available than usual given the covariant nature of some shocks. Evidently, the defences of the poor against covariant and idiosyncratic crises have been weak and unsustainable. This highlights the need to bolster the government's ex-ante and ex-post crisis responses which in turn entail not only quick fixes but also deeper reforms. Increasing the poor's access to formal insurance against risk translates to providing them greater assurance about their chances of escaping the poverty trap.

Notes

1. The authors would like to thank Chhim Chhun for his assistance and contribution to the preparation of this chapter.
2. See Chapter 1 for the definition of covariant and idiosyncratic shocks.
3. Previous studies (Fitzgerald and So 2007, Ballard et al. 2007, Koy and Em 2009) similarly uncovered dominant effects of idiosyncratic shocks on household welfare.
4. Poverty rates are based on the CSES 2004.
5. Five garment workers and two individuals from each of the other groups.
6. Six months to a year before the round in May 2009.

7. Within a period of about six months, before the first FGD round and the SSIs.

8. For instance, pest outbreaks drastically decreased rice yields in Trapeang Prei village in Kampong Speu province, Ba Baong village in Prey Veng province, and Kampong Tnaot village in Kampot province. Third round FGD participants from Trapeang Prei reported that rat infestation caused rice yields to decrease by about 30 per cent relative to 2008. SSI interviewees from the same village complained of widespread lightning strikes. Meanwhile, the first round FGD in Kampong Tnoat reported a 50 per cent decline in rice yields since the 2008. Also during the first FGD round, farmers from Ba Baong complained about the devastation caused by brown plant hoppers. The SSI results placed the harvest loss caused by such infestation at 30 to 50 per cent.

9. For instance, the two villages in Battambang, Andoung Trach and Krasang, experienced too much rain during the wet season and a longer dry season. Harsh weather also affected Don Vong village in Kandal province and Trapeang Prei, Kampong Tnaot and Ba Baong villages.

10. Conversions to USD are based on the exchange rate, US$1 = 4,150 riels.

11. Theng et al. (2005), according to this report, the other two most hazardous occupations that employ child labour in Cambodia are rubber plantation and fishing.

12. See for instance Awad (2009).

13. See for instance Ratha and Shaw (2007).

14. Within the six months before the SSI.

15. Savings groups were reported to have operated in Trapeang Prei, Krasang, Kanhchor, Kampong Tnaot and Ba Baong villages. The very poor, however, lacked access to these institutions given the mandatory payment of a membership fee of 5,000 to 10,000 riels.

16. Loans were owed to ACLEDA, a commercial bank which started as a microfinance institution in Cambodia.

17. This distinction is partly based on the relevant definition in Grosh et al. (2008).

18. LICADHO is a domestic NGO.

19. The assistance for each recipient reportedly included 50 kilograms of milled rice, a tent, some clothes, cotton scarves and 580,000 riels.

20. Assistance from the political parties to each recipient household reportedly included 50 kilograms of milled rice, a sarong, a cotton scarf and/or 50,000 to 100,000 riels.

21. Sub-national elections in Cambodia took place in May 2009.

References

Awad, I. "The Global Economic Crisis and Migrant Workers: Impact and Response". Geneva: ILO, 2009.

Ballard B., C. Sloth, D. Wharton, I. Fitzgerald, K. Murshid, K. Hansen, R. Phim, and S. Lim S. "We Are Living with Worry All the Time: A Participatory Poverty Assessment of Tonle Sap". Phnom Penh: CDRI, 2007.

Fitzgerald, I. and S. So. *Moving Out of Poverty? Trends in Community Well-being and Household Mobility in Nine Cambodian Villages*. Phnom Penh: CDRI, 2007.

Grosh, M., C. del Niño, E. Tesliuc, and A. Ouerghi. *For Protection and Promotion: The Design and Implementation of Effective Safety Nets*. Washington, D.C.: World Bank, 2008.

Kem S. and V. Theng. "Rapid Assessment of the Impacts of the Economic Crisis on Cambodian Households and Vulnerable Workers: Road to Recovery: Third Round". Phnom Penh: CDRI, 2009.

————. "Rapid Assessment of Impacts of Global Economic Crisis on Cambodian Households and Vulnerable Workers: Fourth Round". Phnom Penh: CDRI, 2010.

Koy R. and S. Em. "Building Community Capacity for Poverty Reduction Initiatives". Baseline Survey for the ADB, 2009.

Ministry of Tourism. *Tourism Statistical Report*. Phnom Penh: MoT, 2009.

————. *Tourism Statistical Report*. Phnom Penh: MoT, 2010.

Murdoch, J. and M. Sharma. "Strengthening Public Safety Nets from the Bottom Up". World Bank Social Protection Discussion Paper Series No. 0227. Washington, D.C.: World Bank, 2002.

National Bank of Cambodia. *Annual Report 2009*. Phnom Penh: NBC, 2010.

Ratha, D. and W. Shaw. *South-South Migration and Remittances*. World Bank Working Paper No. 102. Washington, D.C.: World Bank, 2007.

So S. *Informal Risk Management/Safety Net Practices: Experiences of Poor Vulnerable Workers and Households*. Mimeo. Phnom Penh: CDRI, 2009.

So S., Theng V. and S. Kem. "Rapid Assessment of Impacts of Global Economic Crisis on Cambodian Household and Vulnerable Workers' Income, Consumption and Coping Strategies: Second Round". Phnom Penh: CDRI, 2009.

Theng C., M. Seang, and K. Sao. *Experiences and Lessons Learned on Child Labour Monitoring: Rubber, Salt and Fishing Sectors in Cambodia*. Phnom Penh: Ministry of Labour and Vocational Training and ILO, 2005.

Theng V. and S. Kem. "Rapid Assessment of the Impact of the Economic Crisis on Cambodian Households: Focus Group Discussions with Vulnerable Workers and Households: First Round". Phnom Penh: CDRI, 2009.

World Bank. *Sharing Growth: Equity and Development in Cambodia*. Washington, D.C.: World Bank, 2007.

———. *East Asia and Pacific Update — Transforming the Rebound into Recovery*. Washington, D.C.: World Bank, 2009a.

———. *Poverty Profile and Trends in Cambodia 2007*. Washington, D.C.: World Bank, 2009b.

5

THE FOOD AND ECONOMIC CRISES
Impact on Food Security and Agriculture in Cambodia

Hossein Jalilian, Glenda Reyes, and Lun Pide

5.1 INTRODUCTION

The preceding chapters have provided detailed analysis of the impact of global financial and economic crisis (GFEC) on Cambodia's economy and the poor there. However almost a year before the GFEC, the world witnessed an unprecedented increase in prices of food and most agriculture products which was as devastating for the poor as the GFEC was. Although the two crises differ in their origins and breadth of impact, they have endangered food security and therefore setback poverty alleviation efforts, especially among marginalized groups in both rural and urban areas. In this chapter we focus on analysing the impact of the twin crises — GFEC and food price increases that preceded it — on the poor in Cambodia.

The rest of the chapter is structured as follows. Section 2 provides detailed analysis of the impact of food price increases on food security. Given that food security is also affected by the state and pace of change within the agriculture sector, the impact of food prices on agriculture is looked at as well. Section 3 explores the impact of GFEC on food security and agriculture. Finally section 4 offers some recommendations and concludes the chapter.

5.2 IMPACT OF THE FOOD CRISIS ON FOOD SECURITY AND AGRICULTURE

5.2.1 Food Price Trends and Determinants of Impact

What was unique about the food price trends witnessed in 2007–08 was not the price escalation itself. Steep price increases also occurred in 1973–74, chiefly because of the oil crisis. What set the food price movements in 2007–08 apart was that the prices of almost all major food and non-food commodities soared at the same time (FAO 2008) and more importantly, that the confluence of old and new drivers may have started a long trend of higher than average food prices.

The full-blown crisis entailed food price record highs. For each of the first six months of 2008, the international food price index registered a year-on-year increase of more than 50 per cent on average. The world rice price index in particular rose year-on-year by an alarming 118 per cent on average per month during the second and third quarters of 2008. Major international non-food price indices similarly experienced steep increments. For the first six months of 2008, the world energy price index climbed year-on-year by 73 per cent per month on average (see Figure 5.1). These exceptional food price trends have been well scrutinized in the literature. There appears to be consensus that biofuel production, higher input prices (particularly oil) and depreciation of the US dollar were the dominant triggers behind the surge in food commodity prices. There is also consensus that some commodity-specific triggers were at work, including prohibitive policies in the case of rice. The longer term causes of the price escalation are equally, if not more important. Paramount among them has been the stagnation of aid and public investment in agriculture which has stunted agricultural productivity growth (for related studies, see Abbot et al. 2008; Heady and Fan 2008; Timmer 2008; de la Torre Ugarte and Murphy 2008; OECD-FAO 2008). Public investment in agriculture is said to have been flat in the last twenty years (Fan 2008 cited in de la Torre Ugarte and Murphy 2008; World Bank 2008) while simultaneously, aid has steadily declined (FAO and WFP 2009).

FIGURE 5.1
International Commodity Indices

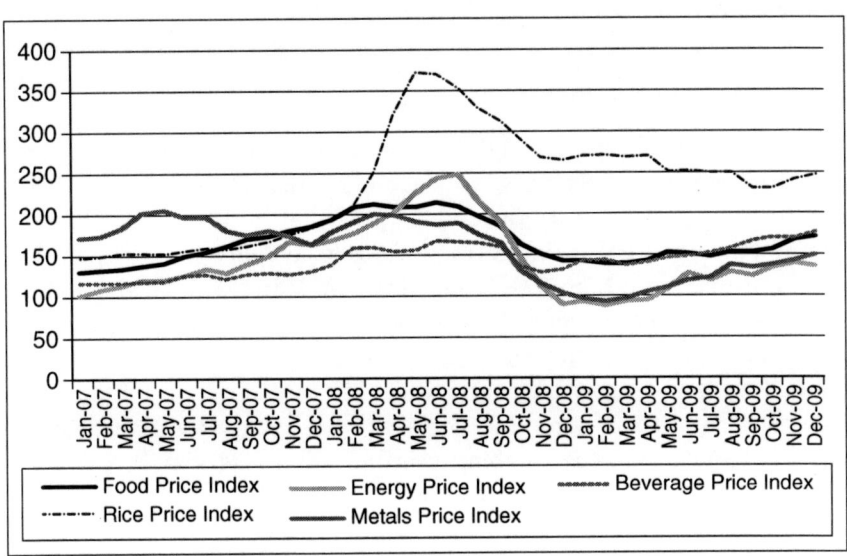

Source: FAO (2008); IMF (2010).

The poor stand to lose the most in a food crisis because the majority of their income is spent on food and they have more limited means of coping with shocks. The estimated 11 per cent (or 80 million) increase in people who were food insecure in 70 developing countries in 2008 largely represented the deterioration in the purchasing power of poor people (USDA 2009). As a result of the food shock, under-nourishment also became more widespread. The number of under-nourished people is estimated to have increased from 873 million in 2004–06 to 915 million in 2008 (FAO and WFP 2009). Even the poor and undernourished, however, are not homogeneous. The global impact also covers nuances in country experiences. Delineating the effects of the food crisis, or any shock for that matter, on food security entails analysis of several determinants including price transmission, household consumption, income and expenditure characteristics, agricultural production status and supply response, and government and non-government responses.[1] It merits stressing as well that the short-run impact of shocks may differ from the long-run impact given how supply responses and government and non-government actions may alter the national and household capacity to deal with crises.

5.2.2 Price Transmission

The food crisis swept through Cambodia with the rise in domestic commodity prices becoming noticeable by the second half of 2007 and reaching full intensity by mid-2008. Overall year-on-year inflation in Cambodia soared to an alarming 36 per cent in May 2008 having averaged not more than 8 per cent per month in 2007. Food inflation soared year-on-year to more than 50 per cent in May 2008, and the rice price index rose year-on-year by a record 106 per cent. Meat, fish and seafood, fruit and vegetable price indices likewise registered exceptional increases. Non-food commodity prices also surged, with transport and utility price indices climbing year-on-year by 24 and 29 per cent, respectively, in May 2008 (see Figures 5.2 and 5.3).

FIGURE 5.2
Domestic Food Commodity-Specific Inflation
(y-o-y)

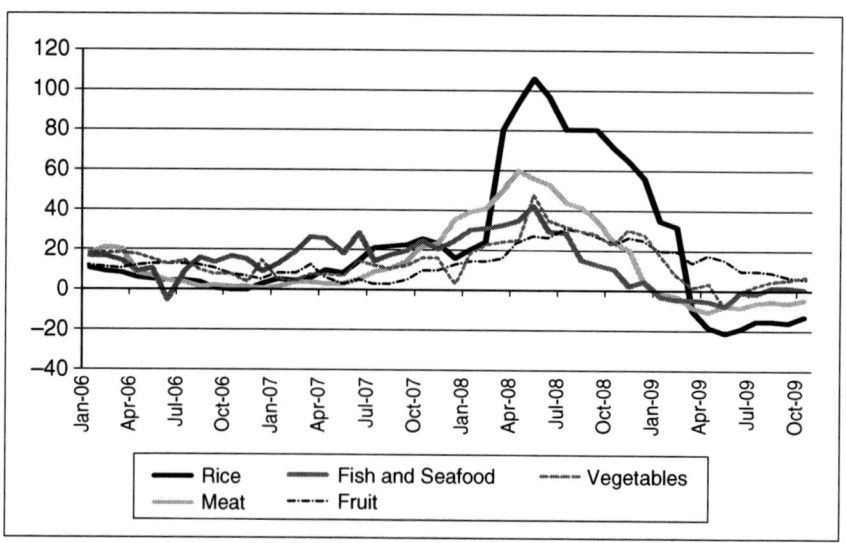

Note: Price indices used have the reference base period October–December 2006.
Source: Authors' calculations based on data from NIS (2008, 2009).

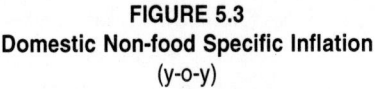

FIGURE 5.3
Domestic Non-food Specific Inflation
(y-o-y)

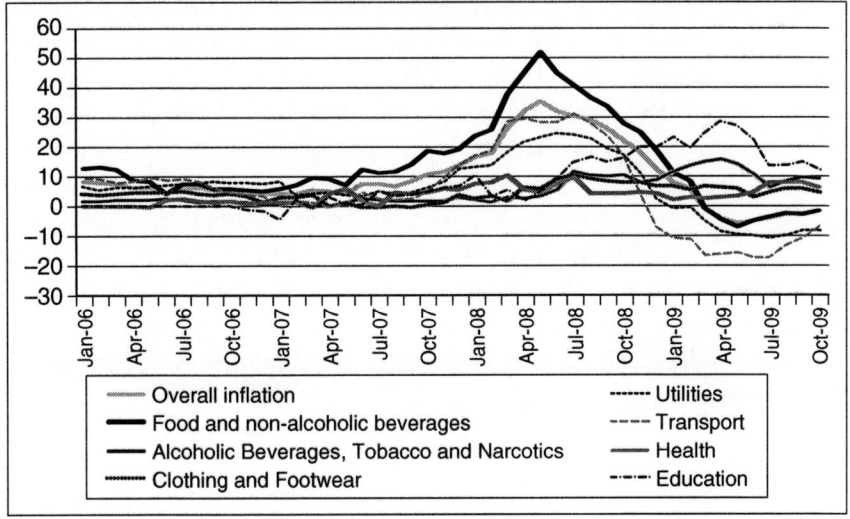

Source: Authors' calculations based on data from NIS (2008, 2009); von Grebmer et al. (2008, 2009).

What would be interesting to find out is the extent to which the domestic food inflation reflected the escalation in international food prices. True, not international but domestic prices are featured in household budgets and expenditures. Timmer (2008) however states that at least 75 per cent of international food price increases are transmitted to domestic price changes in so-called free-trading countries. In so-called stabilizer countries, domestic prices are significantly shielded from world price fluctuations by distortionary government interventions. The strength of the national currency against the U.S. dollar also affects the degree of price increase transmission in that national currency appreciation against the dollar minimizes such transfers (ibid.). Another factor worth mentioning is the general stickiness of prices which causes domestic price adjustments to occur after some time lag.

Given the prominence of rice in Cambodian household consumption, we focus on rice price transmission. Price transmission calculations were based on Dawe's (2008) method.[2] Calculations were also made for maize, pork and beef. As shown later, meat is central to urban diet though domestic demand for meat is largely met by domestic production; the share of imports in total consumption was found to be minimal (see, for example FAO 2008) though imports appear to be rising fast, especially those from neighbouring Thailand. Meanwhile, maize has potential to substitute rice. Fish and vegetables are critical components of the rural Cambodian diet but lack of comparable data precludes calculation of the relevant price transmissions. In relation to non-food items, it was deemed useful to calculate the price transmission for gasoline and fertilizer inasmuch as price trends for these two have bearing on the response of agricultural production to food price inflation. Counterfactual prices were also calculated for rice and gasoline given the hypothesis that government responses to the food and economic shocks significantly influenced the changes in the prices of these commodities.

Food Price Transmission

Based on Dawe's (2008) method, world rice prices are first converted into the national currency. Figure 5.4 maps both actual domestic and international prices in riels. A cursory look gives an idea how, in the middle of 2008, actual domestic rice prices broke away from the previous trend of closely tailing world rice prices. This implies a shift in the characteristic of Cambodia from being more of a free trader to more of a stabilizer upon the peaking of rice prices. Results are presented in Table 5.1.

One finding is that the increases in average actual world and domestic rice prices in riels nearly match each other. This is explained by the stability of the riel-US$ exchange rate and Cambodia's heavy dollarization. The next findings will have to be considered in tandem. Between the fourth quarter of 2007 and third quarter of 2008, about 84 per cent of the rise in average world price was passed to domestic consumers; therefore, Cambodia was more a free trader of rice in this period. This seems to contradict what is clear in Figure 5.4 and what should follow from the fact that Cambodia was among the rice-exporting countries that adopted export restrictions in response to the food shock. As pointed out in Section 3.5, however, the Cambodian rice

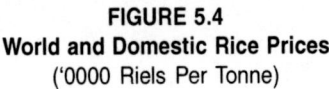

FIGURE 5.4
World and Domestic Rice Prices
('0000 Riels Per Tonne)

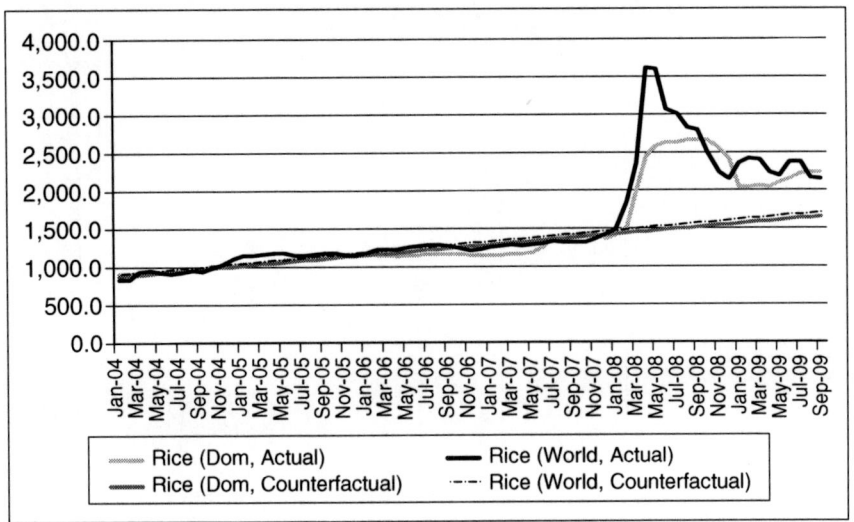

Note: Subject commodities refer to the following (as identified in the sources used): Domestic —
     rice quality #2; International — Thai rice 5 per cent broken.
Source: Authors' calculations based on data from NIS (2008, 2009) (domestic); IRRI (2010)
     (international).

export ban was effective only from late March to May 2008. The gap
that can be seen in Figure 5.4 really pertains to this period. Calculations
show that the pass through was significantly lower for March to
August 2008 (the extended period is to take into account any time lag
effects) than for September 2007 to February 2008. At about 68 per
cent, the pass-through was still significant, however, and not enough to
classify Cambodia as a stabilizer (see Table 5.2). The rice export ban
could not have been that effective because of the limited period of its
enforcement, its exceptions, and the considerable informal rice trade
along the borders.

Counterfactual price calculations show that if it were not for the
food crisis, both world and domestic price increases would have been
minimal. Had rice been freely traded i.e. in the absence of government
response to the crisis, Cambodian prices would have fully absorbed the

TABLE 5.1
Actual Food Price Transmissions during the Food Crisis
(Q4 2007–Q3 2008)

Commodity	World Price (US$ % Change)	World Price (Riels % Change)	Domestic Price (Riels % Change)	Pass Through (3/1) (%)
Rice	104	109	88	84
Maize	44	47	8	19
Pork	16	18	26	165
Beef	7	9	24	335

Note: Subject commodities refer to the following (as identified in the sources used): Domestic — rice quality #2, maize (yellow), pork, beef no. 1; International — Thai rice 5 per cent broken; maize (U.S. no. 2 yellow), U.S. beef export, U.S. pork frozen.

Source: Authors' calculations based on data from NIS (2008, 2009); MAFF (2010) (domestic); IRRI (2010); FAO (2010) (international).

TABLE 5.2
Actual Rice Price Transmissions - Effect of the Rice Export Ban

Period	World Price (US$ % Change)	World Price (Riels % Change)	Domestic Price (Riels % Change)	Pass Through (3/1) (%)
September 2007–February 2008 vs. March–August 2008	109	110	74	68

Note: Cambodia's rice export ban was effective from March to May 2008 but a longer period is selected to account for possible time lag effects; subject commodities refer to the following (as identified in the sources used): Domestic — rice quality #2; International — Thai rice 5 per cent broken.

Source: Authors' calculations based on data from NIS (2008, 2009) (domestic); IRRI (2010) (international).

TABLE 5.3
Counterfactual Rice Price Transmissions during the Food Crisis

Period	World Price (US$ % Change)	World Price (Riels % Change)	Domestic Price (Riels % Change)	Pass through (3/1) (%)
Q4 2007–Q3 2008	7	7	7	108
September 2007–February 2008 vs. March–August 2008	4	5	5	108

Note: Subject commodities refer to the following (as identified in the sources used): Domestic — rice quality #2; International — Thai rice 5 per cent broken.
Source: Authors' calculations based on data from NIS (2008, 2009) (domestic); IRRI (2010) (international).

FIGURE 5.5
Actual World and Domestic Maize Prices
('0000 Riels Per Tonne)

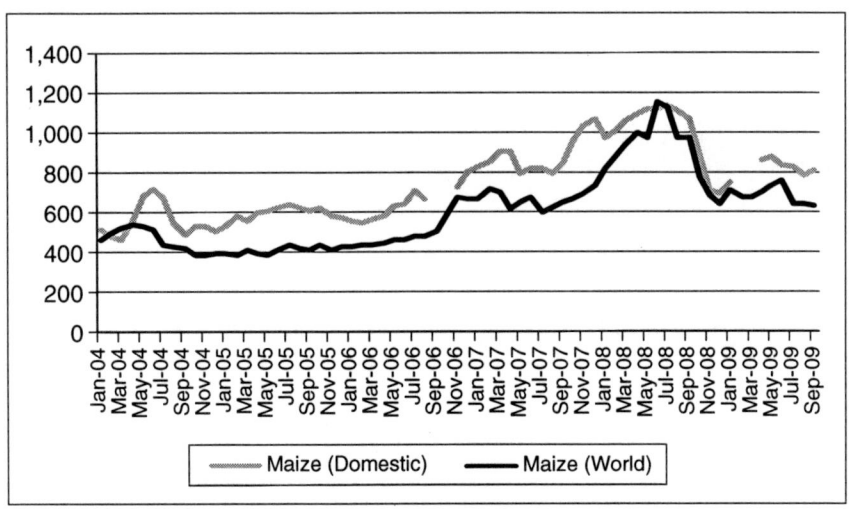

Note: Subject commodities refer to the following (as identified in the sources used): Domestic — maize (yellow);
International — maize (U.S. no. 2 yellow); gaps are due to lack of available data for the periods concerned.
Source: Authors' calculations based on data from MAFF (2010) (domestic); FAO (2010) (international).

changes in international prices; nevertheless, domestic price increases on average would have been only about 7 per cent in the third quarter of 2008 relative to the last quarter of 2007, or 5 per cent during the supposed period of the rice export ban (see Table 5.3). This illustrates clearly the cost of the food crisis on both domestic consumers and the government.

Calculation results for maize, pork and beef show disconnection between actual price movements in the world and local markets (see Table 5.1, Figures 5.5 and 5.6), suggesting significant additional domestic costs in the preparation and sale of these foods in domestic markets. That domestic maize prices are higher than world maize prices invites the thought of increasing maize imports to bring local prices down and make maize more attractive as a daily food item. However, maize prices are already far lower than rice prices in Cambodia, implying that there are non-economic factors inhibiting the use of maize and other cereals for that matter as a substitute for rice.

FIGURE 5.6
Actual World and Domestic Meat Prices
('0000 Riels Per Kg)

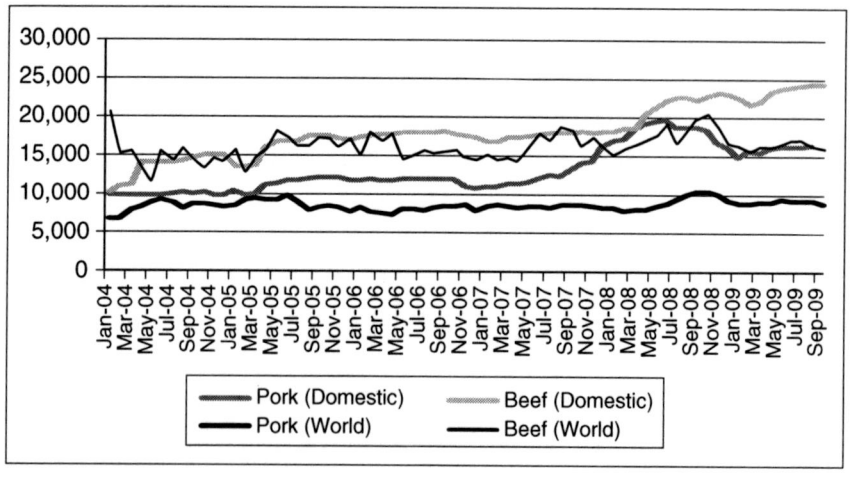

Source: Authors' calculations based on data from MAFF (2010) (domestic); FAO (2010) (international).

Input Price Transmission

Because of their impact on food supply response, we calculated the transmission of gasoline and fertilizer prices. Again, world prices were first converted into riels. Figure 5.7 maps both actual international and domestic prices in the national currency. It immediately shows that domestic gasoline and fertilizer prices were significantly higher than world prices. Factors such as taxes, transport costs and exchange rate movements explain the disparity in prices of petroleum products between international and local markets. The tax component on petroleum imports has been essentially fixed in Cambodia since the government froze the reference prices on which petroleum product taxes are based (World Bank Cambodia 2009; Kojima 2009). This explains the lower volatility and incomplete pass-through of international price changes into domestic gasoline prices. The pass-through was about 78 per cent in the third

FIGURE 5.7
World and Domestic Gasoline Prices
(Riels Per Litre)

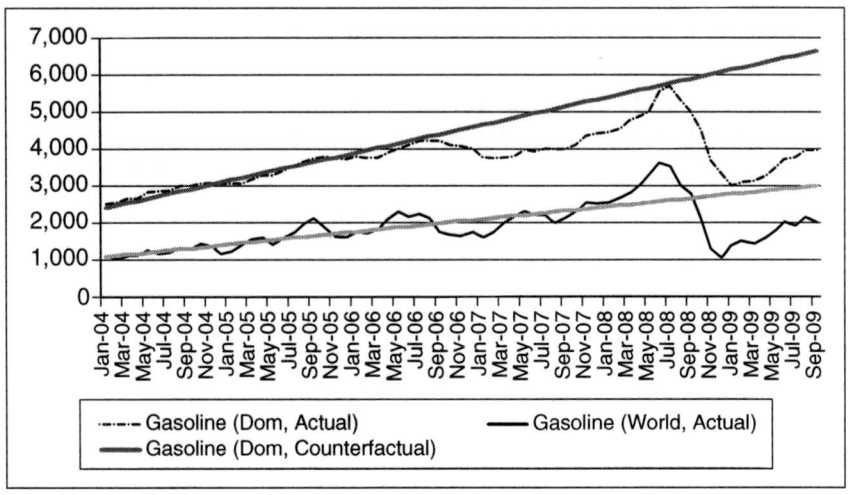

Note: Subject commodities refer to the following (as identified in the sources used): Domestic — gasoline; International — Spot prices FOB for Singapore Conventional Gasoline.
Source: Authors' calculations based on data from NIS (2008, 2009) (domestic); U.S. EIA (2010) (international).

FIGURE 5.8
Actual World and Domestic Fertilizer Prices
('0000 Riels Per Tonne)

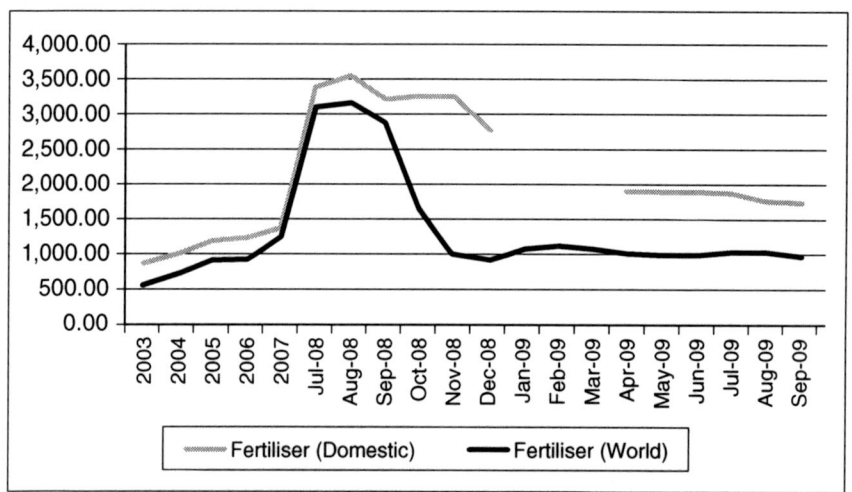

Notes: Subject commodities refer to the following (as identified in the sources used): Domestic — urea; International — urea (international).
Source: Authors' calculations based on data from MAFF (2010) (domestic); IRRI (2010) (international).

quarter of 2008 relative to 2007. Given the stable riel-US$ exchange rate and Cambodia's heavy dollarization, calculations show again that the increments in average world prices in riels and dollars almost mirror each other (see Table 5.4).

Counterfactual price calculations show that if it were not for the food crisis, price transmission might have been complete but international and domestic gasoline price increases would have been just about a quarter of the actual price hikes. The greater effect of the oil subsidy was felt as price increments became steeper over the period of the food shock (see Table 5.5).

The domestic cost of urea, like gasoline, greatly exceeds international urea prices (see Figure 5.8). Calculations indicate that the increase in average actual domestic price surpassed the change in average actual world price. Again, with the riel-US$ rate stability and Cambodia's bi-currency economy, the changes in average world and domestic urea

TABLE 5.4
Actual Non-Food Price Transmissions during the Food Crisis
(2007–Q3 2008)

Period	World Price (US$ % Change)	World Price (Riels % Change)	Domestic Price (Riels % Change)	Pass through (3/1) (%)
Gasoline	43	45	34	78
Fertilizer	141	146	149	106

Notes: Subject commodities refer to the following (as identified in the sources used): Domestic — gasoline; International — Spot prices FOB for Singapore conventional gasoline (Europe).

Source: Authors' calculations based on data from NIS (2008, 2009); MAFF (2010) (domestic); IRRI (2010); US EIA (2010) (international).

TABLE 5.5
Counterfactual Gasoline Price Transmission during the Food Crisis

Period	World Price (US$ % Change)	World Price (Riels % Change)	Domestic Price (Riels % Change)	Pass Through (3/1) (%)
2007– Q3 2008	26	27	27	104

Notes: Subject commodities refer to the following (as identified in the sources used): Domestic — gasoline; International — Spot prices FOB for Singapore conventional gasoline.

Source: Authors' calculations based on data from NIS (2008, 2009) (domestic); US EIA (2010) (international).

prices expressed in riels nearly equalled each other (see Table 5.4). Huge import and informal costs have been pinpointed as mainly responsible for the high cost of fertilizer in Cambodia. The share of fertilizer in production costs is much higher in Cambodia than in neighbouring countries.[3]

5.2.3 Food Consumption, Income and Expenditure Profile

Food consumption, income and expenditure patterns are obvious determinants of a shock's impact on food security. As mentioned earlier, the poor are always at the frontline of a crisis but they are not a homogeneous group. The extent of the blow largely depends on dietary characteristics, spending patterns and income improvements. Profiles presented below delineate data for urban areas, rural areas and the capital, Phnom Penh. True to the dominant trend in developing countries, majority of the Cambodian poor are concentrated in rural areas. In 2007 the poverty incidence in rural Cambodia was 34.7 per cent compared to only 4.6 per cent in Phnom Penh and 25.8 per cent in other urban areas (World Bank 2009*a*).

Cambodian Consumption Basket

One obvious consideration in the appraisal of a shock's impact on food security is the share of food to total consumption. Groups with higher food consumption shares are bound to feel the impact more. In this regard, Cambodian households are no different from those in other developing countries. Food consumption shares are found to have a negative relationship with per capita income; poorer households have higher shares than richer households. In 2007 food represented more than two-thirds of the poorest 20 per cent's total consumption but less than half of that of the richest 20 per cent. As majority of the poor in Cambodia live in rural areas, it follows that food consumption shares are higher in rural than in urban areas (World Bank 2009*b*).

What food items dominate the consumption basket is the next important consideration, the determination of which informs us whether these items were among those that showed sharp price increases in 2007–08. Another purpose is to identify existing or potential food substitutes that could help those affected better cope with food security shocks. The results of a 2008 CDRI survey confirmed the role of rice as the key staple food in Cambodia, in both rural and urban areas, and that there is no ready substitute for it (see Table 5.6). Rice also represents about 65 per cent of total calorie intake in Cambodia (Johansson and Backlund 2005 cited in CDRI 2008). The lack of a ready substitute therefore has serious implications for the nourishment of Cambodians in the event of a supply or price shock.

Using this information on the structure of household consumption and setting it against dietary diversity requirements, it was estimated that in 2008, the number of food insecure people during the lean season was about 2.75 million or around 20 per cent of the population; the highly food insecure, those whose consumption rarely, if at all, meets dietary requirements, were about 37 per cent of the total food insecure; and the borderline food insecure, those whose consumption roughly meets minimum requirements, comprised the rest. About 91 per cent of food insecure people live in rural areas (see Figure 5.9).

FIGURE 5.9
Number of Food Insecure People

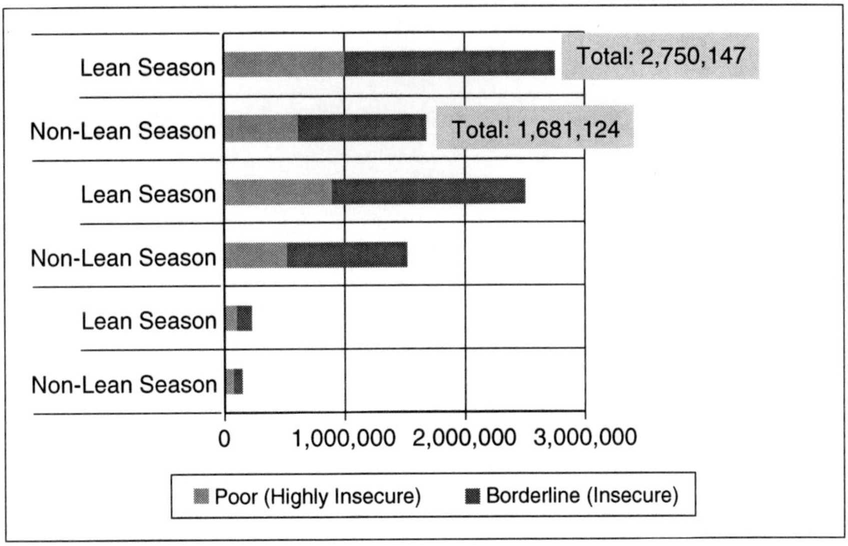

Source: CDRI (2008).

TABLE 5.6
Average Weekly Household Food Consumption

Food Commodity		Cambodia	Rural Areas	Urban Areas	Phnom Penh
Cereals and tubers	Rice	7.0	7.0	7.0	7.0
	Maize	0.2	0.2	0.3	0.4
	Bread	0.4	0.2	0.8	1.2
	Cassava/yam	0.2	0.2	0.1	0.3
	Sweet potato/potato	0.2	0.2	0.3	0.5
Pulses	Beans/groundnuts	0.4	0.3	0.3	0.4
Meat and fish	Fish	4.1	4.1	4.2	3.6
	Other aquatic animals	1.0	1.2	0.3	0.4
	Meat (beef, pork, chicken)	1.8	1.5	2.9	3.5
	Wild meat	0.1	0.1	0.0	0.1
	Eggs	1.7	1.5	2.0	2.9
Vegetables		5.7	5.6	6.0	6.0
Fruits		1.5	1.2	2.5	3.1
Sugar and sweets		2.2	2.2	2.4	1.9
Oils/fats	Vegetable oil or animal fat	4.1	4	4.8	3.9
Milk	Milk products	0.4	0.2	1.0	1.7

Source: Adapted from CDRI (2008).

Income and Expenditure Profile

Net Food Spending

There is a vital distinction between net food sellers (food surplus households) and net food buyers (food deficit households). A rise in commodity prices may be a boon for net sellers but a bane for net buyers. Studies have found that among the poor, even those in rural areas which are largely agriculture-based, there are more net food buyers than net food sellers. Food deficit households are predominant in urban areas, tend to have higher income than net food sellers, and also comprise many rural non-farming households (see, for example Aksoy and Isik-Dikmelik 2008). Food price inflation can therefore have income multiplier and distributive effects across different groups.

Calculations based on the results of the CSES 2007 show that, in the case of rice, net sellers predominate in rural areas (about 59 per cent of surveyed rural households), while net buyers predominate in urban areas (about 77 per cent) (see Table 5.7). For food overall, it has been found that 25.8 per cent of smallholders, 11.5 per cent of the rural

TABLE 5.7
Sources of Food Consumption (Percentage of Households)

	Cambodia	Rural	Urban	Phnom Penh
Rice				
Own production	47.0	59.3	13.3	8
Purchase	50.2	35.3	81.1	90
Fish				
Own production	3.4	4.2	1.2	1
Fishing/hunting/gathering	14.1	19.2	3.8	1
Purchase	82.5	76.6	95.0	98
Vegetables				
Own production	9.7	12.5	8.1	1
Gathering	18.6	25.0	5.6	2
Purchase	70.5	61.8	84.1	96

Note: Figures may not total 100 per cent given minor sources of food consumed.
Source: Authors' calculations (except for Phnom Penh data and rice - own production) based on data from CDRI (2008).

landless and 8.4 per cent of the urban poor in Cambodia are net purchasers (Brahmbhatt and Christiaensen 2008).

Another important consideration is the intensity of net food sales or purchases, i.e. the share of households that are significant net sellers/buyers and the share that are marginal participants. The impact of food price shocks is expected to be significant for the former and only marginal for the latter. Cambodian net food sellers usually have only small surplus to sell. CDRI (2008) observes that only 35 per cent of rural farmers have potential surplus to sell at market. Among the food deficit households, many are only marginal net buyers and are likely to be rich urban households that spend a small share of their income on food (Aksoy and Isik-Dikmelik 2008).

Income Improvements

It is important to consider per capita improvements which can cancel any inflationary impact. This was shown in the results of the CSES 2004 and 2007; despite the increase in food prices between the surveys (37 per cent for Phnom Penh, 45 per cent for other urban areas and 41 per cent for rural areas), per capita consumption and poverty indicators improved across all groups. Per capita real daily consumption increased by 13 per cent in rural areas, 36 per cent in Phnom Penh and 27 per cent in other urban areas, while the poverty headcount against the food poverty line decreased by 1.3 per cent in rural areas, 2.4 per cent in Phnom Penh and 2 per cent in other urban areas (World Bank 2009b). These trends are attributable to the 9 per cent average increase in per capita income between 2004 and 2007, when Cambodia's real output grew by a remarkable 11 per cent on average.[4]

5.2.4 Production Balance Sheet

Looking at food production data is important because a shock's ultimate impact on food security is contingent on the supply response to the shock's price related effects. Because primary sector inputs are mostly invariable in the short term, any notable positive supply response from high food prices is expected to occur in the longer run.

Due to scarcity of data, this sub-section focuses only on rice. Cambodia became a net rice exporter in 2004 (World Bank 2009*a*), with rice exports reaching about 450,000 tonnes in 2008/09 (Guzman 2008). Given the considerable informal rice trade at the borders, this figure is likely an underestimate. The rise in exports has been made possible by growth in production. In the decade 1998–2007, annual paddy and milled rice production each grew by about 8 per cent on average (USDA-PSD 2010; FAOSTAT 2010). This growth rate was well below potential however. Comparisons with its rice-exporting neighbours reveal that rice yields in Cambodia have lagged behind those of Thailand and Vietnam (see Figure 5.10). This illuminates the otherwise puzzling fact that Cambodia, unlike Vietnam, has not yet been able to penetrate the Philippine rice market, which is the biggest in the world. A rise in rice yield to Vietnam's level would increase Cambodia's rice production by 7 per cent on average over a ten-year period (Yu and Fan 2009).

Well-known constraints that bar yield improvements in Cambodia include low mechanization, poor fertilizer use, inadequate irrigation and poor infrastructure (see Table 5.8). Landlessness and land insecurity also remain a problem (see Table 5.9). The majority of the poorest

FIGURE 5.10
Comparative Yields for Paddy
(Kg Per Ha)

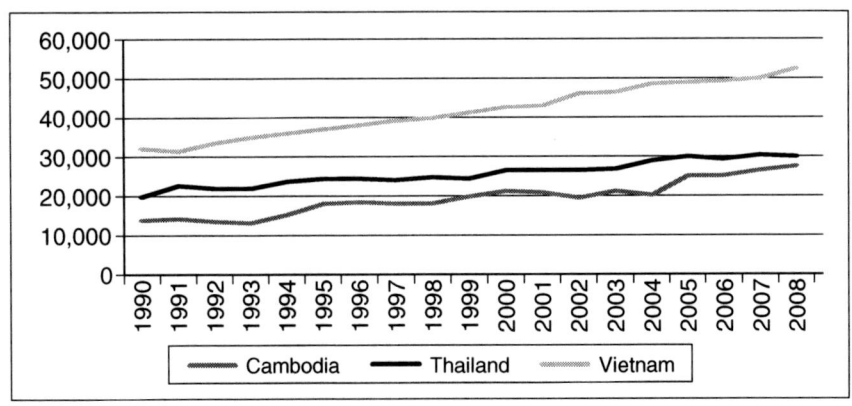

Source: FAO (2009*b*).

TABLE 5.8
Requirements of Agricultural Production Growth

Factor	Cambodia	Thailand	Vietnam
Modern technology			
Tractor (per ha, 1999–2003)	0.6	14.2	24.9
Fertilizer (kg per ha) (kg/ha, 2002–04)	5.0	132.6	324.4
Irrigation (% of arable land, 1998–2002)	7.0	31.0	45.0
Roads paved (% of total roads)	6.3	9.8	25.0

Source: Yu and Fan (2009); World Bank (2009a).

TABLE 5.9
Land Ownership and Security

	Poorest			Richest		
	2004	2007	% Change	2004	2007	% Change
Per cent of households owning or farming agricultural land	83.1	89.1	7.22	48	39.1	−18.54
Median value of land per ha (riels)	1,893	4,000	111.30	3,913	9,000	130.00
Land secured by government title as per cent of land owned	14.3	29.5	106.29	29.2	44.2	51.37

Source: World Bank (2009b).

landowning households in Cambodia are smallholders, and the median area of land-owned is less than one hectare. Among those with land, many are threatened by insecure tenure or ownership. According to the CSES, only about 30 per cent of the poorest land-owning households and 40 per cent of the richest land-owning households had official

TABLE 5.10
Top Natural Disasters in Cambodia, 1990–2009

Disaster	Date	Total No. of Affected People	Damage (US$ million)
Typhoon (Ketsana)	September 2009	*	284
Flood	August 2002	1,470,000	0.1
Flood	August 2001	1,669,182	15
Flood	July 2000	3,448,053	160
Flood	June 1996	1,300,000	1.5
Drought	June 1994	5,000,000	100

Note: * There is not enough accessible information on the total number of people affected by Typhoon Ketsana.
Source: Adapted from World Bank and ISDR (2009); Bernama (2010).

land titles in 2007 (World Bank 2009*b*). Another serious problem has been the very low level of public investment in agriculture: 3 per cent of agricultural GDP compared with more than 10 per cent in Thailand (World Bank 2009*a*). Adverse weather conditions also challenge production (Table 5.10).

Such constraints limit supply responses to price signals. The sharp rise in the prices of intermediate inputs such as gasoline and fertilizer compounded the problem during the food crisis. Assuming that at least fertilizer is variable in the short run, Yu and Fan (2009) estimated the short-run elasticities of supply with respect to a percentage change in output price in Cambodia at 0.26 for wet season paddy and 0.33 for dry season paddy. Assuming that other production constraints are loosened in the end, the long-run elasticities were estimated at 1.15 per cent for wet season paddy and 1.45 per cent for dry season paddy.

5.2.5 Government and Development Partner Responses

Government responses are obviously important considerations in gauging the impact of food price hikes because they can distort food prices and increase the ability of the poor to cope with higher prices. Like other aid-dependent countries, Cambodia has relied on development partner assistance to finance a huge part of its budget deficit and discharge timely automatic stabilizers. Table 5.11 summarizes the

TABLE 5.11
Government Responses to the Food Shock

Trade Policy Measures	Domestic Market-based Measures
Rice export restrictions	Release of stock at subsidized prices
Lifting of pork import restrictions	Reduction of food grain taxes

Social safety nets (with donor support)	Income and credit
Food for Work	Increase in civil service wages
School Feeding Programme	Soft loans by Rural Development Bank

Emergency Food Assistance	

Source: Jalilian et al. (2009); MAFF (undated); Naron (2008).

government's responses to the food shock (other government responses were implemented to address the impact of both the food and economic shocks; see Table 5.12).

The most prominent government response to the run on food prices was the rice export ban imposed in late March 2008 to shore up internal supplies and contain domestic inflation. A large part of the increase in international rice prices by 2008 was due to such export curbs (FAO 2009b). However, Cambodia's export restrictions may not have had as large an impact on world prices as prohibitions imposed by such major exporting countries as India, China and Vietnam. Exceptions to the Cambodian export ban were made for three of the country's provinces along the Vietnamese border (Morning 2008; UN Cambodia 2008). The government lifted the quantitative restrictions after just two months, knowing that the ban came at the cost of preventing farmers and others in the value chain from profiting from higher prices. Reports indicated that while the ban was able to temper price increases, it did so only slightly and only for select areas and varieties (Arnst 2009). A less discussed trade policy response was the lifting of the restrictions on pork imports imposed in August 2007 in reaction to outbreaks of pig-borne diseases abroad. The removal of the import ban was aimed at helping bring down prices of pork products (Xinhua 2007, 2008). The government also provided oil subsidies by fixing the reference prices on which petroleum product taxes are based. Through its company Green Trade, it also distributed rice from its stocks at subsidized prices.

TABLE 5.12
Immediate Government Responses to Economic Shock

Agriculture	Garment Sector
Agriculture Support and Development Fund	Suspension of advance profit tax payment
3-year tax holiday for agricultural investment projects	Reduction of employer contribution to social security
Zero-tariff on import of agricultural inputs	
Vat exemption for agricultural inputs	

Tourism Sector	Construction Sector
Visa fee waivers	Removal of the cap on real estate lending
International advertising campaigns	
Opening of new border checkpoints and waterways	
Showcasing activities	

Trade Policies and Domestic Support	Other Social Safety Nets
Import oil subsidy	Government Fund for Short-term Vocational Training
Electricity subsidy	Fund for Self-Employment
Reintroduction of pork imports	Food Security Programme
	Food Facility
	Food for Work
	School Feeding Programme
	Emergency Food Assistance

Note: This summary is based on collated information and is by no means exhaustive. It does not include the government's longer-term strategies.
Source: Jalilian et al. (2009); MAFF (undated); Naron (2008).

Green Trade reportedly sold about 300 tonnes of rice to local markets at approximately 70 per cent of market price (Arnst 2009; UN Cambodia 2008; Oxfam International 2008). The government also suspended taxes on food grains (ADB 2008; Brahmbhatt and Christiaensen 2008).

Moreover, the government, with support from development partners, utilized automatic stabilizers in the form of several social safety nets.

Government strategy involved mobilizing existing safety nets — primarily the government's school feeding and food-for-work programmes implemented in partnership with the World Food Programme (WFP) — and instituting new ones, primarily the Emergency Food Assistance Project funded by the ADB (Jalilian et al. 2009; ADB 2009a). The importance of food aid in Cambodia is clearly demonstrated by the drop in student attendance in receiving schools whenever school feeding programmes are suspended (CARD and FSN 2009). Affected especially by the spikes in rice prices, WFP Cambodia was forced to scale-down support in the second quarter of 2008, resulting in the temporary suspension of its school feeding programmes to the detriment of about 450,000 primary school pupils (FAO and WFP 2008).

Aware of the decline in real incomes due to higher food prices, the government also raised civil servants salaries and allowances (UN Cambodia 2008; Naron 2008; Demeke et al. 2009). The state-owned Rural Development Bank also released soft loans to Green Trade and private sector rice millers to help them boost their stockpiles (Arnst 2009; UN Cambodia 2008).

5.2.6 Impact

Based on Cambodia's Global Hunger Index (GHI) scores (see Figure 5.11), the status of hunger in the country has risen to alarming levels though the problem has been tempered over the years. About 25 per cent of the country's total population is undernourished, a share that may be significantly higher than its neighbours' but nonetheless reflects a huge improvement over the situation ten years ago when it was close to 40 per cent. Under-five mortality improved from 12 per cent in 1990 to 9 per cent in 2007, while the prevalence of underweight children under five declined from about 45 per cent a decade ago to 28 per cent in 2005 (FAO and WFP 2009; von Grebmer et al. 2008; UNICEF Cambodia 2009). The poverty headcount was significantly brought down from 45–50 per cent in 1993–94 to 30 per cent in 2007 (Jalilian et al. 2009; CDRI 2009). Exceptional growth in national and per capita incomes prior to the food and economic crises made all these welfare improvements possible. The first-hand impact of the food shock was to bar further progress. Ultimately, it made it much easier for the financial economic crisis to counter decade-old achievements.

FIGURE 5.11
Cambodia's Global Hunger Index

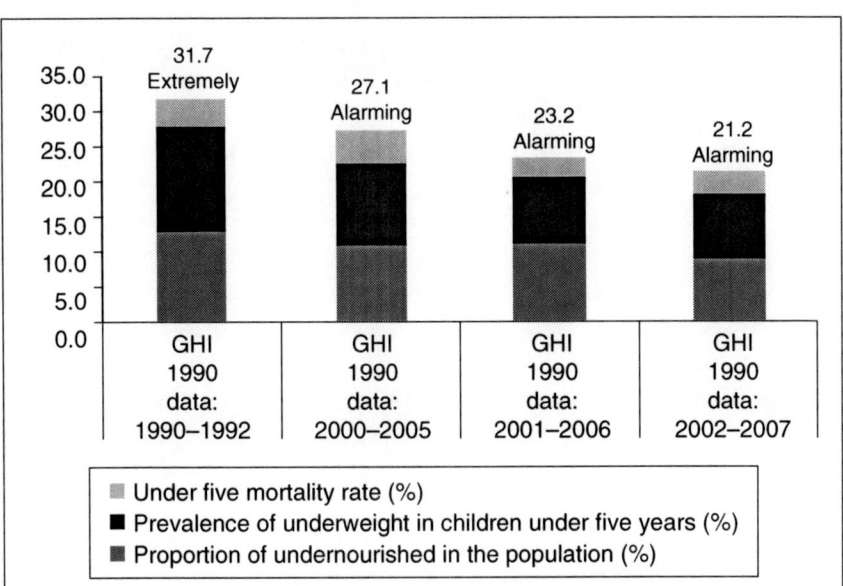

Source: Authors' calculations based on GHI data from Weismann et al. (2007); von Grebmer et al. (2008, 2009).

Three factors are worth mentioning at the outset. First, the impact of the world price shock in Cambodia was moderated due to incomplete price transmission, particularly in relation to rice. Second, the effects of the price escalations were actually differentiated at the micro-level due to varying household characteristics. Third, the constraints impeding immediate and significant supply response to the price hikes prevented Cambodia from optimizing terms of trade gains from the higher prices.

To recap, rice has remained the primary staple food and source of calorie intake across all geographical groups in Cambodia, with no ready substitute. Thus, rice price increases have the most important implication for food security in the country. Calculations on the impact of earlier (2005–07) food price increases on poverty in Cambodia reveal that the rice price increase accounted for virtually all of the food price impact

(Ivanic and Martin 2008). Taking into account diverse dietary requirements, food insecurity was found to be concentrated in rural areas. Yet earlier descriptions also show that rural households are mostly net rice sellers while urban households are mostly net rice buyers. Therefore, the rice price shocks must have affected urban households more than rural households. The deterioration in food security must have been greater in urban areas, though in terms of total the prevalence of poor food consumption in rural areas dwarfed that in urban areas. Because many urban net rice buyers are the richer marginal rice deficit households, the aggravation of food insecurity in urban areas must have fallen more on the urban poor. As net rice sellers, many rural households stood to benefit from the price escalation. But because many of them often have little surplus to sell, with production increase barred by constraints that are invariable in the short run, only a limited number of farming households would have benefited significantly from higher prices; the least benefit likely accrued to the poor, the landless and credit-short farming households.

Results of CDRI surveys support some of the above inferences. Using PDS data, Tong (2009) found that the food crisis led to a reduction in household consumption of both food and non-food items. Between March and September 2008 in particular, household food consumption on the whole declined by about 8.4 per cent . The poorest 20 per cent , however, were found to have cut back less on food than the other groups. The decline in consumption was also found to be less in the case of those with credit (see Table 5.13).

Meanwhile, results of a CDRI study in 2008 show that more than half of the surveyed households reported consuming lower quality and quantity of food as well as buying food on credit (see Table 5.14). The frequency of cutbacks and credit purchases varied across groups. Food insecure households needed to use these coping strategies more often, suggesting further deterioration in their welfare. Another inference is that the decrease in the quantity and quality of food consumed was greater in rural areas. Notwithstanding survey limitations, this may have captured what was cited earlier: that many rural households are net food buyers and many food deficit urban households are only marginal net food buyers. Partly compelled by greater indebtedness, sale of assets was another coping strategy identified in the survey. The sale of

TABLE 5.13
Household Consumption Per Capita Per Day by Group
(Riels)

Group	Category	March 2008	September 2008	% Change
All		2,676.40	2,451.60	−8.40
Income	Poorest	1,674.80	1,571.60	−6.16
	Next poorest	2,190.50	2,030.60	−7.30
	Middle	2,605.40	2,394.00	−8.11
	Next richest	3,039.10	2,795.50	−8.02
	Richest	3,906.80	3,496.00	−10.51
Gender	Male	4,136.80	3,622.48	−12.43
	Female	3,466.54	3,233.14	−6.73
Education	No school	3,651.50	3,337.33	−8.60
	Elementary	3,839.89	3,528.66	−8.11
	Secondary	4,818.62	3,778.70	−21.58
	Tertiary and higher	4,579.35	3,916.18	−14.48
Labour	Not active labour	3,651.37	3,316.55	−9.17
	Active labour	4,040.75	3,577.25	−11.47
Loan	With loans	3,999.94	3,561.32	−10.97
	Without loan	3,978.39	3,517.23	−11.59

Source: Tong K. (2009) using PDS data.

land and other productive assets is associated with high risk because it jeopardizes future livelihoods. It was found that the crisis also pushed those whose livelihoods depended on something other than crop production into a serious situation. It made the poor reduce spending on healthcare, education and agricultural inputs, which in turn undermines future food production and income.

So (2008) conducted a survey on rural households in nine villages in Cambodia and found that the food crisis struck the poor hardest because most of them are net food buyers and possess small farm plots (only 24 per cent of households in the sample owned two hectares or more). The seasonality and irregularity of jobs also made it hard for the poor to generate enough income to cope with rising food prices. The increase in the price of other commodities such as oil and agricultural inputs placed the poor in an even more difficult position.

TABLE 5.14
Household Coping Strategies

Coping Strategy	Proportion of Households that Used the Strategy, Any Frequency	Frequency of Use (Lower Figures = More Frequent)				
		Food Insecure Households	Cambodia	Rural Areas	Other Urban Areas	Phnom Penh City
Rely on less preferred and cheaper food	71	2.6	3.4	3.3	3.8	3.8
Purchase food on credit	60	3.5	3.9	3.8	4.2	4.2
Reduce daily food consumption	53	3.6	4.0	4.0	4.2	3.8
Decrease expenditure on healthcare	35	4.4	4.5	4.3	4.9	5.0

Note: In relation to the frequency of use, ranking is from 1 (everyday) to 5 (never) (a score of 2.4 means between "often and sometimes"); thus, the higher the score, the lower the frequency. See CDRI (2008) for the methodology.
Source: Adapted from CDRI (2008).

As discussed earlier, supply response to price surges is constrained by a number of formidable problems. Yu and Fan (2009) found a small but positive relationship between change in output price and supply in the short run, but this is based on the assumption that at least fertilizer use is increased. According to CDRI (2008), at least 3 per cent more households reported plans to cultivate land rather than leaving it idle or renting it out in the next season; the fruition of these plans, however, was challenged by long-standing impediments to agricultural intensification, the high price of fertilizer being one of them. As mentioned earlier, even without the price hike, fertilizer costs in Cambodia are much higher than in neighbouring countries. Supply responses may have become more realizable in the longer run. This topic is therefore revisited in Section 5.4 to check for any lag in response.

FIGURE 5.12
Child Nutrition Status

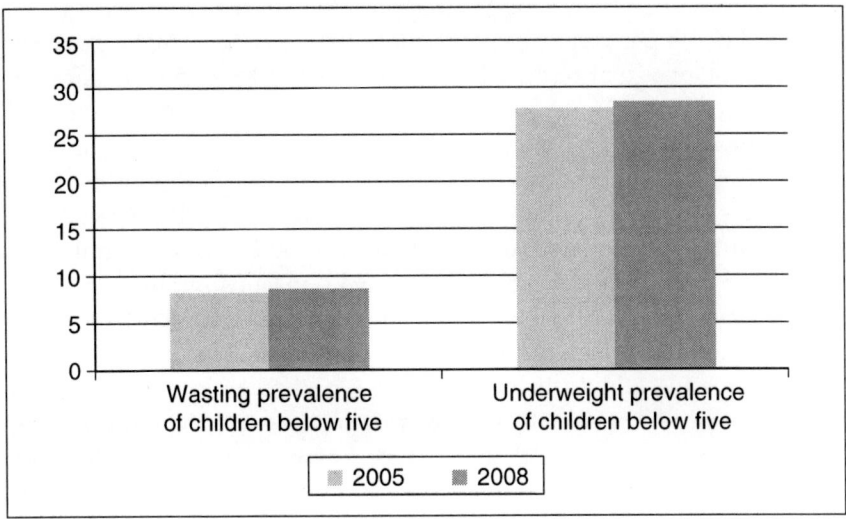

Source: UNICEF Cambodia (2009).

FIGURE 5.13
Prevalence of Diarrhoea among Children below Five

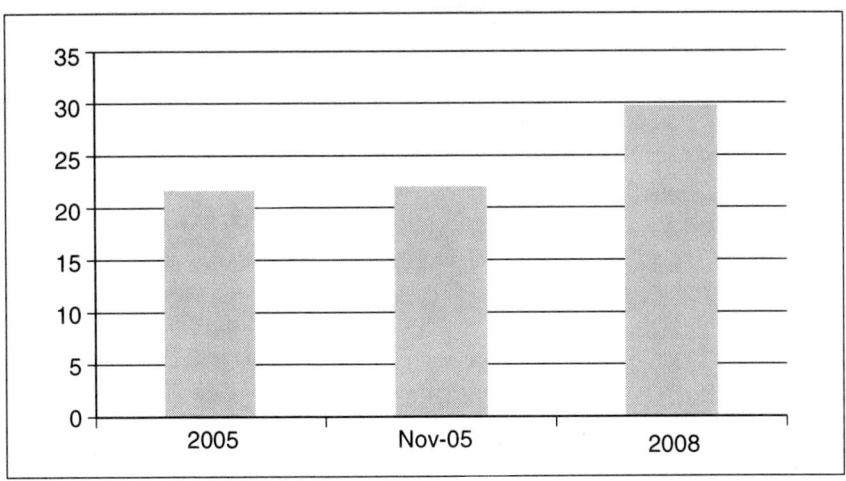

Source: UNICEF Cambodia (2009).

While production had not necessarily intensified, soaring prices were found to have enhanced agricultural incomes. Again, CDRI (2008) shows that even though gross profit margins from selling rice increased by 38 per cent, rice production costs increased by 50 per cent. Gross profit margins increased by 82 per cent for maize, 46 per cent for soybeans and 176 per cent for cassava. Given that many net food sellers only have small surplus to sell, consequent income improvements due to higher prices likely benefited few households. This renders the impact of higher food prices on rural poverty uncertain.

In contrast, the negative impact of the food shock on nutrition must have been serious given the cutbacks in consumption in terms of both quantity and quality. Data limitations make it hard to gauge the nutritional impact more precisely. At least, the prevalence of wasting among children below five was found to have increased from 8.4 to 8.9 per cent, while the prevalence of underweight among the same group was found to have increased from 28.2 to 28.8 per cent between 2005 and 2008 (UNICEF Cambodia 2009). The prevalence of diarrhoea among children below five also reportedly climbed alarmingly, from 22 to 30 per cent over the same period (see Figures 5.12 and 5.13).

5.3 IMPACT OF THE GFEC ON FOOD SECURITY AND AGRICULTURE

5.3.1 Transmission into Food Prices and Security

The global crisis proved how the financial and real sectors and food and non-food commodity markets have become much more interlinked. It showed how a crisis of confidence in financial systems can easily translate into a crisis of confidence in the real economy and how these twin crises can aggravate food insecurity. It is true that the global recession dampened prices brought to a peak by the food crisis. While this allayed some food security concerns, the sudden decline in prices was just as much a shock to those who had benefited from the run-up in prices, borrowed money and invested in production on the expectation that the trend of higher prices would continue. Just as the food price spikes had winners and losers, so did the deflationary trend set off by the global recession. Food prices have also remained higher than their historical averages over the period of the GFEC and in fact have started rising rather rapidly again in recent months. This volatility poses serious risks for food security.

As discussed in Section 5.2, the brunt of the crisis was felt mainly through the slowdown in trade and FDI. This in turn triggered a slump in three of Cambodia's four growth drivers. While agriculture withstood the crisis and helped cushion the blow to the economy, the sector and food security were by no means immune to the shock. For one, growth linkages rendered them unable to escape the crisis. The drying up of capital flows also curbed much needed investment in food production. Terms of trade losses were also suffered due to the decline in agricultural export prices and, more so, the decline in garment prices. However, the lower import bill due primarily to lower petroleum prices did help mitigate these income losses. That key sectors were hit by the downturn also meant losses to government revenue that otherwise could have been channelled as public investment in food production or used to intensify social safety net provision to those most affected. Further, aid budgetary pressures from the crisis intensified sectoral competition for donor assistance. The slump in business and gloomier economic prospects also led to record high unemployment and underemployment which depressed household incomes. Cutbacks in remittances compounded the pressure on household budgets. Although food prices have since declined from their mid-2008 levels, income losses have made the situation of households no better than during the food crisis. The GFEC in fact made things worse and spread adversity to a broader population. This is notwithstanding its differentiated effects based on the same determinants discussed in Section 5.3.

Given the nature and extent of changes generated by the GFEC, fully capturing all its effects is not an easy task and thus requires a general equilibrium framework that links all the changes in economic activities, income generation, distribution and household earnings. There are various general equilibrium macro modelling tools that can be used to achieve this, including Social Accounting Matrices (SAM) and Computable General Equilibrium models (CGE); the latter however mostly uses SAM as the database for analysis.

The application of macro models of any type has substantial require-ments with regard to data availability and reliability. In the context of Cambodia, there are serious constraints to meeting such requirements; data availability is very limited and the reliability of what is available is an issue. It is understood that an Input Output table, a SAM as well as a simple CGE model for Cambodia are under construction. None of these are yet available and therefore quantitative assessment of the impact of GFEC on various components of the economy as well as foodsecurity along a macro model of any sort is not possible at this stage. A more descriptive analysis of the impact of GFEC on food security with focus on the household level follows. Consistent with the preceding section, price transmission and the effects of GFEC on agricultural production are also looked at.

5.3.2 Food Price Trends

As mentioned above, the global crisis essentially halted the commodity price boom, though food prices remained above average both in nominal and real terms over the period of the crisis. The food price index kept falling from the second quarter of 2008 until March 2009 when it started rising again. The rice price index averaged 240 in the final quarter of 2009 after peaking at about 372 in May 2008. Still, as with other food commodities, rice prices remain higher than their pre-crisis levels (see Figure 5.3).

The exceptional price increases in 2008 and the more recent price resurgence have raised concerns that the higher price environment has assumed a greater degree of permanence because of how food price dynamics have become more strongly influenced by such non-traditional factors as developments in the energy sector due to heightened competition between food and biofuel production, volatility in capital and currency markets, and even abnormal weather conditions and lower productivity allegedly due to climate change.[5] The OECD-FAO Agricultural Outlook 2009–18 argues that there still appears to be no primary restructuring in food price dynamics. The fundamentals governing food supply still outweigh the non-traditional influences on demand as evidenced by the recent supply responses to price signals (OECD-FAO 2009).

5.3.3 Price Transmission

Following international trends, inflation in Cambodia eased as the country's economy started feeling the effects of the GFEC. Overall inflation year-on-year went as low as –5.6 per cent in May 2009, after peaking at 36 per cent a year earlier. As the economy recovered and expansionary policies affected prices, inflation began to pick up again, climbing to –1.3 per cent by October 2009. Food inflation went as low as –6.7 per cent in May 2009 before rebounding to –1.5 per cent in October. The domestic rice price index followed the same pattern, as did non-food inflation (see Figures 5.2 and 5.3).

Again, what would be interesting to know is how much of the domestic price changes reflect changes in international prices. Select counterfactual prices are also calculated to appraise the impact of the crisis on prices. Calculations were made for the same commodities looked at earlier in this section.

Food Price Transmission

As shown in Figure 5.4, actual movements of rice prices, both world and domestic, were downwards over the period of the crisis. But while the decline in international prices was marked by several fluctuations, that in domestic prices was smooth, suggesting the effects of domestic interventions. Still based on Dawe's (2008) method, calculations of price transmissions show that the reduction in average domestic price exceeded that in average international price in the fourth quarter of 2008 relative to the third quarter of 2009. What this suggests is that prices were not only pushed down by the pass-through effect but also by influences such as government intervention. Another finding from the calculations is that the increases in average world and domestic prices in riels almost matched each other (see Table 5.15). Again, this is explained by the stability of the riel-US$ exchange rate and Cambodia's heavy dollarization.

Counterfactual price calculations show that if it were not for the GFEC, both world and domestic rice prices would not have decreased. In the third quarter of 2009 relative to the fourth quarter of 2008, the average domestic rice price would have increased by about 7 per cent, fully reflecting the increase in average international price (see Table 5.16).

Earlier, it was noted how there appears to be little relationship between world and domestic maize and meat prices. This was true for

TABLE 5.15
Actual Food Price Transmissions, GFEC Period
(Q4 2008–Q3 2009)

Commodity	World Price (US$ % Change)	World Price (Riels % Change)	Domestic Price (Riels % Change)	Pass Through (3/1) (%)
Rice	−4	−3	−12	276
Maize	−11	−9	6	−58
Pork	−9	−7	−4	46
Beef	−13	−12	6	−46

Note: Subject commodities refer to the following (as identified in the sources used): Domestic — rice quality #2, maize (yellow); pork, beef no. 1; International — Thai rice 5 per cent broken grains; maize (U.S. no. 2 yellow), U.S. beef export, U.S. pork frozen.
Source: Authors' calculations based on data from NIS (2008, 2009); MAFF (2010) (domestic); IRRI (2010) FAO (2010) (international).

TABLE 5.16
Counterfactual Rice Price Transmissions, GFEC Period

Period	World Price (US$ % Change)	World Price (Riels % Change)	Domestic Price (Riels % Change)	Pass Through (3/1) (%)
Q4 2008–Q3 2009	6	7	7	108

Note: Subject commodities refer to the following (as identified in the sources used): Domestic — rice quality #2; International — Thai rice 5 per cent broken grains.
Source: Authors' calculations based on data from NIS (2008, 2009) (domestic); IRRI (2010) (international).

maize and beef during the GFEC period as international prices declined but domestic prices increased. Local pork prices however decreased (see Table 5.15); given the reintroduction of pork imports, this has been attributed to the surge in imports specifically from Thailand (such imports are however quota-bound) (*Phnom Penh Post*, 21 December 2009, p. 7).

Non-Food Price Transmission

Between the final quarter of 2008 and third quarter of 2009, both world and domestic gasoline prices increased, though they were not as high as during the peak of the food crisis. The change in average domestic price was more muted, with the pass-through calculated at only 6 per cent. This reflects the effect of the oil subsidies. The changes in average world and domestic prices expressed in riels nearly match each other as well (see Table 5.17), reflecting the overall stability of the riel against the dollar over the period of the crisis.

Counterfactual price calculations indicate that were it not for the GFEC, domestic gasoline prices would have increased far more than they actually did. In the third quarter of 2009 relative to the fourth quarter of 2008, the counterfactual average domestic price increase would have been 9 per cent while the actual was only 2 per cent (see Table 5.18).

In contrast to gasoline price movements, fertilizer prices between the last quarter of 2008 and third quarter of 2009, both in international

TABLE 5.17
Actual Non-Food Price Transmissions, GFEC Period
(Q4 2008–Q3 2009)

Commodity	World Price (US$ % Change)	World Price (Riels % Change)	Domestic Price (Riels % Change)	Pass Through (3/1) (%)
Gasoline	36	39	2	6
Fertilizer	−17	−16	−43	246

Note: Subject commodities refer to the following (as identified in the sources used): Domestic — gasoline, urea; International — Spot prices FOB for Singapore conventional gasoline, urea (Europe).
Source: Authors' calculations based on data from NIS (2008, 2009); MAFF (2010) (domestic); IRRI (2010) US EIA (2010) (international).

TABLE 5.18
Counterfactual Gasoline Price Transmission, GFEC Period

Period	World Price (US$ % Change)	World Price (Riels % Change)	Domestic Price (Riels % Change)	Pass Through (3/1) (%)
Q4 2008–Q3 2009	9	9	9	104

Note: Subject commodities refer to the following (as identified in the sources used): Domestic — gasoline; International — Spot prices FOB for Singapore conventional gasoline.
Source: Authors' calculations based on data from NIS (2008, 2009) (domestic); IRRI (2010) (international).

and domestic markets, went down. Again, however, the change in the average domestic fertilizer price more than reflected the full change in average international price (see Table 5.17), possibly reflecting the impact of such government response to the crisis as the imposition of zero tariff on import of agricultural inputs.

5.3.4 Effects on Household Income

As already mentioned, the economic downturn adversely affected food security, albeit inflationary pressures were temporarily relieved. The impact was largely channelled via its effects on household income. In real terms, the crisis generally tightened incomes and led to adverse changes in consumption. There were also differentiated effects based on variations in household characteristics. Four reasons for income deterioration are discussed here: higher unemployment and underemployment, lower wages, reduced remittances, and greater difficulty in accessing credit.

Employment and Wage Effects in Growth Sectors

Unemployment rate in the country reportedly stood at 3.5 per cent in 2007 (World Bank 2009a). The dearth of data precludes making definitive statements about national unemployment changes, but sectoral information suggests that unemployment must have gone up and the economy's ability to absorb new market entrants must have diminished as a result of the recession. CDRI's focus group discussions (FGDs) and semi-structured interviews (SSIs) found a general reduction in job availability in both urban and rural areas of approximately 30 to 40 per cent. That said, again it must be noted that factors other than the crisis were also responsible for the overall welfare deterioration observed during the crisis (Theng and Kem 2009a, 2009b; So 2009).

The garment industry has been a critical source of household income for its 300,000 or so workers, about 90 per cent of whom are female and mostly come from poor rural households (Nathan Associates 2006). As an effect of the crisis and fiercer competition in the post-quota environment, approximately 52,000 garment sector jobs were shed from September 2008 to August 2009 (see Figure 5.14). More recent accounts report that in the first eleven months of 2009, 93 garment and shoe factory closures resulted in 38,190 job losses.

FIGURE 5.14
Monthly Job Losses/Gains in the Garment Industry

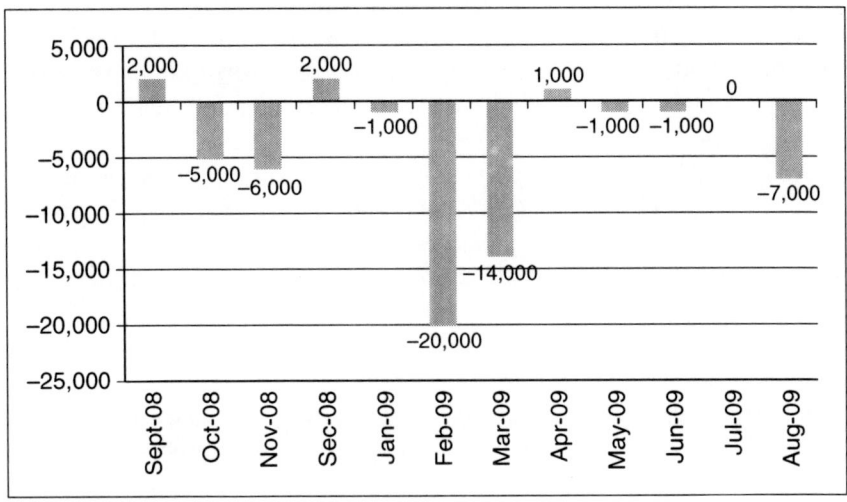

Source: Cham (2009).

Temporary suspension of 60 factories over the same period affected 35,337 additional jobs (*Phnom Penh Post*, 15 December 2009, p. 9). Underemployment in the industry also increased. Some garment workers reportedly had as few as 10 days work in a month (World Bank 2009*d*). CDRI's FGDs and SSIs revealed cuts in overtime work and working hours. Some factories also reportedly shifted from base salaries to quota-based salaries, which, given flagging orders during the crisis, must have resulted in lower individual earnings (Theng and Kem 2009*a*, 2009*b*). The total monthly payroll in the garment sector reportedly went down by about US$3.4 million, or about 13 per cent of the average total, between September 2008 and August 2009 (Cham 2009).

The lull in construction also resulted in lay-offs and greater under-employment. The scarcity of systematic data again precludes assigning a precise number to job losses in the sector, but available information suggests that the employment impact of the downturn in construction was considerable. CDRI's interviews revealed an approximately 70 per cent reduction in construction job availability (Theng and Kem 2009*a*, 2009*b*). A December 2009 news report placed the number of construction job losses at a huge 100,000 (Pou 2009).

In the tourism sector, surveys also found an increase in unemployment and underemployment. A survey of 72 hotels showed that 30 to 50 per cent of workers in 12 hotels were laid off while working hours decreased by 30 to 50 per cent in the remaining hotels (*Phnom Penh Post*, 30 July 2009, p. 14). Given sectoral linkages, these employment and income effects in the growth sectors must have had spillover effects on other sectors.

Adverse impacts on employment in the garment, construction and tourism industries must however have been tempered by the absorption of laid-off workers in the agriculture sector and the informal economy. Again, lack of available data makes it hard to assign a number to the workers absorbed into agriculture but this was probably not as significant as some would like to assume. With 60 per cent of the workforce already competing for jobs in agriculture, an area already with lagging productivity, the sector has hardly any extra capacity to absorb additional job seekers. Additional labour supply also further lowers wages in the agricultural sector. CDRI's FGDs and SSIs even reported accounts of people accepting payments in kind in order to be able to compete. Further, these FGDS and SSIs revealed that another strategy to cope with employment loss during the crisis was to shift to the informal sector. The informal economy in Cambodia is large, with paid employees accounting for only 25 per cent of the total workforce in 2007 (NIS 2008). Earnings from working in agriculture and many jobs in the informal sector however have not likely been on a par with earnings from working in the other growth sectors. Shifting from the industrial to the services sector has been another strategy and this seems to have been popular among laid-off female garment workers, many of whom noticeably ended up in the entertainment industry.

CDRI's vulnerable workers surveys (Tong et al. 2009) provide additional evidence of widespread reduction in earnings among the vulnerable. They found that eight of the ten surveyed vulnerable worker groups experienced substantial declines in average real daily earnings over the period of the crisis, though these reductions occurred at different times. Interestingly, the two groups reliant on agriculture, rice field workers and vegetable traders, experienced a notable increase in average real daily earnings between November 2007 and November 2008, the period of the food price spikes, and a notable fall in earnings between November 2008 and November 2009, the period of recession and overall decline in food prices (see Figure 5.15).

FIGURE 5.15
Average Real Daily Earnings, Percentage Change

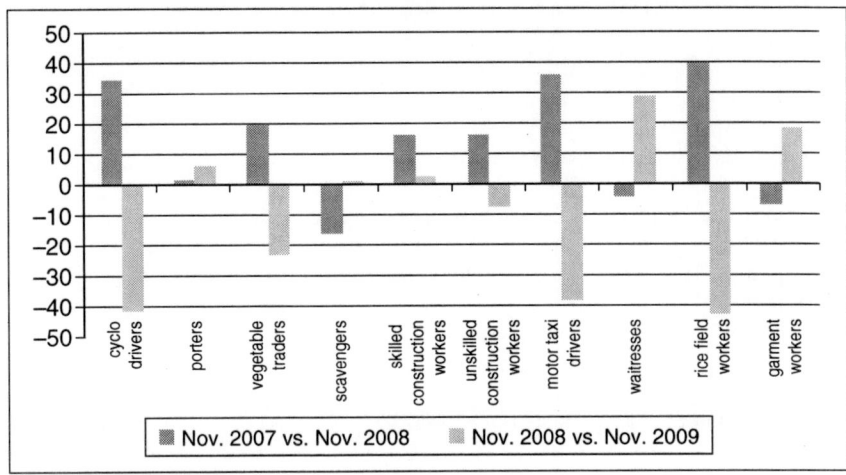

Source: Adapted from Jalilian and Reyes (2010).

Effects of Slowdown on Remittances

A significant share of Cambodian households across all income groups receives remittances. According to the CSES, about 17 per cent of the poorest and 20 per cent of the next poorest households received domestic remittances in 2007, compared to 19 per cent of the middle income and 18 per cent of the richest groups (World Bank 2009b). Smaller percentages of households across all groups also receive international remittances (see Figure 5.16). While remittances to richer groups are larger than those to poorer groups, it is safe to assume that remittances generally comprise a bigger part of the latter's incomes.

Again, lack of data prevents exact quantification of the impact of the crisis on domestic remittances; however, available information suggests consequential decline. CDRI's FGDs and SSIs revealed that not only was there a sharp decline in remittance transfers from urban workers to their families in rural areas, but also that reverse flows, transfers from rural households to their members' working in urban areas, also occurred. This was noted to be especially true for workers of the hard-hit garment industry. In relation to international remittances, the top two

FIGURE 5.16
Per Cent of Households Receiving Remittances

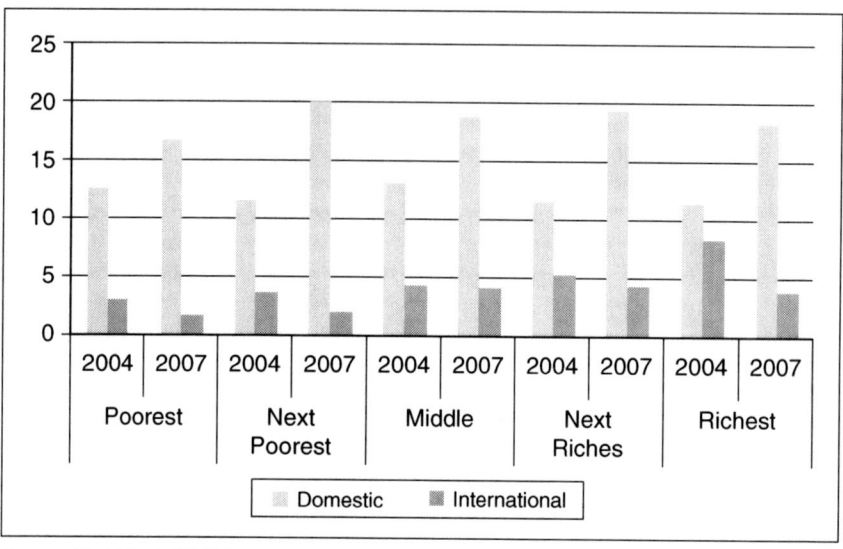

Source: World Bank (2009*b*).

destination countries for Cambodian migrants, Thailand and Malaysia, were also severely hit by the world crisis, resulting in increased populist pressure for migrants to be kept out of jobs. New regular migration flows from Cambodia to these countries were either limited or capped. Crackdowns on migrant workers and their employees were also intensified. Although this did not necessarily cause droves of migrants to return to Cambodia, it must have decreased remittances to the country.

More Limited Credit

Figure 5.17 shows that nearly half of the poorest households have outstanding credit compared with only 20 per cent of the richest, that 88 per cent of the latter are able to borrow compared to 70 per cent of the former, and that the values of loans extended to the richest households are three times as high as those to the poorest families.

As briefly recounted in Section 5.2, the crisis resulted in a substantial squeeze on private sector credit in Cambodia. It also nudged up the

FIGURE 5.17
Credit Access, Per Cent of Households, 2007

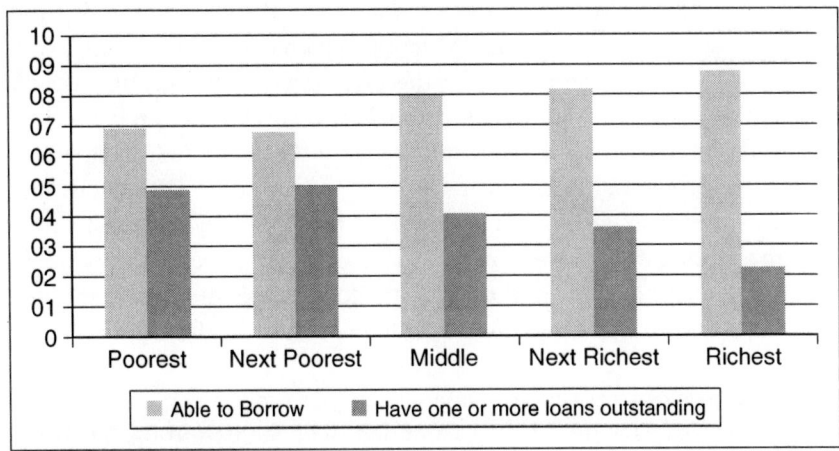

Source: World Bank (2009b).

cost of borrowing as liquidity evaporated. While this adverse turn of events affected both well-off and poorer households, the setback in welfare must have been greater for the latter given their higher dependence on credit and fewer income alternatives. CDRI's interviews found increased indebtedness among interviewed households, while credit became scarcer and more difficult to obtain. The narrowing of household income and dwindling savings and assets drove households to seek credit not only from micro-finance institutions but also from private lenders, who charge higher interest, and from social networks. Borrowed funds were used to finance migration of family members, repay outstanding debt, and even purchase basic consumption items such as food. The intensified scramble for credit consequently upped its cost, which aggravated the debt burden of borrowing households.

5.3.5 Impact on Agricultural Production and Export

Agriculture may have made erratic and smaller contributions to growth prior to the world crisis, but it served as a buffer to the shock, managing to grow at 5 per cent while the other growth sectors contracted in 2009.

The fall in agricultural prices engendered by the global recession may have been a boon for food insecure households but it proved painful for those who had invested in greater production on the expectation that the surge in prices would continue. While rice production in Cambodia was mostly able to buck the impact of the price decline, the fall in cassava and rubber demand and prices proved devastating for growers and exporters. As industrial demand for rubber and cassava fell, their prices nosedived; rubber prices in particular fell to record lows. Ultimately, this most hurt the incomes of farmers because they have the smallest profit margins among the players in the cassava and rubber value chains. Given that many of them had taken loans to increase investment in their smallholdings, the price shock pushed them into greater debt (Jalilian et al. 2009).

That prices of staple foods remained higher than average and prices of commodities such as rubber rebounded over the period of the GFEC means that the opportunity to revive the agricultural sector persists. As argued in Section 5.3, however, there are a number of obstacles to exploiting this opportunity. Given such constraints, no significant positive supply response was observed immediately after food prices peaked. It is suspected, however, that there could have been a time lag in the response as players sought to address the constraints in order to profit from higher prices.

It appears that there indeed was such a lagged response. As mentioned in Section 5.2, while rice export values and volumes shrank year-on-year by more than 50 per cent between April and June 2008, the period when world rice prices peaked, they nonetheless registered consistent increases in the following months. Monthly year-on-year growth of rice export values averaged 430 per cent and volumes averaged 280 per cent from July to November 2009. Also, according to an FAO brief on Cambodia (FAO-GIEWS 2009), at the time of writing a record rice surplus was expected given the bumper harvest in December 2009 to February 2010. The exportable surplus was estimated to reach 1.6 million tonnes, 6.6 per cent higher than in the previous year. Given normal rainfall in 2009, much of the improvement is attributed to the expansion of the cultivation area encouraged by higher rice prices. It was estimated that paddy areas cultivated for harvesting in December 2009–February 2010 reached about 2.28 million hectares, 126,500 hectares more than the year before. However, Yu and Fan (2009) suspect that factors such as government interventions and past investments account for a larger part of the anticipated increase in surplus.

5.3.6 Government and Development Partner Responses

Agriculture is a pillar of the government's poverty reduction strategy. This is at odds with the historically low public investment and aid in the sector. Between 1998 and 2006, only 1 per cent of GDP on average was devoted to agriculture, compared with 7 per cent to core government (which includes defence), 2.7 per cent to health and 2.7 per cent to education. Rural development was provided with about 1.6 per cent of GDP while spending on infrastructure (transport), which has important bearing on agricultural and rural development, averaged about 1.9 per cent (see Table 5.19). Nor has there been any clear trend of increasing budget allocations to the Ministry of Agriculture, Forestry and Fisheries (MAFF) and Ministry of Rural Development (MoRD) (see Table 5.20). Available information on the 2010 budget law passed at the end of 2009 indicates no notable ramping up of public expenditure on agriculture despite the alarm sounded by the food crisis. In the almost US$2 billion budget programmed for 2010, defence has a 14 per cent share, while agriculture and rural development have meagre shares of 1.7 per cent each (*Phnom Penh Post*, 2 December 2009, p. 2).

It was briefly discussed in Section 5.2 how running a bigger budget deficit for 2009 was the government's key means of helping to stimulate the economy. The deficit was financed mainly by external funding and drawdown of deposits, eliciting concern about the potential effect on

TABLE 5.19
Public Expenditure by Sector
(Percentage of GDP)

	1998	1999	2000	2001	2002	2003	2004	2005	2006
Core government	9.4	7.2	8.4	7.7	8.7	7.1	5.5	5.3	5.5
Agriculture	0.6	0.9	1.5	1.3	1.3	1.2	1.2	1	0.9
Rural development	2.1	1.8	1.9	1.8	1.6	1.2	1.5	1.1	1.0
Health	2.4	3.0	2.6	2.5	2.6	2.7	2.7	3.1	2.8
Education	2.7	2.3	2.3	2.5	3.3	3.2	2.9	2.5	2.5

Source: Adapted from World Bank (2009).

TABLE 5.20
Ministry Recurrent Budget Allocation
(Constant US$ million)

	2004	2005	2006	2007	2008
MAFF	15.2	14.9	16.1	14.6	13.1
MoRD	7.5	7.3	9.4	9.1	8.3

Source: NGO Forum (2008).

FIGURE 5.18
Broad Money Growth
(y-o-y Percentage Change)

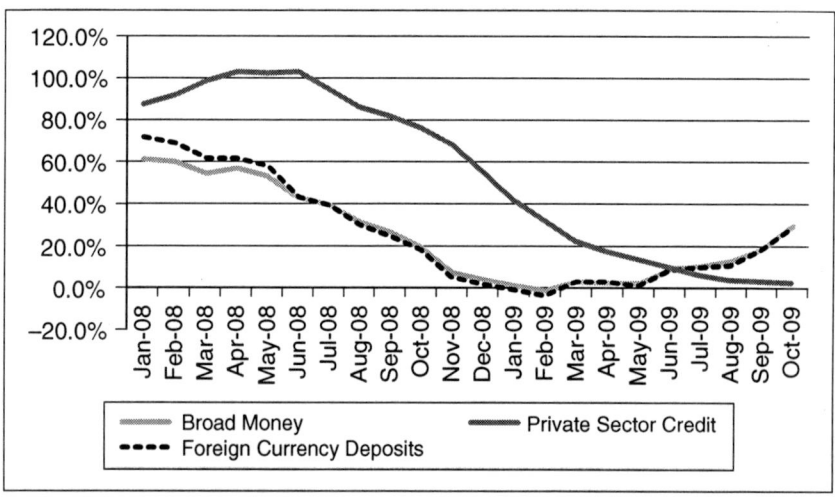

Source: Adapted from Jalilian and Reyes (2010a).

debt sustainability, inflation and exchange rate stability. The GFEC directly impacted on revenue collection, challenging the commendable improvements in tax administration made by the government in the past years. Figure 5.18 again shows how revenues collected for the first eleven months of 2009 were down 7 per cent compared to the same period in 2008. Financing pressures intensified sectoral competition for funds. One resounding issue has been the prioritization of

TABLE 5.21
Sectoral Composition of Aid
(Percentage of Total)

	2005	2006	2007	2008
Social Sectors				
Education	11.4	11.2	11.2	7.6
Health	18.1	15.3	14.1	11.9
HIV/AIDS	4.2	5.0	5.2	5.0
Economic Sectors				
Agriculture	5.5	17.3	5.5	6.0
Rural development	8.2	7.0	9.0	8.0
Manufacturing, mining and trade	1.6	3.4	2.0	3.3
Urban planning and management	0.6	0.1	0.2	0.5
Banking and business services	2.1	1.4	2.0	1.3
Infrastructure				
Transportation	12.1	7.7	12.5	19.2
Water and sanitation (urban)	4.0	2.6	2.2	3.0
Energy, power and electricity	2.6	1.9	1.6	3.5
Information and communications	0.1	1.4	4.0	0.2
Services and cross-sectoral	22.0	23.9	27.4	22.5
o.w. environment and conservation	2.0	2.0	1.1	0.8
Emergency and food aid	0.5	0.1	0.3	1.2
Others	6.9	1.9	2.9	6.7
Total disbursements (US$)	610.0	713.2	790.4	887.9

Source: Adapted from CDC-CRDB (2008).

increased spending on the military and defence rather than on priority sectors, topping which is agriculture and rural development.

Table 5.21 shows that the share of agriculture in total yearly (except for 2006) aid has been about 5.5 per cent on average, noticeably behind the shares of social sectors, while that of rural development was about 8 per cent (CRC-CRDB 2008). It important to recognize however that other sectoral allocations, to transport infrastructure for instance, have significant beneficial feedback effects on agriculture and agri-business. Again lack of available data precludes giving definitive statements about how aid for agriculture fared in 2009. Aid commitments for the

TABLE 5.22
Immediate Government Responses to the Economic Shock

Agriculture	Garment Sector
Agriculture Support and Development Fund	Suspension of advance profit tax payment
3-year tax holiday for agricultural investment projects	Reduction of employer contribution to social security
Zero-tariff on import of agricultural inputs	
Vat exemption of agricultural inputs	

Tourism Sector	Construction Sector
Visa fee waivers	Removal of the cap on real estate lending
International advertising campaigns	
Opening of new border checkpoints and waterways	
Showcasing activities	

Trade Policies and Domestic Support	Other Social Safety Nets
Import oil subsidy	Government Fund for Short-term Vocational Training
Electricity subsidy	Fund for Self-Employment
Reintroduction of pork imports	Food Security Programme
	Food Facility
	Food for Work
	School feeding programme
	Emergency food assistance

Note: This summary is based on collated information and is by no means exhaustive. It does not include the government's longer-term strategies.
Source: Jalilian et al. (2009); MAFF (undated); Naron (2008).

year do not seem to have been cut back; difficulty in meeting funding targets for priority sectors was reported, but this appears to have been due more to typical disbursement problems than the impact of the crisis.

Table 5.22 summarizes the immediate government responses to the economic shock, some of which were backed by donor funding. Growth sector-specific responses are discussed in detail in Jalilian et al. (2009)

and Jalilian and Reyes (2010) and will therefore not be recounted here; nonetheless, they are included in Table 5.22 because they have directly affected household employment and income prospects and thus had bearing on household food security. While there was no notable progress in enlarging the agricultural budget, the government was quick to put in place other measures intended to exploit the potential of agriculture to cushion the impact of the economic shock and deterioration in food security. These measures include the creation of the Agriculture Support and Development Fund, a three-year tax holiday for agricultural investment projects, and suspension of tariffs and value-added tax on agricultural inputs (Jalilian et al. 2009). Other policies were put in place to address the challenge of higher food and non-food prices and tighter household budgets. These include the oil import subsidy, the effect of which was seen in the results of the price transmission calculations, and electricity subsidy. Food for work, school feeding and the Emergency Food Assistance programmes continued while new programmes sprang up, including the Government Fund for Short-term Vocational Training, Fund for Self-employment[6] and the EU-supported Food Security Programme and Food Facility.[7]

5.3.7 Impact

The crisis was mostly bad news for household food security, though one good result of the recession was the cooling down of food and non-food commodity prices. With help from government interventions, the reduction in domestic prices, particularly rice, was smooth and without the volatility that marred the decline in world prices. Still, this has not necessarily made commodities cheap for the poor: the prices of meat, for instance, remain high, as do the prices of intermediate inputs such as fertilizer and gasoline. Not everyone emerges as a winner from a deflationary trend. The losers are defined by the food balance sheets of Cambodian households. Also, as already pointed out, food prices have hovered at levels higher than their historical averages and are on the rise again. Most importantly, income deterioration resulting from the impact of the crisis on employment, earnings, remittances and credit seriously challenged the ability of households to retain or progress towards acceptable levels and quality of consumption.

Earlier discussions reveal how the regression of Cambodia's economic growth sprung mainly from the downturn in the country's three growth sectors, garments, construction, and tourism, which in turn exerted pressure on the income of workers in these sectors and their dependants. Growth sector activities have been mainly concentrated in urban areas. Therefore the slump in them directly affected mainly vulnerable workers and groups in urban areas, who are largely net food buyers. It goes without saying that the recession in the growth sectors was painful for richer urban groups as well, but these groups were found to be marginal net food buyers in general and their income status provides them more means of coping with the shock including access to more credit. It is also true that many workers, notably in the garment sector, are migrants from rural areas whose families rely on their remittances which dwindled in the crisis. Thus, the slowdown in urban activity had spillover effects on rural food security. This line of impact joins the GFEC's effect on agriculture in determining how the food security of rural groups ultimately fared in the face of the world crisis, taking into account the distinction between net food sellers and net food buyers.

The combined findings of CDRI research present strong evidence that there was a serious deterioration in food security, particularly of vulnerable groups, during the recession. CDRI's FGDs and SSIs found that reductions in income affected the quantity but more so the quality of food consumption. The crisis also led to sacrifices in consumption of non-food items such as cigarettes and alcohol. The multiplier effect also connotes that the worsening in consumption was not limited to the individuals and households directly affected. While not robust, the linkages between the growth sectors and other sectors imply that the crisis must have had cross-sectoral effects.

Focusing on rural households, data collected in September 2009[8] for the Poverty Dynamic Study reveals the same trend of reductions in food consumption. Between September 2008 and September 2009, real consumption of key items in the Cambodian diet declined as follows: rice, −31 per cent; fish, −13 per cent; vegetables, −14 per cent; and pork and beef, −50 per cent[9] (see Table 5.23).

Cuts in the quantity of food consumed and the shift to goods of inferior quality must have aggravated the setback in health and nutrition

TABLE 5.23
Household Consumption by Food Item

Food Item	2008	2009	Percentage Change
Rice	852.25	586.65	−31.16
Other cereals	107.66	63.49	−41.03
Fish	487.00	425.81	−12.56
Vegetables (fresh)	119.41	102.23	−14.39
Pork and beef	114.35	125.43	9.69
Fruit	88.66	44.6	−49.70

Source: PDS data (consumption); NIS (2008, 2009) (commodity price).

experienced during the food crisis. The nutritional effects of the economic shock on women and children must have been worse given their special nutritional needs (UN-SCN 2009). Studies quantifying the impact of the economic crisis on health and nutrition in Cambodia have yet to be updated. Because they really capture the impact of the food shock rather than the economic meltdown, results of the latest studies were presented in Section 5.2.

Government interventions must have played down the harsh impact of the crisis on household food security. However, given funding limitations and problems with the administration of social safety nets, the reach of such interventions could not have been that widespread. Their sustainability is also at risk. According to CDRI's survey round of FGDs and SSIs in May 2009, there had been no intensification in the provision of formal social safety nets. In Cambodia, informal safety nets are just as important as formal ones, if not more so. Further, there had been no reported intensification in the provision of informal safety nets. Assistance from contacts in social networks, for instance, narrowed because they were also hurt by the recession. Assistance from non-profit organizations on the other hand continued, but this entailed mostly one-time emergency support (to help victims of calamities, not economic crisis) with limited geographical scope (see Jalilian et al. 2009; Theng and Kem 2009*a*, 2009*b*; So 2009).

Increased production and higher profit margins due to higher food prices present a silver lining, but mainly for the net food sellers with significant surplus to sell at market. The big players in the value chain are expected to reap more benefits than the smallholders struggling to remove the constraints to enhancing their production. In the longer run, however, if profits are translated into investments, the benefits could be more widely spread and national food sufficiency enhanced.

The world crisis, in sum, reversed Cambodia's achievements in poverty reduction. In 2007 Cambodia's poverty headcount stood at approximately 30 per cent. The World Bank estimated that the crisis could increase this figure by 1 to 4 percentage points by 2010 (World Bank 2009c). Earlier, it was discussed how per capita income improvements can cancel higher prices. Based on the estimate of a 2.2 per cent contraction in Cambodian output in 2009 (IMF 2009a, b), per capita income is estimated to have declined by 2 per cent between 2008 and 2009.

5.4 CONCLUSIONS AND RECOMMENDATIONS

The decade closed on a gloomy note as the food and economic shocks caused setbacks in economic development and poverty reduction. There is now also the constant threat of another crisis occurring and trouncing development plans. The impact of the shocks on poverty and hunger was most painful for least developing countries like Cambodia, and the threat of another crisis may mean economic doom. How the food crisis of 2007–08 led to cutbacks in both the quantity and quality of consumption in spite of government measures aimed at moderating transmissions of international price changes into domestic prices and averting food shortages is shown above. The GFEC, causing sharp contractions in the growth sectors, resulted in the same painful sacrifices in consumption. Even as it temporarily relieved inflationary pressures, the blow to the real economy resulted in substantial declines in real income. Some groups, the net food sellers in particular, had the opportunity to benefit from the price hikes during the food crisis or from the above average food prices during the economic recession. However, such opportunity was lost specifically for the many Cambodian smallholders struggling against constraints to agricultural production growth. Counterfactual price calculations illustrated that were it not for the food shock, increase in the price particularly of rice, sufficient consumption of which is used to define food security in the country, would have been very modest. Were it not for the economic recession, rice prices would not have gone down. The overriding lesson from Cambodia's experience with the food and economic shocks is to revive agriculture, a sector neglected as the country pushed for structural transformation towards export-oriented manufacturing. That agriculture buffered the country against the GFEC emphasizes the fact that the growth contribution of the sector has yet to be optimized.

As Cambodia looks forward to the resumption of growth, a re-evaluation of the country's agricultural and rural development strategy must be made so that the benefits of such growth can be shared more equitably by all Cambodians and so that agriculture can become not only a stronger cushion to shocks but, more importantly, a stronger force supporting longer-run growth. The first priority is to increase the amount and efficiency of public spending in agriculture, which would be consistent with the priority granted to the sector in the government's development plans. Agricultural spending must be based on a pragmatic assessment of what the sector's needs are given its characteristics. Another priority is to define clearer directions for agricultural development. Given the overall aim of poverty reduction and the fact that the majority of the country's poor are based in agricultural rural areas, the first goal is to promote smallholder development. Such a strategy necessitates dealing with the problems primarily in land security, low productivity, and access to finance and information. An entity akin to the Garment Manufacturers Association (GMAC) in agriculture would go far in pushing progress in these areas.

Another imperative is to pursue food sufficiency in tandem with agricultural export development. When talking about agriculture, it is easy to forget about urban residents, most of whom are net food buyers. The goal of food sufficiency should not miss this important linkage. How to bring food to urban areas more cheaply is a key question. Rice export development on the other hand has been the key demand of those who should have benefited from higher international food prices. One resounding complaint is that most of Cambodia's rice is sent to Thailand and Vietnam for milling, so the higher profits that come with higher value-added are missed. How to loosen the constraint is straightforward: invest more in milling capacity. The problem lies in attracting private investment. In this regard, the government has a lot of work to do. The high cost of electricity is widely acknowledged as a top constraint to doing business in Cambodia, along with corruption.

As there is restrained optimism that the Doha development agenda can move forward to achieve its aims, Cambodia also has to turn to exploiting the benefits from regional trade initiatives such as the Early Harvest Programme under the Framework Agreement on Comprehensive Economic Cooperation between ASEAN and China. Cambodia stands to benefit greatly from this set-up, but only if it stays competitive. One other goal given urgency by the food and economic crises is the establishment of a comprehensive social safety net system that can be readily mobilized in the event of a shock. Funding limitations are one of the biggest hurdles, and securing regular budget allocations and greater development assistance is the only way to resolve the problem.

Notes

1. Determinants of impact are also mentioned in Ivanic and Martin (2008) and World Bank (undated). Heady and Fan (2008, Figure 4) also illustrate the factors conditioning the transmission of price impacts on household welfare.
2. Calculations used nominal exchange rates.
3. This share is about 29 per cent in Cambodia and 7 per cent in Thailand (IFC-MPDF 2004).
4. Based on data from NIS (2008, 2009); MoEF (various years).
5. The food crisis, GFEC and climate change have been collectively called the triple crises. Climate change is said to reinforce food price inflation by lowering agricultural productivity and prompting greater bio-energy production (Addison et al. 2010).
6. See Jalilian et al. (2009) for brief descriptions of these initiatives.
7. See Hem (2009) and FAO-GIEWS (2009) for descriptions of these initiatives.
8. Note however that this pertains to a smaller sample of only ninety households.
9. Real figures were generated by deflating nominal figures by respective commodity price indices or their proxies over the period of coverage.

References

Abbott, P., C. Hurt, and W. Tyner. *What's Driving Food Prices?* Oak Brook, IL: Farm Foundation, 2008.
ADB. *ADB's Response to the Food Crisis*. Manila: ADB, 2008.
———. "Protecting Cambodia's Most Vulnerable from Food Crisis". Manila: ADB, 2009a.

————. *Asia Economic Outlook Update*. Manila: ADB, 2009*b*.

Addison, T., C. Arndt, and F. Tarp. *The Triple Crisis and the Global Aid Architecture*. UNU-WIDER Working Paper No. 2010/01. Helsinki: UNU-WIDER, 2010.

AFP. "China Boosts Cambodia Aid after Uighurs Deported". Available at <http://www.channelnewsasia.com/stories/afp_asiapacific/view/1026199/1/.html> (accessed 15 January 2010).

Aksoy, M.A. and A. Isik-Dikmelik. *Are Low Food Prices Pro-Poor? Net Food Buyers and Sellers in Low-Income Countries*. Policy Research Working Paper 4642. Washington, D.C.: World Bank, 2008.

An, C. "Towering Folly?" *Economics Today*, vol. 2, no. 45 (2009).

Arnst, R. *Businesses as Usual: Responses within ASEAN to the Food Crisis*. Occasional Papers 4. Bangkok: Focus on the Global South, 2009.

Bernama. "Typhoon Ketsana Costs Cambodia $284 Million Damages". Available at <www.bernama.com/bernama/v5/newsworld.php?id=467879> (accessed 28 January 2010).

Brahmbhatt, M. and L. Christiaensen. *Rising Food Prices in East Asia: Challenges and Policy Options*. Washington, D.C.: World Bank, 2008.

CDC-CRDB. *The Cambodia Aid Effectiveness Report 2008*. Phnom Penh: CDC-CRDB, 2008.

CDRI. *Impact of High Food Prices in Cambodia (Survey Report)*. Phnom Penh: CDRI, 2008.

————. "Cambodia Country Report". Prepared for the International Conference on East Asian Economy in Beijing, 22–23 October 2009.

Cham P. "The Impacts of a 2-Tiered US LDC Policy". Presentation, Washington, D.C., 17 November 2009.

Council for Agricultural and Rural Development (CARD) and Technical Working Group on Food Security and Nutrition (FSN). "Social Safety Net in Cambodia". Background paper for the Government-Development Partner Coordination Committee Meeting No. 14, 28 April 2009.

Dawe, D. *Have Recent Increases in International Cereal Prices Been Transmitted to Domestic Economies? The Experience in Seven Large Asian Countries*. Working Paper 08-03, FAO-ESA, 2008.

de la Torre Ugarte, D. and S. Murphy. *The Global Food Crisis: Creating an Opportunity for Fairer and More Sustainable Food and Agriculture Systems Worldwide*. Ecofair Trade Dialogue Discussion Papers, No. 11. Berlin: Ecofair Trade Dialogue, 2008.

Deloitte. "The Economic Case for the Visitor Economy". Final Report. New York: Deloitte, 2008.

Demeke, M., G. Pangrazio, and M. Maetz. "Initiative on Soaring Food Prices (Country Responses to the Food Security Crisis: Nature and Preliminary Implications of the Policies Pursued)". Rome: FAO, 2009.

Fan, S. *Public Expenditures, Growth and Poverty in Developing Countries: Issues, Methods and Findings*. Baltimore: Johns Hopkins University Press, 2008.

FAO. "Soaring Food Prices: Facts, Perspectives, Impacts and Actions Required". Rome: FAO, 2008.

———. *Food Outlook: Global Market Analysis*. Rome: FAO, 2009b.

———. "International Commodity Price Database". Available at <http://www.fao.org/es/esc/prices> (accessed 1 February 2010).

FAO and WFP. "Cambodia — Initiative on Soaring Food Prices Final Report". FAO/WFP Consultation Mission. Rome: FAO, 2008.

———. "The State of Food Insecurity in the World (Economic Crises — Impact and Lessons Learned)". Rome: FAO, 2009.

FAO-GIEWS. "Country Brief on Cambodia". Available at <http://www.fao.org/giews/countrybrief/country.jsp?code=KHM> (accessed 28 January 2010).

FAOSTAT Production. Available at <http://faostat.fao.org/site/339/default.aspx> (accessed 1 February 2010).

Guzman, R.B. *The Global Food Crisis: Hype and Reality*. Penang: People's Coalition on Food Sovereignty and Pesticide Action Network Asia and the Pacific, 2008.

Heady, D. and S. Fan. "Anatomy of a Crisis: The Causes and Consequences of Surging Food Prices". IFPRI Discussion Paper 00831. International Food Policy Research Institute, 2008.

Hem, C. "Upcoming EC Food Security Assistance to Cambodia". Presentation to the Food Security Forum, 39th Session, Phnom Penh, 1 February 2009. Available at <http://www.foodsecurity.gov.kh/otherdocs/FSA-EC.pdf> (accessed 25 January 2010).

Hun Sen. "Keynote Address to the Third Cambodia Economic Forum". Phnom Penh, 5 February 2008.

IFC-MPDF. "Constraints to the Competitiveness of Cambodia's Private Sector". *Business Issues Bulletin Cambodia*, No. 3, 30 January 2004.

IMF. *Country Report No. 07/291 (Cambodia: Statistical Appendix)*. Washington, D.C.: IMF, 2007.

———. *Country Report No. 09/48 (Cambodia: Statistical Appendix)*. Washington, D.C.: IMF, 2009a.

———. *Country Report No. 09/325*. Cambodia: 2009 Article IV Consultation — Staff Report; Staff Supplement; and Public Information Notice on the Executive Board Discussion. Washington, D.C.: IMF, 2009b.

———. "Primary Commodity Price Database". Available at <http://www.imf.org/external/np/res/commod/index.asp> (accessed 1 February 2010).

IRRI. "World Rice Statistics". Available at <http://beta.irri.org/solutions/index.php?option=com_content&task=view&id=250> (accessed 1 February 2010).

Ivanic, M. and W. Martin. "Implications of Higher Global Food Prices for Poverty in Low-Income Countries". *Agricultural Economics* 39, Supplement (2008): 405–16.

Jalilian, H. "Food Price Changes and Their Consequences for Vulnerable Groups: What Lessons Can Be Learned?" *Annual Development Review 2008–2009*. Phnom Penh: CDRI, 2008.

Jalilian, H., S. Chan, G. Reyes, C.H. Saing, D. Pon, and D. Phann. *Global Financial Crisis Discussion Paper Series 3: Cambodia*. London: ODI, 2009.

Jalilian, H. and G. Reyes. *Global Financial Crisis Discussion Paper Series 4: Cambodia*. London: ODI, 2010.

Johansson, S. and S. Bäcklund. "A New Set of Poverty Estimates for Cambodia 2004 Based on the CSES 2004 Diary Data". Unpublished report, 2005.

Keane, J. "The Great Unravelling? The Impact of the Global Financial Crisis on Differentiated Commodity Exporters — the Evidence from Sub-Saharan Africa". Presentation to the Development Studies Association annual conference, University of Ulster, 2–4 September 2009.

Kojima, M. "Government Response to Oil Price Volatility". Extractive Industries for Development Series # 10. Washington, D.C.: World Bank, 2009.

Ministry of Agriculture, Forestry and Fisheries. "Agricultural Marketing Office Price Reports". Available at <http://www.camis-kh.org/?q=en/node/79> (accessed 1 February 2010).

———. "Global Economic Crisis: Impact, Issues and Opportunities for Agriculture and Food Security (Cambodia Presentation)". Available at <http://www.foodsecurity.gov.kh/otherdocs/Global-Financial-and-economic-crisis-Eng.pdf> (accessed 19 January 2010).

Ministry of Economics and Finance. "Recent Macroeconomic Performance". Available at <http://www.mef.gov.kh/> (accessed 4 January 2010).

———. *Economic and Monetary Statistics Issues*. Phnom Penh: MoEF, various years.

———. *Monthly Bulletin of Statistics*. Phnom Penh: MoEF, various years.

Morning, Z. "Rice Tumbles as Cambodia Lifts Ban on Exports". *Market Watch*, 27 May 2008. Available at <http://www.marketwatch.com/story/rice-tumbles-as-cambodia-lifts-ban-on-exports> (accessed 19 January 2010).

Naron, H.C. "Macroeconomic Management in Response to Financial Crisis". Presentation to the Second Cambodia Development Cooperation Forum, Phnom Penh, 4 December 2008.

Nathan Associates Inc. *Cambodia Garment Industry Workforce Assessment*. Phnom Penh: Cambodia GIPC-USAID, 2006.

National Bank of Cambodia (NBC). *Balance of Payments Statistics Bulletins*. Phnom Penh: NBC, various years.

National Institute of Statistics. *Statistical Yearbook of Cambodia 2008*. Phnom Penh: NIS, 2008.

————. *General Population Census of Cambodia 2008*. Phnom Penh: NIS, 2009.

NGO Forum. "2009 National Budget Should Favour Farmers". Phnom Penh: NGO Forum, 2008.

OECD-FAO. *Agricultural Outlook 2008–2018*. OECD-FAO, 2008.

————. *Agricultural Outlook 2009–2018*. OECD-FAO, 2009.

Oxfam International. *Double-Edged Prices — Lessons from the Food Price Crisis: 10 Actions that Developing Countries Should Take*. Briefing Paper 121. Oxfam International, 2008.

Pou S. "How Cambodia Can Recover from the Global Financial Crisis". Available at <www.iseas.edu.sg/viewpoint/ps25dec09.pdf> (accessed 22 January 2010).

Ratha. D. and S. Mohapatra. "Migration and Development Brief 9 — Revised Outlook for Remittance Flows 2009–2011". Washington, D.C.: World Bank, 2009.

Reuters. "World Trade Contracted 12 Percent in 2009 — WTO's Lamy". Available at <http://www.reuters.com/article/idUSTRE61N2AO20100224> (accessed 12 March 2009).

Roodman, D. "History Says Financial Crisis Will Suppress Aid". Global Development: Views from the Centre, 2008. Available at <http://blogs.cgdev.org/globaldevelopment/2008/10/history-says-financial-crisis.php> (accessed 1 March 2010).

Sea, K. "Statement of the Permanent Representative of the Kingdom of Cambodia to the United Nations during the High-Level Event on the MDGs". 63rd Session of the UN General Assembly, 2008.

So S. *Impacts of Rising Prices on Poverty in Nine Study Villages: Some Preliminary Findings*. Phnom Penh: CDRI, 2008.

————. *Informal Risk Management/Safety Net Practices: Experiences of Poor Vulnerable Workers and Households*. Phnom Penh: CDRI, 2009.

Srun, D. and P. Kauffman. "Food Security in Cambodia: Update against the Background of Food Price and Economic Crisis". Presentation for the European Commission workshop, Phnom Penh, 22 April 2009.

te Velde, D.W. and I. Massa. *Donor Responses to the Global Financial Crisis: A Stock Take*. London: ODI, 2009.

Theng V. and Kem S. "Rapid Assessment of Impacts of Global Economic Crisis on Cambodian Households: Effects and Coping Strategies". *Cambodia Development Review*, July–September 2009. Phnom Penh: CDRI, 2009*a*.

————. "Rapid Assessment of Impacts of Global Economic Crisis on Cambodian Household and Vulnerable Workers' Income, Consumption and Coping Strategies (Second Round)". Phnom Penh: CDRI, 2009b.

Timmer, C.P. "Causes of High Food Prices". *Asian Development Outlook 2008 Update*. Manila: ADB, 2008.

Tong K. *How Did Cambodian Rural Households Cope with Shocks from Food and Oil Price Increases?* Phnom Penh: CDRI, 2009.

Tong K., S. Khieng, D. Phann, M. Hem, and D. Pon. "Vulnerable Workers Survey in Phnom Penh, Kandal, Kompong Speu, Siem Reap and Battambang". Phnom Penh: CDRI, 2009.

Tong K. and D. Pon. "Vulnerable Workers Survey in Phnom Penh, Kandal, Kompong Speu, Siem Reap and Battambang: Third Round". Phnom Penh: CDRI, 2009.

UN Cambodia. "Rising Food Prices Discussion Paper". Available at <http://www.un.org.kh/index.php?option=com_content&view=article&id=103:rising-food-prices-discussion-paper-&catid=46:rising-food-prices> (accessed 19 January 2010).

UNCTAD. "Keeping ODA Afloat: No Stone Unturned". UNCTAD Policy Briefs, 7 March 2009. Geneva: UNCTAD, 2009b.

UNICEF Cambodia. *Cambodia Anthropometrics Survey Report (English Supplement)*. Phnom Penh: UNICEF Cambodia, 2009.

UN Standing Committee on Nutrition. "Global Recession increases Malnutrition for the Most Vulnerable People in Developing Countries". Geneva: UN SCN, 2009.

USDA Economic Research Service. "Food Security Assessment 2008–2009". Washington, D.C.: USDA, 2009.

US Department of Commerce Office of Textiles and Apparel. Available at <http://otexa.ita.doc.gov/msrpoint.htm> (accessed 15 February 2010).

USDA Production, Supply and Distribution (PSD) Online. Available at <http://www.fas.usda.gov/psdonline/psdQuery.aspx> (accessed 1 February 2010).

US Energy Information Administration. "Spot Prices: Conventional Gasoline". Available at <http://tonto.eia.doe.gov/dnav/pet/pet_pri_spt_s1_d.htm> (accessed 1 February 2010).

von Braun, J. *Food and Financial Crises: Implications for Agriculture and the Poor*. Washington, D.C.: IFPRI, 2008.

von Grebmer, K., B. Nestorova, A. Quisumbing, R. Fertziger, H. Fritschel, R. Pandya-Lorch, and Y. Yohannes. *Global Hunger Index 2009*. Bonn: IFPRI, Welthungerhilfe, Concern Worldwide, 2009.

von Grebmer, K., H. Fritschel, B. Nestorova, T. Olofinbiyi, R. Pandya-Lorch, and Y. Yohannes. *Global Hunger Index 2008*. Bonn: IFPRI, Welthungerhilfe, Concern Worldwide, 2008.

Vong, S. and P. Kaufmann. "Food Security and Nutrition in Cambodia — CARD's Role and Achievements". Presentation to the inception workshop Emergency Food Assistance Project — Strengthening Institutional Capacities for Emergency Response to Food Crisis and Improving Food Security. Phnom Penh: CARD, 2009.

Weismann, D., A.K. Sost, I. Schöninger, H. Dalzell, L. Kiess, T. Arnold, and S. Collins. *Global Hunger Index 2007*. Cologne: IFPRI, Welthungerhilfe, Concern Worldwide, 2007.

Weiss, J. and H. Khan, eds. *Poverty Strategies in Asia: A Growth Plus Approach*. Cheltenham, UK; Northampton, MA: ADBI & Edward Elgar Publishing, 2006.

Willenbockel, D. and S. Robinson. "The Global Financial Crisis, LDC Exports and Welfare: Analysis with a World Trade Model". MPRA Paper No. 15377. Brighton: University of Sussex, 2009.

World Bank. *Rising Food Prices: Policy Options and World Bank Response*. Washington, D.C.: World Bank, undated.

———. "More and Better Investment in Agriculture". Agriculture for Development Policy Brief. Available at <http://siteresources.worldbank.org/INTWDR2008/Resources/2795087-1191440805557/4249101-1191602454982/Brief_MoreBetterInvest_web.pdf> (accessed 16 January 2010).

———. World Development Indicators 2008 CD-ROM. Washington, D.C.: World Bank, 2008.

———. *Sustaining Rapid Growth in a Challenging Environment: Cambodia Country Economic Memorandum*. Phnom Penh: World Bank Cambodia, 2009a.

———. *Poverty Profile and Trend in Cambodia: Findings from the 2007 Cambodia Socio-Economic Survey (CSES)*. Washington, D.C.: World Bank, 2009b.

———. *East Asia and Pacific Update — Transforming the Rebound into Recovery*. Washington, D.C.: World Bank, 2009c.

———. World Development Indicators Online Database. Available at <http://web.worldbank.org/WBSITE/EXTERNAL/DATASTATISTICS/0,,contentMDK:20535285~menuPK:1390200~pagePK:64133150~piPK:64133175~theSitePK:239419,00.html> (accessed 1 February 2010).

World Bank Cambodia. "Rockets and Feathers? Petroleum Products Price Movements". *Petroleum Sector Briefing Note No. 17* (Special Supplement), August/September 2009. Phnom Penh: World Bank Cambodia, 2009d.

World Bank and ISDR. "Disaster Risk Management Programs for Priority Countries". Washington, D.C.: World Bank, 2009.

Xinhua. "Ban on Pork Imports Creates Windfall for Cambodian Pig Farmers", 19 September 2007. Available at <http://ki-media.blogspot.com/2007/09/ban-on-pork-imports-creates-windfall.html> (accessed 19 January 2010).

————. "Cambodia Lifts Ban on Importing Pigs, Pork to Curb Soaring Prices", 27 March 2008. Available at <http://ki-media.blogspot.com/2008/03/cambodia-lifts-ban-on-importing-pigs.html> (accessed 19 January 2010).

Yanara, C. "Priority Project Monitoring and the Joint Monitoring Indicators". Summary presentation to the GDCC meeting, 29 September 2009.

Yu B. and S. Fan. "Rice Production Response in Cambodia". Paper presented at the International Association of Agricultural Economists Conference, Beijing, 16–22 August 2009.

6

ROAD TO RECOVERY
Responses, Risks and Opportunities

Hossein Jalilian and Glenda Reyes

6.1 WAKING UP FROM THE DARK SPELL

All over the world, revival from the long spell of economic slump had begun by the second half of 2009. East Asia was at the forefront of global recovery, with some of the hard-hit industrialized countries finally managing positive quarterly output growth and the Chinese economy regaining its pre-crisis robustness. The road to recovery certainly did not come easily. Countries recognized that go-it-alone strategies would have been ineffective in battling the recession given its nature. Thus, they needed to synchronize remedial action as far as possible. Countries were also confronted with serious policy dilemmas. Aggressive policy interventions came with a high price that needed to be settled afterwards. This settlement would be painful but failure to stem the tide of the crisis with Keynesian-type strategies would have depressed economies further. Everywhere, it was recognized that while economic rebound rested on quick fixes, a more sustainable recovery depended on re-orientation of development strategies and structural reforms. Economic risks remain aplenty, heightening the pressure to act on such imperative decisively.

Cambodia started to emerge from the crisis along with the rest of the world. The global upturn served as a beneficial push factor that stimulated trade and capital inflows, while government actions served as a pull factor that helped rein in investor flight and keep the growth sectors afloat. Recovery for the country was also a struggle, not least because its crisis response was undermined by the fact that it is one of the poorest nations in the world. Some quick fixes facilitated economic rebound but there was also the recognition that deeper reforms were needed to ensure a recovery that could better address existing and imminent risks, better exploit growth opportunities and better withstand another crisis that might not be far away. Such thrust rests on the thesis broached in Chapter 1 and is reflected in the discussions in the other chapters. The nature of Cambodia's post-conflict economic development shaped the impact of the global crisis. Some features of the post-conflict milieu heightened the country's exposure to the meltdown and undermined its crisis response. It follows then that improving the country's resilience to shocks necessitates reforms in its safeguards.

This chapter deals with Cambodia's crisis responses and the risks and opportunities impinging on its socioeconomic recovery. Section 2 mentions the quick fixes and longer-term responses promulgated by the government to contain the effects of the crisis at the macro, sectoral and micro levels. Section 3 briefly describes the signs and bases of economic recovery. Section 4 discusses the risks, opportunities and directions for reform in line with the thesis cited above. Section 5 concludes.

6.2 RESPONSES

Keynesian strategies clearly dominated policy responses to the global economic downturn. This was somewhat remarkable given that pro-cyclical policies were strongly disapproved of during the Asian financial crisis. Fiscal deficits across developing East Asia all widened (see Figure 6.1). Countries like China, Vietnam, Malaysia and Thailand put together huge fiscal stimulus packages which included expansionary budgets, public infrastructure investments, tax breaks, social safety net

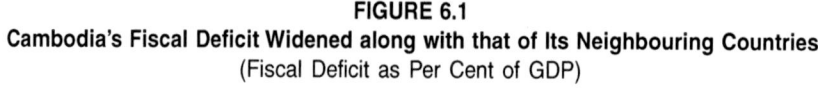

FIGURE 6.1
Cambodia's Fiscal Deficit Widened along with that of Its Neighbouring Countries
(Fiscal Deficit as Per Cent of GDP)

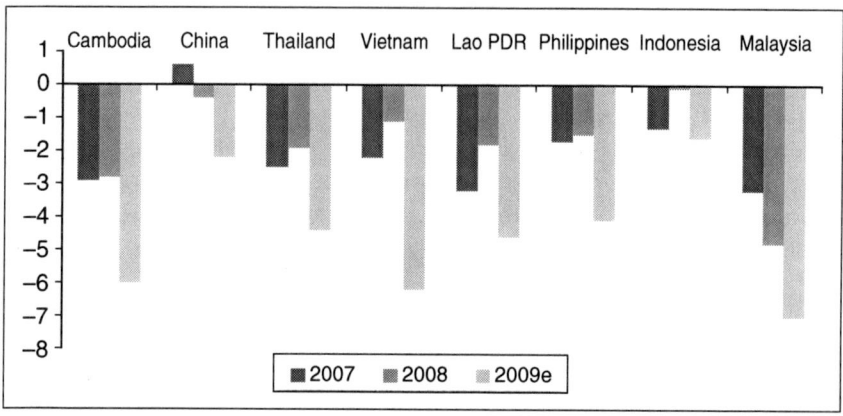

Source: World Bank (2010).

spending, subsidies and rebates among others. With its fiscal resources already stretched, the Cambodian government was able to execute only a limited set of interventions. As mentioned above, a swift rebound from the crisis needed quick fixes but a more sustainable recovery from the shock necessitates longer-term and structural improvements given how some aspects of Cambodia's post-conflict milieu heightened its exposure to the meltdown. The government moved to administer both types of responses. However, not only were its hands effectively tied by financial constraints, the soundness of some of its remedial actions was also questionable.

6.2.1 Fiscal Easing

Fiscal policy was the main crisis management tool available to the Cambodian government. The heavy dollarization of the country since the initial transition phase effectively prevented the use of monetary policy to contain the impact of the shock. With inflation at bay, the government had room for a looser fiscal stance. The 2009 fiscal deficit was set to widen from 2.8 to 4.3 per cent of GDP. In the end however, actual fiscal balance swelled to approximately –8.1 per cent of GDP

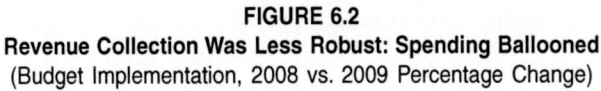

FIGURE 6.2
Revenue Collection Was Less Robust: Spending Ballooned
(Budget Implementation, 2008 vs. 2009 Percentage Change)

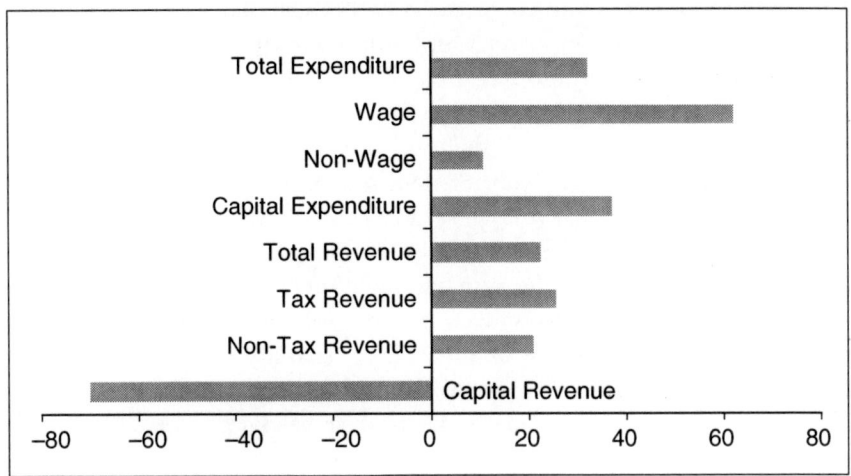

Source: Authors' calculations based on data from MoEF (various).

(World Bank 2010). Figure 6.2 shows that total spending ballooned by 32 per cent relative to 2008. Total revenues may have managed to exceed 2008 revenues but that for the period January–November 2009 actually showed a decline of 7 per cent relative to the same period in 2008. Financial management reforms may have led to improvements in tax collection but the lack lustre economic environment caused tax and non-tax revenues to suffer. The offer of tax incentives in the hope of priming the economy also contributed to the decline in revenues. As can be seen in Figure 6.2, it was capital revenue in particular that declined remarkably by about 70 per cent between 2008 and 2009. Collections in December managed to hoist revenues up.

Echoing past critiques of the government's budgeting, objections were raised regarding how its fiscal action during the crisis prioritized military and civil service spending at the expense of expenditure on supposedly priority areas, primary of which are agriculture, rural development and social protection. Spending on priority sectors increased by 39 per cent between 2008 and 2009, which is significant compared to the 2 per cent increase in 2008 relative to 2007; on the other hand, wage expenditure rose by a much higher 62 per cent. In fairness, the 2009 budget programme was prepared in view of the more dominant concerns at the time, specifically the higher cost of living due to the food and energy shocks and the mounting border conflict. As explained in Chapter 2, initial opinions on how the crisis would affect Cambodia were optimistic. The hike in military budget met little opposition. When it became evident that the shock was severely affecting the economy, a more pro-poor expansionary budget would have helped mitigate the adverse impact on employment and help alleviate the hardship of poor and vulnerable groups.

Another critique was the part domestic financing of the budget deficit as this imperilled price and exchange rate stability. Also, while Cambodia's current level of external indebtedness is sustainable, warning against increasing borrowing was raised given slower capital inflows and the weak state of the economy. The possibility that, after the long post-conflict gush in aid, less donor support (except perhaps for Chinese assistance) might flow to Cambodia cannot be discounted as reforms within the donor community take effect and Cambodia's economy is expected to progress more in the medium-term and thus decrease its reliance on official external financing.

6.2.2 Monetary Easing

The easing of inflation gave the NBC needed leeway to loosen monetary policy and complement the government's crisis recovery efforts. The bi-currency economy limited its range of possible interventions. Further, while on the upside the underdeveloped state of the financial sector shielded Cambodia from the first-round effects of the crisis, on the downside it prevented the government and private financial institutions from raising more funds to bolster the national coffers.

The NBC's remedial actions consisted of both quick fixes and longer-term measures. The central bank slashed the reserve requirement from 16 to 12 per cent to help enhance liquidity in the financial system and eliminated the cap on real estate lending to inject some relief into the property sector. It put up an overdraft facility, though backed by a limited amount, to help banks that were solvent but temporarily struggling with liquidity shortfalls. The NBC also issued tougher regulations on asset reclassification and provisioning so as to more accurately diagnose the NPL problem, and on banks' obligations to better detect and report credit risk exposures. Alongside these, the central bank strengthened off-site and on-site surveillance of banks. It also started granting deposit-taking licences to qualified MFIs to ease their reliance on foreign capital. One well-known factor that inhibits the effectiveness of the central bank's crisis response is its overstretched capacity. The institution has been undertaking capacity building measures to address this long-standing problem.

Notwithstanding the significant post-conflict financial liberalization, Cambodia's financial infrastructure remains immature. The inter-bank market is underdeveloped and there are a limited number of financial instruments. Additionally, there are no deposit insurance and rating agencies and the credit information system is relatively new. In recent years, the foundations of a capital market have been gradually laid in accordance with the government's Financial Sector Blueprint 2001–2010; supporting laws have been passed and the Securities and Exchange Commission was created. The plan was to reportedly launch the bourse in 2008 but the crisis got in the way. Despite the publicity and the groundwork, the stock exchange plans still did not take off in 2009, nor was the launch feasible in May 2010 as anticipated at the time.

6.2.3 Sectoral Responses

Garments

The rebound in the garment sector mainly underpinned the rebound in the export industry, garments being the leading export since the latter years of the initial transition phase as discussed in Chapter 1. This rebound rested as much on private sector responses as it did on government-provided relief. Given again the fiscal constraints that constrain its options, the government could only execute limited interventions to aid the crisis-hit garment industry. Two major measures that it undertook were the suspension of the payment of the advance profit tax and reduction in employers' social security contributions. Garment factories reportedly found some degree of relief from the first measure (Jalilian and Reyes 2010); however, other tax incentives could have arguably been more effective such as investment tax credit or tax credit on training expenditures. Another issue related to this was how some garment factories used the economic downturn as a pretext to close down only to reopen under a new name so as to qualify for tax breaks, evade tax obligations and wage payments, and re-negotiate labour contracts.

In Chapter 2, it was discussed how the loss of preferential access cost the domestic garment sector a major aspect of its competitiveness in the garment business. The government and the Garment Manufacturers Association in Cambodia (GMAC) have been jointly negotiating for substitute preferential arrangements or improvements in existing schemes. In particular, they have been lobbying for duty-free access to the U.S. market and greater flexibility in the Rules of Origin Requirement of the EU's Everything but Arms initiative. In May 2010, the so-called Cambodian trade bill, which grants duty-free access to Cambodian-made garments, was introduced in the US House of Representatives. Already, it has met opposition (Lewis 2010).

Construction

Responses to the slowdown in the real estate sector were expected to likewise stimulate construction activities given the close linkage between the two sectors. As earlier mentioned, the NBC slashed the cap on real estate lending in the hopes of limiting the seriousness of the real estate bust. However, as raised in Chapter 2, this policy appears to have had little impact. One longer-term redress to the slump was said to be the granting of permission for foreign ownership of real estate. This spurred the drafting of the Foreign Property Bill. With the approval of the bill by the Cambodian parliament, the law is expected to be promulgated soon. The bill allows foreigners to own property, but only above the ground floor. The allowable extent of foreign ownership, however, is yet to be decreed (Meas and Finch 2010). Land also remains off-limits to foreigners. Alongside this greater liberalization of the property market is the tightening of the regulatory framework covering real estate developers who were obliged to apply for a licence by April 2010 at the latest in accordance with a sub-decree passed at the end of 2009. Property buyers were hurt by the crisis-induced flight of developers that left building projects unfinished. The sub-decree is said to be aimed at strengthening buyer protection. Aside from the licensing require-ment, it also requires developers who use customer financing to deposit 2 per cent of their estimated project value with an Inter-ministerial Working Group, open an account with a commercial bank in Cambodia, and complete projects or risk forfeiting assets. As of March 2010, only a few had applied for the licence, prompting the government to issue an admonishment (Soeun 2010).

Tourism

Strategies to quell the downturn in the tourism sector were probably the most visible of the remedial policies aimed at the growth industries. Given concerns about the long-term situation of tourism in the country discussed in Chapter 2, these strategies aptly comprised quick fixes and longer-term measures targeting sectoral sustainability. The short-term responses seem to have been directed at increasing the quantity of visitors and mainly entailed three types of strategy. The first involved travel facilitation measures, particularly: visa-fee waivers for neighbours, Vietnam and Laos and other selected ASEAN members; operation of the national carrier, Cambodia Angkor Air and the start of direct flights between Cambodia and the Philippines; and opening of new border checkpoints and waterways. The second type entailed marketing strategies, particularly the launch of international advertising campaigns, tourism branding (Cambodia: Kingdom of Wonder), institution of provincial tourism offices, and organization of showcasing activities. The third type was composed of cost reduction measures undertaken by the private sector with encouragement from the government; for example, prices of tourism services, including accommodation, food and transport, were reportedly slashed by 10 to 20 per cent while discounts on package tours were also reportedly offered by 30 to 40 per cent of travel agencies operating in Cambodia (MoT 2009).

The long-term responses, on the other hand, seem to have been directed at enhancing the quality of tourism in the country and mainly comprised four different strategies. Two of these strategies involved improvements in regulatory framework and tourism infrastructure, rightly addressing the two major reasons for the country's inferior competitiveness broached in Chapter 2. The Tourism Law was passed by the Cambodian National Assembly in April 2009 and three major features of this law are on licensing requirements, penalties on errant industrial operators, and enhanced standards on customer service and tourist products. Improvements in tourism infrastructure included rehabilitation and better maintenance, particularly of roads leading to key border checkpoints. The third and fourth strategies dealt with the diversification of markets and tourist attractions, respectively. Market diversification was a widely supported strategy having seen how tourism receipts significantly suffered even though the increase in tourism traffic from less developed countries compensated for the decline in tourists from more developed nations. The Middle East, Europe, Russia, non-traditional ASEAN markets and the Cambodia expatriate community have been eyed as potential strong markets. The diversification of tourist attractions is an enormous challenge given the entrenched interests in the status quo. The huge underdevelopment of alternative tourist sites and the uncertain outlook for tourism are also serious stumbling blocks to attracting investment away from Angkor Wat in particular and the Sihanouk-Phnom Penh-Siem Reap triangle in general. Nevertheless, at least there is verbal consensus that Cambodia's rich natural endowment could potentially make the country an excellent choice for eco-tourism.

Agriculture

As discussed in Chapters 1 and 2, the agriculture sector buffered the impacts of the shocks. It helped cushion the pinch of the Asian financial crisis and recently, the blow of the global economic crisis. The price deflation that accompanied the slump, however, hurt agricultural workers who had banked on the previous price spikes to make their increased investments and production profitable. Notably, the incomes of rubber and cassava farmers plummeted as product prices tumbled in the markets. As one of the priority economic sectors, agriculture was unfairly affected by the prioritization of civil service and defence wages in the allocation of the national budget. Despite its determination as the key to poverty reduction in the country, the sector's share of the budget has remained unchanged and its share of aid has declined. The government, however, did undertake three measures with the aim of stimulating agricultural growth and harnessing its mitigating influence on the downturn: the establishment of the Agriculture Support and Development Fund to provide credit, the grant of a three-year income tax holiday for qualified agriculture and agro-industry projects, and the imposition of zero-tariffs on imports of agricultural inputs and equipment.

6.2.4 Social Protection

The economic upheaval brought the debilities in Cambodia's formal social protection system to the fore. It strengthened the impetus for articulating a strategy that addresses the fragmented, geographically limited, episode-driven and unsustainable nature of official social interventions in the country. The crisis demanded a swift and effective administration of safety nets to soften the blow of the crisis on the poor but the state of the social protection system prevented the government from meeting such demand. Chapter 4 emphasizes the FGD and SSI findings about the lack of intensification in social safety net provision over the period of the crisis. Informal safety nets may play a central, if not sometimes superior, role in risk mitigation in the Cambodian context but they cannot substitute formal safety nets.[1] Chapter 4 further reveals the weakness of informal safety nets as coping mechanisms. Covariant shocks have widespread impact; being likely victims of the crisis themselves, social networks may be unable to provide insurance as they would under more normal circumstances.

Mandated by the government at the end of 2008, the Council for Agriculture and Development (CARD) undertook a gap analysis, set up a working group that completed a concept note by June 2009, and organized the National Forum on Social Safety Nets the month after. The end goal was to develop the National Social Protection Strategy. The Strategy was initially expected to be finished by the end of 2009, but it was still in progress as of June 2010 (CARD 2010; CARD, WFP and World Bank 2009). The government dispensed two safety net schemes in specific response to the crisis: the Government Fund for Short-term Vocational Training which targeted dismissed workers from the growth sectors; and the Fund for Self-employment which targeted the accomplished trainees wishing to set up their own business or any other initiative. These schemes were backed by donor funding, though this was limited in actual amount. Financing has always been a challenge to programme sustainability. Like agriculture, social protection was unfairly affected by the prioritization of the defence and civil service wages in the allocation of the bigger budget in 2009.

6.3 SIGNS AND BASES OF RECOVERY

Cambodia's real output growth in 2009, as mentioned in Chapter 2, reached a measly 0.1 per cent according to the government and an average of –2 per cent according to other estimates. If not for the improvements in the second half of 2009, the country's year-end performance would have been worse. The rebound witnessed in said period was not all-inclusive, however. Strong upturn was seen in some areas but upsets continued in others. Cambodia's former high-growth economy is not expected to be resurrected soon. Mirroring the outlook for global recovery, the country's economic growth in 2010 as well as the year after will be modest. This assessment is shared by both the government and international institutions. Real output is specifically projected to grow by an average of 4.7 per cent in 2010 and 6 per cent in 2011 (see Figure 6.3).

FIGURE 6.3
Recovery Has Been Made
(Real GDP Growth, Per Cent)

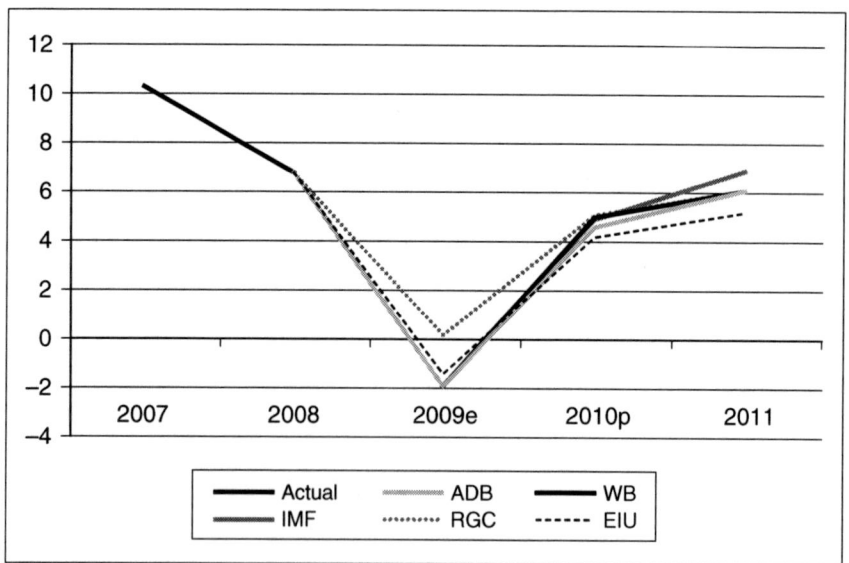

Source: NIS for 1998–2008; for 2009 and 2010 projections, MoEF, IMF (2010*b*), ADB (2010*a*). World Bank (2010) and EIU (2010).

Recovery has been anchored on renewed trade and investment flows, which in turn are facilitated by the government's crisis response discussed above. Year-on-year growth in export values bounced back in the final quarter of 2009 after witnessing its worst slump in the previous quarters. It had regained its pre-crisis strength by early 2010. Although already recovered, import values have yet to reach pre-crisis levels (see Figure 6.4). A key reason for this has been the lower fuel import prices. Fuel imports continually increased in terms of volume but declined in terms of value. In spite of the price escalation, import values in the first quarter of 2010 were still 15 per cent lower than in the first quarter of 2009. Both volumes and values of durable imports had recovered by 2010. The easing of petroleum prices in particular and overall inflation in general helped stimulate transport equipment sales. The current account balance was expected to widen in 2010 after shrinking in 2009 due to the revival in exports and stronger turnaround in imports.

FIGURE 6.4
Export and Import Growth Recovered after Experiencing Their Worst Slump
(3mma Values, y-o-y Percentage Change)

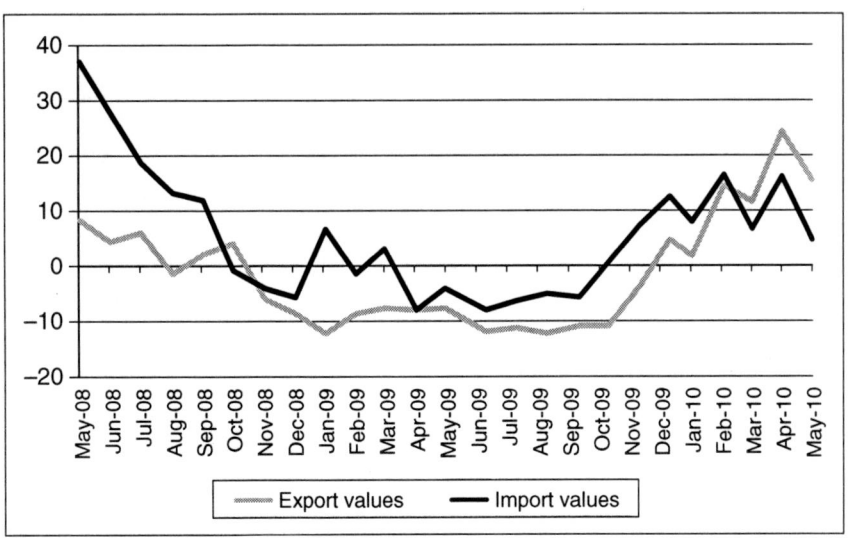

Source: Authors' calculations based on data from MoEf.

Chapter 2 shows a 36 per cent decrease in net FDI from about US$795 million in 2008 to US$511 million in 2009. Much of the drop occurred in the first half of the year. Net FDI flows in the last two quarters experienced fewer declines relative to the same quarters in 2008. By the first quarter of 2010, they had already managed positive growth *vis-à-vis* the same period in 2009. By year-end, they were expected to regain some of their pre-crisis lustre and reach US$639 million (World Bank 2010), which is about 25 per cent higher than in the previous year. International remittances exhibited greater resilience than FDI, as intimated in Chapter 2. Total remittance inflows to Cambodia recovered quickly following a slight decline in 2008. The lack of systematic data on informal transfers, which comprise the bulk of remittance flows to Cambodia, precludes assessment on how they fared during and after the crisis; anecdotal evidence described in Chapter 4 suggests however that cross-border remittances have yet to pick up pace. More aid was committed for 2010. Breaching the US$1 billion mark, at the time of writing it looked likely to be about 10 per cent higher than disbursements in 2009 (see Figure 6.5). Japan, at least based on its

FIGURE 6.5
More Aid Was Committed for 2010
(US$ Million)

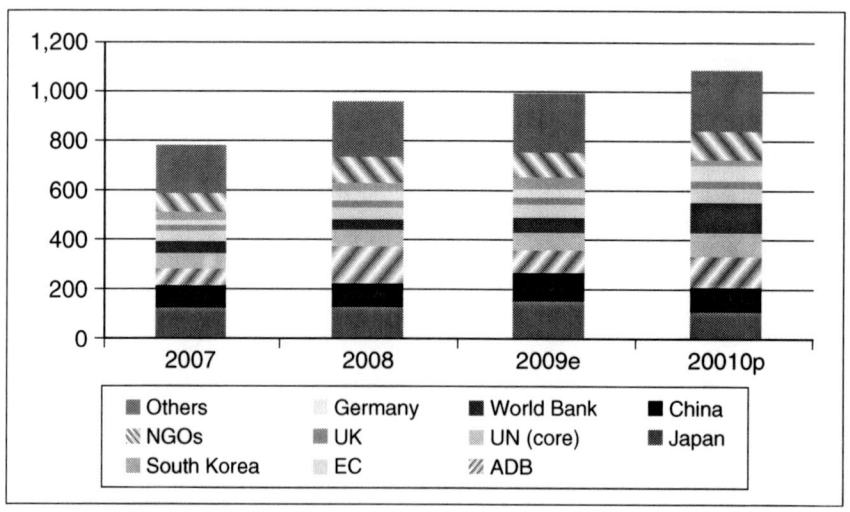

Source: CDC-CRDB (2009).

pledges, has kept its position as the leading bilateral donor, with China tailing it closely. Notably however, the share of Japanese assistance in total aid has fallen from about 15 to 10 per cent. Aid reforms induced by the crisis are also expected to affect Cambodia, albeit (all things considered) not significantly. Shaken by the economic meltdown, an announcement was made that the United Kingdom is to close its office and gradually withdraw its financial assistance to Cambodia by 2011. The bilateral donor is to channel more of its aid away from high-growth economies towards fragile countries.[2] Any diminution in traditional aid is expected to be filled by non-traditional assistance, however.

Among the crisis-hit growth sectors, tourism was the first to recover. Year-on-year international visitor arrivals grew again by June 2009 and were nearly back to pre-crisis levels by 2010 (see Figure 6.6). Tourism traffic from Japan, China and Thailand resurged though that from South Korea remained slow and visits from the U.S. and the United Kingdom significantly contracted. The burst of tourism from Laos and Vietnam, which supported the industry at its worst, also eventually quieted down. In terms of tourism receipts, year-end revenues failed to equal those of the preceding year because of the deceleration in tourism from more developed countries in the first half of 2009.

FIGURE 6.6
Tourism was the First to Recover among the Crisis-hit Growth Sectors
(International Visitor Arrivals, y-o-y Percentage Change)

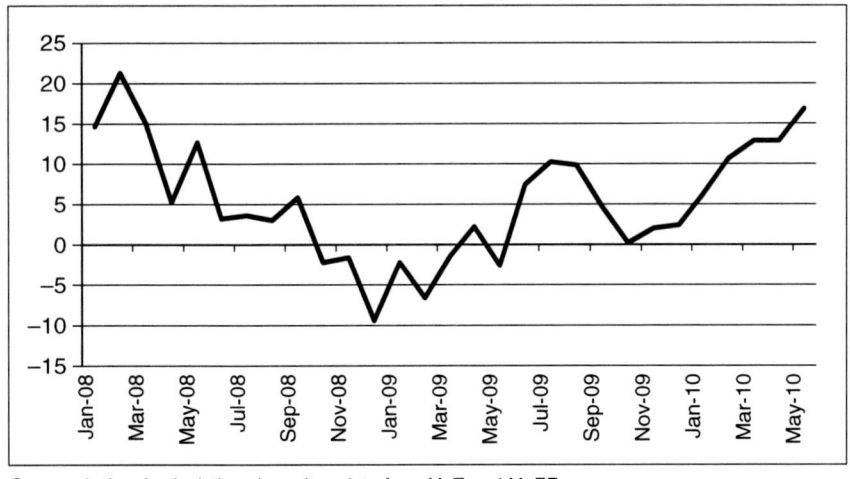

Source: Authors' calculations based on data from MoT and MoEF.

The pull-through in the garment sector came later. Clothing exports had begun their recovery by the last quarter of 2009. Almost a year of negative year-on-year growth finally ended by 2009-end (see Figure 6.7), mainly due to holiday sales and stronger exports to non-U.S. markets. Garment exports to the U.S. only registered positive year-on-year growth again by the second quarter of 2010. U.S. import data show that though garment shipments from Bangladesh eventually contracted, they had recuperated by the second quarter of 2010. Chinese and Vietnamese garment exports showed greater resilience (see Figure 6.8).

Recovery in the construction sector was similarly later in coming. Import volumes of construction equipment had improved by the third quarter of 2009 but were yet to reverse their negative year-on-year growth as of the first quarter of 2010 (see Figure 6.9). The drag in construction reflects the lull in real estate development. The property sector overall is not expected to regain its pre-crisis buoyancy till 2011 at least. Results of a 2010 study reveal that more than half of the survey's respondent investors would consider buying property, but

FIGURE 6.7
Garment Exports Have Recovered from Their Year-long Slump
(Total Monthly Clothing Exports, 3mma y-o-y Percentage Change)

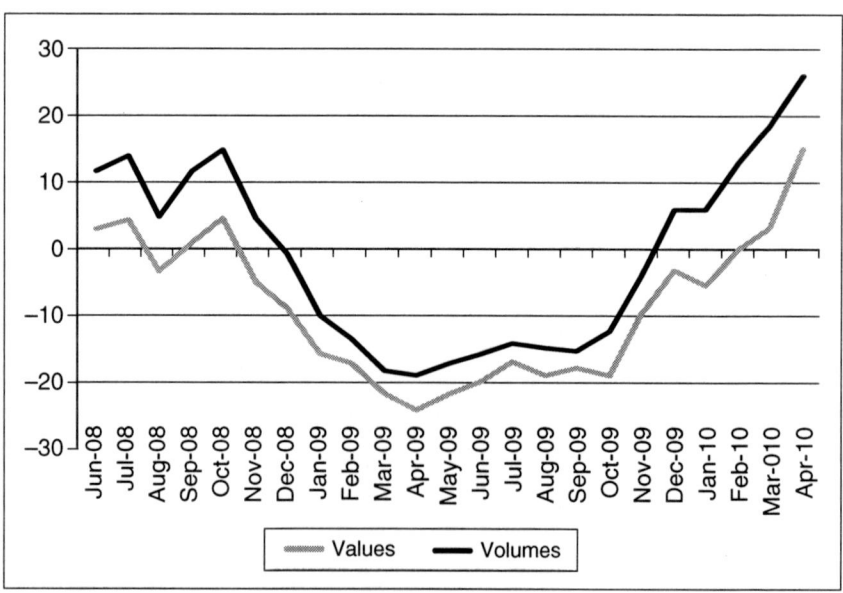

Source: Authors' calculations based on data from MoEF (various).

FIGURE 6.8
Garment Exports to the U.S. Regained Pre-crisis Vigour
(Comparative Values of Garment Exports to the U.S., 3mma y-o-y Percentage Change)

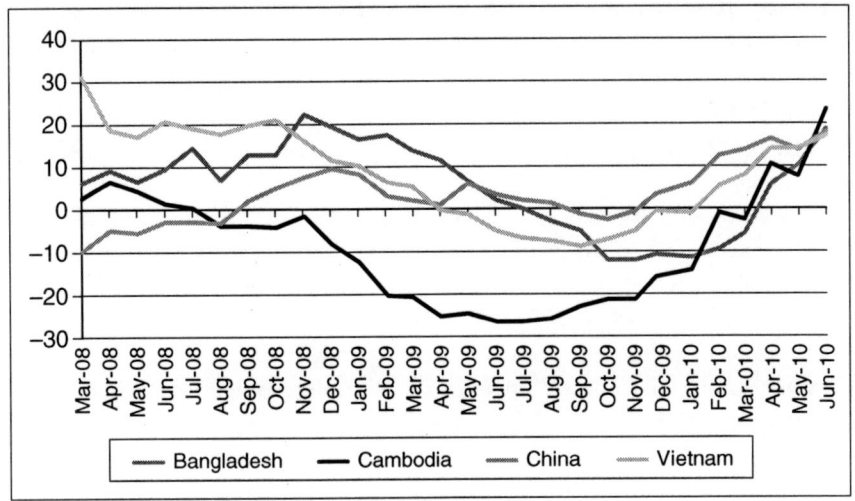

Source: Authors' calculations based on data from USITC.

FIGURE 6.9
Construction Suffered a Blow so Severe that It Took the Longest Time to Recover
(Import Volumes, 3mma y-o-y Percentage Change)

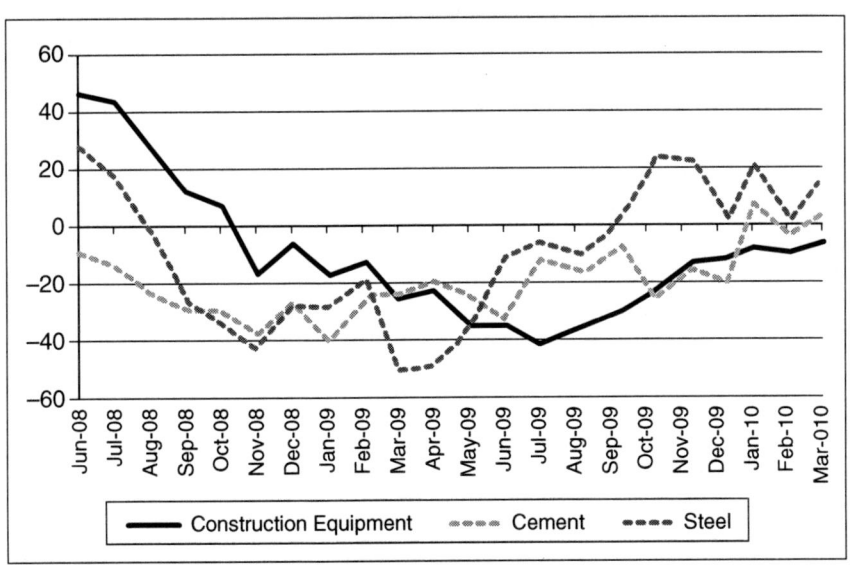

Source: Authors' calculations based on data from MoEF.

only after more than two years; a mere 11 per cent of them had been mulling over whether to purchase property in 2010.[3] As of June 2010 compared to the same period last year, the prices of premium commercial properties in Phnom Penh were still down by 15 to 20 per cent while those of prime residential real estate in the capital were still down by 25 to 35 per cent (Cambodia Estate Agent 2010).

Agricultural output was expected to rise by 5 per cent in real terms in 2010, continuing the stable growth of the previous year. The year-on-year surge in milled rice exports carried over to the first five months of 2010, specifically by nearly 300 per cent in terms of value and 155 per cent in terms of volume on average (see Figure 6.10). Rice prices in the international market appeared to have stabilized at levels lower than the peak prices in 2007–08 (stimulating imports) but were higher than pre-food crisis prices (stimulating production).[4] As mentioned in Chapter 2, actual Cambodian exports of milled rice are however way below potential due to limited milling capacity. Informal paddy exports dominate rice trade, resulting in significant revenue loss for the government. Earlier projections expected rice production to increase to 7.25 million tonnes and exportable paddy to 3.1 million tonnes in 2010 (Commodity Online 2010). Unfortunately, this optimistic outlook

FIGURE 6.10
Milled Rice Exports Continued to Rise
(3mma y-o-y Percentage Change)

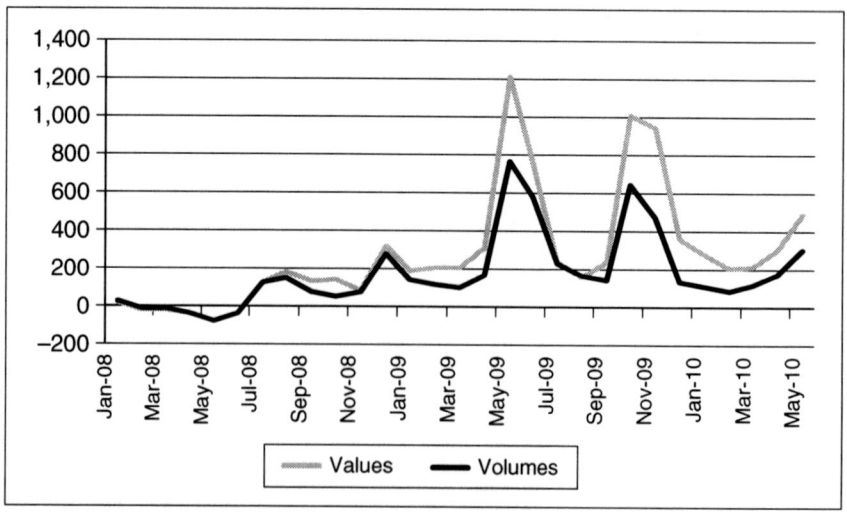

Source: Authors' calculations based on data from MoEF (various).

was thwarted by abnormal weather. Chapter 4 reports the FGD and SSI findings on the adverse livelihood impacts of drought on the one hand and too much rainfall on the other. The delayed rainy season and record low rainwater levels in 2010 also hurt farming and fishing prospects. Reversing its former view, the FAO placed Cambodia's total estimated rice production at 6.6 million tonnes in 2010, which is 13 per cent lower than the previous year. Exportable paddy was estimated at about 1 million tonnes (FAO-Global Information and Early Warning System 2009, 2010). Rubber exports from Cambodia had recovered from their year-on-year declines at the time of the food shock. Renewed trade has consequently driven up prices.[5] Like rice, however, rubber production in Cambodia has been hurt by erratic weather, which explains the lower export volumes in early 2010 relative to the same period in 2009.[6]

Reflecting the upturn in the economy, broad money growth had resurged to double-digit levels by the second half of 2009. Ample liquidity has been restored, though most of it has been concentrated in big banks which means that smaller institutions may still be in danger of serious liquidity shortfalls or even insolvency. Foreign currency deposits year-on-year growth averaged about 40 per cent in the first five months of 2010. Credit, by contrast, has remained tight overall. It grew by just 4 per cent in the second half of 2009 and 13 per cent in the first five months of 2010 on average (see Figure 6.11). With lending still reined in, the problem seems to have changed from liquidity squeeze to liquidity overhang. NBC reportedly has held most new bank deposits as excess reserves. Bank profitability has been harmed in that these reserves have been earning close to zero per cent. Interest rates on both dollar and riel deposits have thus been trimmed; those on loans, riel or dollar, went up as banks continued with their more stringent lending policy. Several banks have reportedly been self-insuring against any more liquidity pressures by bringing down loan-to-deposit ratios. This is a risky move given the negative spread between the central bank rate and deposit rates.[7] As far as the NPL ratio is concerned, the official figure — below 6 per cent at 2009-end (NBC 2010) — is small. This may be an underestimation, however. There are concerns that bank balance sheets are being window dressed to escape the determination of loan losses. This clearly only delays, not solves, the problem.

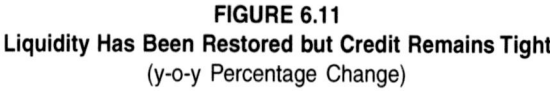

FIGURE 6.11
Liquidity Has Been Restored but Credit Remains Tight
(y-o-y Percentage Change)

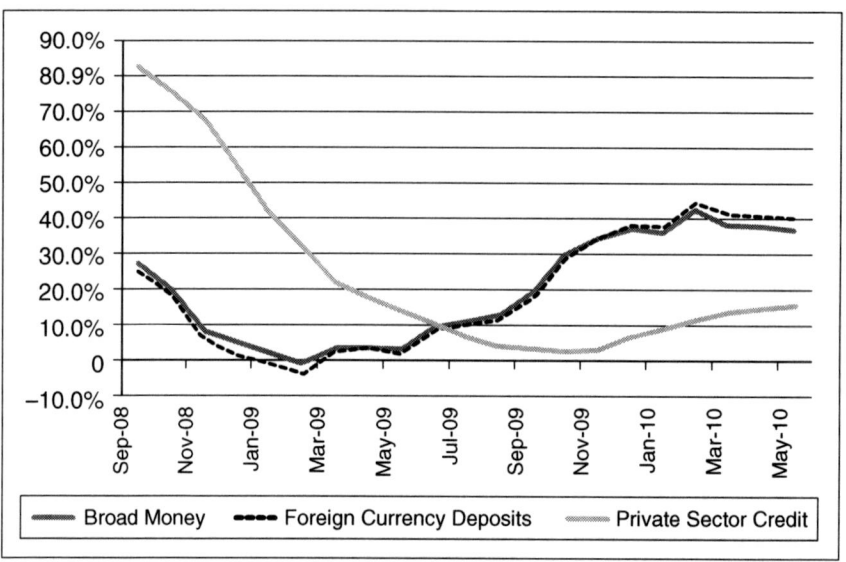

Source: Authors' calculations based on data from NBC (2010).

6.4 RISKS, OPPORTUNITIES AND DIRECTIONS

The conclusions of the earlier chapters all converge on one thesis and on one recommended general policy direction: that exposure to the crisis was heightened by debilities in the country's post-conflict milieu; hence, these debilities must be addressed in order to attain a more sustainable and crisis-resistant recovery. Even with a stronger-than-expected global recovery, risks in the external environment remain, explaining the gradual implementation or even postponement of exit strategies worldwide. Cambodia, being a small economy, has little control over these exogenous risks. Fortifying its crisis response therefore rests more on taking advantage of growth opportunities and reversing inner weaknesses that undermine its international competitiveness as well as its poor people's capacity to cope with shocks.

Garments are expected to continue dominating the country's export basket. The Diagnostic Trade Integration Strategy (DTIS)

2007 (MoC and UNDP Cambodia 2007) and Revealed Comparative Advantage (RCA) analysis by the World Bank (World Bank 2009) affirm the still high export potential of garments. This potential though is significantly contingent on addressing the bottlenecks to sectoral growth and exploiting opportunities. The possibility of a double economic dip obviously puts the sector at risk once again but, on closer analysis the bigger risk is lagging further behind in competitiveness as other exporters do better in the vertical development and diversification of the industry. Strengthening backward and upward linkages (textiles, accessories and packaging) allows reduction in delivery time and unit cost. Diversifying markets and output increases receipts and helps ensure against slowdowns in some export markets or products. The global economic crisis amassed interest in the implementation of these strategies in Cambodia. But the greater interest may not all translate into action. As discussed in Chapter 2, about 90 per cent of the industry's capital has been foreign-financed. About two-thirds of the garment firms are CMT factories. Decision-making regarding industrial upgrading or diversification thus largely rests on parent companies overseas. Given that some countries have a more established reputation in other aspects of the textile and garment business, it is possible that Cambodia's garment industry may not progress further up the value chain. A consequential difference between the garment sectors in Bangladesh and Cambodia is that the latter's mostly operates on local capital. Strategies on how to attract more local investment in the industry while keeping the generous investment climate that has made Cambodian trade flourish should be considered. Accessories, trimming and packaging production entail relatively less investment and thus there is room for more local participation given appropriate and provisional incentives. Further, serious debate has centred on the contribution of the labour standard compliance to garment export competitiveness as touched upon in Chapter 2. The reputation of the garment industry in Cambodia as a model of corporate governance has certainly attracted patrons from the ethical market but this has come at a cost. As the diminution in preferential arrangements has intensified price wars, exporting firms have questioned the net returns from such a reputation. Strong unionism in the sector and associated activities were criticized as costly and a disincentive for investment. Tension in industrial labour relations climbed to worrying levels even with the dissipation of the crisis as garment workers clamoured for higher wages and employers suspended union delegates and fired workers while awaiting court ruling on the legality of strikes launched in September 2010.[8] It is maintained, however, that labour standard compliance as a key source of product differentiation must be sustained as public valuation of corporate governance strengthens. Other major Asian garment exporting countries, particularly China and Bangladesh, have more restrictive policies on unionism and trade unions, but they also have been dealing with strong worker pressure for wage hikes. Competitiveness needs to be reined in on other factors. Two possible opportunities for the garment sector pertain to the passage of the Cambodian trade bill of 2010 by the U.S. government and the relaxation of the ROR requirement under the European Union's EBA. However, in spite of the serious lobbying on these two matters, the prospect of victory is slim. Reception to the Cambodian trade bill was soured by the government's deportation of Uighur asylum seekers to China at the end of 2009 (Lewis 2010). While preferential access was thus responsible for the earlier cultivation of and industrial dominance of the garment sector in Cambodia, the sector's future progress, again, must be made to hinge more on other aspects of competitiveness.

Diversification is likewise a key challenge for the tourism industry. Easing the dependence on Angkor Wat and directing efforts to developing other tourist areas serve both equally important aims of insuring against any future slump in tourism and helping ensure the physical sustainability of the Angkor temples. Already, there have been warnings about the potential instability of the ground on which the temples stand due to the siphoning off of the groundwater by hotels and businesses in the area (Follmer 2010). These disconcerting warnings must be heeded and current planning concerning the sustainability of the cultural heritage site must be translated into action. Developing tourist sites out of the Siem Reap-Phnom Penh-Sihanoukville triangle in general would not only again strengthen the country's resilience to crisis but would also help widen the distribution of receipts from and thus the poverty impact of tourism. Needless to say, eco-tourism is a viable alternative to cultural tourism, which is already heavily depended on, and beach tourism, which cannot be as strong as that in other countries. The country's natural resources, often described as rich and abundant, support the viability of eco-tourism. Eco-tourism development should not be considered exclusive and ignore the imperatives of environmental conservation and poverty reduction. Community-based tourism development is a tested strategy to ensuring the harmonization of these three objectives. Koh Kong is a province with good potential for eco-tourism but further tourism development will have to be considered in tandem with the massive hydropower constructions in the area. In terms of market, the experience with the crisis demonstrated the benefits of promoting sub-regional and domestic tourism. Sub-regional and local tourists may not be the biggest spenders but, with the cost and ease of travel being the lowest for them, they can be effective shock absorbers. Looking at the findings of the travel competitiveness ranking discussed in Chapter 2, tourism infrastructure and regulatory quality need to be upgraded. Diversification away from the Siem Reap-Phnom Penh-Sihanoukville triangle calls for the rehabilitation of roads towards other provinces. The overhaul of rail transport must also follow-through, travel by train being an attractive alternative to travel by bus, waterway and plane. The Tourism Law's attention to quality control is on the right track. Enforcement of the standards must be fully implemented if Cambodia wishes to compete with the major visitor economies in the world, known for their excellent tourist services.

The construction industry is evidently in a precarious situation due to the longer time it is taking for property sector recovery to set in. The impending promulgation of a foreign property act should be a sure booster, but probably not until supporting regulations and overall business prospects are more defined and investors move from their wait-and-see approach. Till then, public sector investments must fill the lull in private investments. For greater effectiveness, this action entails not only an increase in the amount of public spending. It also requires rethinking the direction of such spending. More specifically, it involves increasing the construction industry's linkages with sectors other than garments and tourism and its concentration in urban areas. Naturally, more risk-averse private investment tends to shun less developed sectors and areas. Public investment must take leadership in this regard.

Agriculture's role in the long-term development of Cambodia has been downplayed. At the maximum, it is projected that the sector could grow at only 5 per cent per year, contribute 2 percentage points to yearly output, and account for 20 per cent of annual GDP by the time annual GDP per capita rises to US$1,000 (World Bank 2009). This by no means discounts agriculture's primary role in poverty reduction or the role that it could play in crisis management. The negative relationship between agriculture and poverty is widely supported on both theoretical and empirical fronts. Given the concentration of poverty in largely agriculture-based areas and the highly segmented nature of the economy, growth in agriculture as opposed to non-agricultural sectors is likely to have greater impact on reducing the poverty rate.[9] For the same reasons, agriculture can be a very helpful shock absorber, both ex ante and ex post, especially at the household level. This is evidenced in the experience with the global economic turmoil. There are certainly a number of major risks facing agriculture, three of which are price volatility, climate change, and land security. The precarious state of the global economic recovery promises more ups and downs in agricultural commodity and input prices, posing a menace to investment and income stability, hence to the growth and capacity of agriculture as a crisis coping mechanism specifically for the benefit of the poor. Climate change, which is a cross-cutting underlying factor of the "triple crises"[10] and itself a cause of price instability, is an equally, if not a greater, threat to agricultural production, income and food security in general. Nearly all the provinces in Cambodia, particularly those reliant on farming and fishing income in the Tonle Sap basin, are reported to be vulnerable to climate change due to their low adaptive capacity and reliance on climate-sensitive livelihoods (Wingqvist 2009). Managing the risks posed by price fluctuations and climate change is not only difficult, but also prone to controversy. Price interventions can enable countries to stem the transmission of international price hikes to domestic prices but these inevitably create distortions. These distortions, however, will be worth it if their gains advantage the poor rather than those who can insure themselves against price instability. Public purchase programmes based on local procurement from peasant households coupled with food aid has proven to be a win-win strategy.[11] The facts and implications of climate change are still being debated and full appreciation of the issue has yet to permeate public consciousness in Cambodia. Cambodia is a party to the United Nations Framework Convention on Climate Change and the Kyoto Protocol.

As the country contributes little to climate change, the pressing task before it is countering the livelihood, health and other effects of climate hazards. It needs to strengthen institutional and research capacity and work in partnership with donors for sustainable funding. The lack of resolution to widespread land insecurity in Cambodia is another key risk. Apart from being considered constitutive of the right to a decent living standard, land security is widely acknowledged as having a stimulating effect on agricultural investment.[12] Obvious imperatives include the acceleration of land titling and the distribution of more social land concessions, but these are preceded by the need for improved governance in the institutional arrangements that implement them. On the upside, a great opportunity for Cambodia's rice exports has come with the further liberalization of its ASEAN neighbours' rice markets starting in 2010. This is in accordance with the ASEAN Free Trade Agreement (AFTA). Thailand, one of the ASEAN member countries and also the world's biggest rice exporter, has been dealing with some public backlash following said liberalization. However, with Vietnam already able to markedly increase its rice exports by allowing paddy imports from Cambodia for instance, it has been goaded to quickly consider the same policy. It is bound to implement stricter quality control and import timing, however, to ensure farmer protection against the pending inroad of imports (Pratruangkrai 2010*a*, *b*). Hence, to be able to fully capitalize on this opportunity, Cambodia must enhance the quality of its rice exports without losing sight of the need to upgrade its milling capacity.

Diversification and scaling-up within leading sub-sectors would serve the country well, but diversification away from them and scaling-up in other sub-sectors with high export potential are equally pressing tasks. This is a key lesson from the country's experience of the global economic downturn. The narrow economic base failed to provide adequate insurance against the shock. A blasé approach to the problem reinforces the vulnerability of the economy to crises or stagnation. It is thus necessary to cultivate new growth drivers, building up in the process the country's ex-ante crisis coping mechanism at the broader level. The DTIS 2007 and the World Bank's RCA analysis have effectively identified likely candidates for such role. In the case of agriculture, both demand conditions in the world market and domestic supply capacity were found to be high for cassava and rubber, currently still accounting for low export shares. The two prerequisites were found to be medium for fruits and vegetables and wood products, and high for fisheries produce; all three sub-sectors presently have low export shares. The profitability of building up the fruits and vegetables, wood and wood products, and fishing sectors significantly rests on their high product density or high probability of intensive and extensive diversification.[13] Better established fruit and vegetable production could more easily spur development of the processing industry; the same goes for wood and fish. Diminishing the concentration on a single (rice in the case of Cambodia) or few primary commodity exports has benefits that are strongly touted in the literature critical of the classic theories on trade. Higher concentration has been found to be associated with higher vulnerability to commodity shocks, price and income volatility, deteriorating terms of trade and low growth (Prebisch 1950; Singer 1950; Carrère, Strauss-Kahn and Cadot 2007). Global demand and domestic supply capacity were also found to be medium for light manufacturing assembly (including motorcycle and bicycle) and labour export (particularly construction and domestic workers). Even when extensively researched, moves towards diversification are still a gamble; increasing the chances of success involves clear identification and resolution of key common and product-specific export constraints. The DTIS 2007 has rightly identified four priority targets for improvement: trade facilitation, investment facilitation, technical barriers to trade, and sanitary and phyto-sanitary control.

Concerning private external transfers, reflections in the aftermath of the crisis must not only be on how to resuscitate the capital flows but also on how to increase the country's regional share in the face of intense competition and maximize the direct and indirect benefits of the transfers. Acceleration in FDI flows must not rest solely on improving push or exogenous factors. Such strategy comes with great risks. Rather, substantial concrete progress must be aimed at improving the pull factors. As mentioned in Chapter 2, these factors are present at both the country and firm levels. Some necessary firm-level improvements have already been touched upon in the preceding discussions. At the macro level, investment climate surveys (World Bank-IFC 2009; Guimbert 2010) provide useful insights into the major bottlenecks to investment. That corruption has been consistently identified as the top investment constraint is enough justification for a more aggressive approach to ousting corruption in the government and the private sector. This problem is revisited in the discussion on positive peace below. Macroeconomic and regulatory uncertainties have also been identified as top constraints, along with the high cost of electricity. Continuing with the government's public financial management reform would significantly help address the former while speeding up the construction of the national grid and hydropower development would help address the latter. Exploiting more of the direct and positive spillover effects of investment would entail, among others, human resource development and financial deepening. The intergenerational and technological transfers that could be had from hosting FDI are currently limited by the shortage of skilled labour in the country. Meanwhile, the still relatively shallow financial markets are not helping to retain profits which could otherwise be put to productive purposes.

Enabling the poor to better cope with crises, covariant or idiosyncratic, requires overhauling the public social protection system. Informal means of assistance are ingrained in the Cambodian social fabric, but they are not and must not be taken as adequate substitutes for formal schemes. An overhaul of the national social protection system is in progress. Three aspects in particular must weigh on such a task: the coverage of protection, the type and design of schemes, and the sustainability of funding. Studies such as the Vulnerable Worker Survey and the Rural Household Survey are helpful in significantly informing decision-making in this regard. The social protection strategy must rest on two types of programmes: permanent and transitory. Deciding which programmes are required for which groups must be based on the country's poverty profiles on the one hand and crisis assessments on the other. Also, the crisis appears to have rightly increased the demand for safety nets, though it must be remembered that social protection is so much more than safety nets. Other vital forms of social protection such as a mandatory health insurance system remain absent or considerably under-funded. Resource constraints importantly explain the immature state of the social protection system in the country. Crucial crisis coping mechanisms such as access to food aid have been highly dependent on donor funding and NGO administrative capacity. This question about funding sustainability forms part of the overall question about the government's fiscal capacity and prudence which in turn cannot be separated from the overall question about positive peace in Cambodia.

Making progress in the attainment of positive peace, which is basically the elimination of economic and political inequality, chiefly hinges on making progress in governance. The government's rectangular strategies on which the former and current NSDPs are based place good governance at the centre. This is a correct acknowledgement of the need to enhance the institutional framework that processes and implements plans in order to make sure that such plans are effectively administered and their benefits do not get monopolized. The government's fiscal capacity is burdened by the sheer number of pressing needs. The revenue envelope remains small and the possibility of declining aid flows from traditional sources is a looming challenge. Reforms in revenue collection, helped by the implementation of the Public Financial Management Reform Programme (PFMRP) in the past years, have of course led to the expansion of the tax base and improvement in revenue collection. The completion of the PFMRP must be seen through. Its aspects seeking to increase transparency and reduce red tape must especially be strongly committed to in order to combat the most daunting challenge to governance in the country, which is corruption. As mentioned above, corruption has been consistently identified as the most serious constraint to investment. Helped by the lack of transparency, it is tantamount to robbery of the state coffers and cheating many Cambodian people of their growth dividends. The prioritization in budgeting and budget implementation of defence and security at the expense of pro-poor sectors such as agriculture and social protection has been a rightful target of public criticism. The threat of civil war has long passed while the worthiness of pursuing military action in relation to the Thai-Cambodian border conflict must be carefully contemplated. A wilful clamp down on corruption could however bolster fiscal capacity and free up more budget for the priority sectors. In March 2010, the Anti-Corruption Law was passed. This should have been welcome news but its contentious provisions and the lack of public consultation and debate preceding its approval seems to have reinforced the long-standing concerns of some groups. The state coffers are expected to benefit from the discovery of offshore and onshore oil and gas in years to come, though the size of gains cannot yet be ascertained. Whatever the case, the rise of the oil and gas sector holds significant promise for broadening the country's development base, enhancing the spread of growth dividends and fortifying safeguards against external shocks. Guarding against corruption and lack of transparency is imperative to ensure pro-poor and crisis-ready petroleum revenue management. It is key to ensuring that the oil and gas revenues help the country develop and prosper rather than stagnating.

6.5 THE PROMISE OF A BETTER MILIEU

The Cambodian economy started its journey to recovery in the second half of 2009. Government responses of both quick fixes and longer-term remedial actions helped contain the crisis transmission and placed the economy on the road to recovery. Fiscal easing enabled greater spending though the sectoral prioritization of budgeting was questionable and revenue collection was weakened by the economic slump. Monetary easing helped alleviate the strain on the banking sector even though the economy's heavy dollarization limited the crisis response of the central bank. The garment sector benefited from quick fixes but these were few and longer-term solutions seemed to be more focused on regaining preferential access. Construction was expected to be stimulated by responses hoping to revive the real estate sector and enhance foreign property ownership, yet investor response has so far been limited. Tourism benefited from a strong set of both short-term and long-term remedial measures but was held back by the difficulty of diversifying the industry and reaping benefits in the short term. Agriculture and social assistance benefited from newly established schemes but these were few and had limited funding to the greater detriment of the poor. Similarly to world output, Cambodia's output is projected to register modest growth in 2010 and 2011. Trade and capital inflows are expected to regain some of their pre-crisis robustness, thus resuscitating garments, construction and tourism. The risks to recovery are plentiful, however. Overcoming these risks and thus ensuring a more sustainable recovery rests on exploiting growth opportunities and addressing the inherent debilities in Cambodia's post-conflict milieu. The resounding conclusion from the discussions in all the chapters is that the gravity and nature of the blow of the global financial and economic crisis in Cambodia were importantly determined by vulnerabilities cultivated in the country's post-conflict history. Cambodia may have little control over exogenous risks but it can certainly improve on the inner weaknesses that have evolved and undermined its external competitiveness. In brief, policy directions aligned with this mission are: greater diversification, sophistication and differentiation, both intra-sectoral and economy-wide; further progress in removing structural bottlenecks particularly poor infrastructure, regulatory uncertainty and shortage of skilled capital; maximization of the potential and greater pro-poor orientation of the agriculture sector; and the elimination of corruption to bolster fiscal capacity and make the distribution of growth dividends more equitable. The experience of dealing with the triple economic crises has strengthened post-conflict Cambodia. The country's future is promising, more so for everyone when key weaknesses of the post-conflict milieu are overcome.

Notes

1. See Chapter 4 for definition of formal and informal safety nets.
2. See DFID official website: <http://www.dfid.gov.uk/Where-we-work/Asia-East--Pacific/Cambodia/>.
3. The survey results were jointly released by C.B. Richard Ellis, AN Royal Bank and Indochina Research (Meas and Finch 2010; Dyer 2010).
4. See IMF Commodity Price Database for relevant data.
5. See the price database of the Malaysian Rubber Board for the rubber export prices.
6. Based on MoEF (various years) data.
7. For more on this, see IMF (2010).
8. Nearing the end of September 2010, the garment unions and manufacturers were able to agree on and sign a Memorandum of Understanding (MOU) which prohibits lock-outs, strikes and claims during the term of the negotiated collective bargaining agreement. See the MOU downloadable at <http://www.ilo.org/asia/decentwork/lang--en/docName--WCMS_145234/index.htm>.
9. See for instance Cervantes-Godoy and Dewbre (2010), Ligon and Sadoulet (2008), Christiaensen and Demery (2007), and DFID (2004).
10. Based on Addison, Arndt and Tarp (2010), the triple crisis refers to the financial crisis, food crisis, and climate change.
11. See Blein and Longo (2009).
12. See for instance Feder and Nishio (1998), Deininger and Binswanger (1999), and Lipton (2009).
13. Product density refers to the number of products that are related to each other or are in the same cluster or the so-called "product space". Intensive diversification, which can be alternatively called vertical diversification, pertains to diversification and movement from primary commodities to

higher value-added products within the same product space; meanwhile, extensive diversification, which can be alternatively called horizontal diversification, pertains to diversification towards another product space. See Hausmann and Klinger (2007), and World Bank (2009).

References

Addison, T., C. Arndt, and F. Tarp. *The Triple Crisis and the Global Aid Architecture*. UNU-WIDER Working Paper No. 2010/01. Helsinki: United Nations University, World Institute for Development Economic Research, 2010.

Blein, R. and R. Longo. "Food Price Volatility: How to Help Smallholder Farmers Manage Risk and Uncertainty". Discussion Paper for Roundtable 1. Governing Council, Rome, 18–19 February 2009.

Cambodia Estate Agent. "Property Market Overview in 2010". Available at <http://www.cambodiaestate.com/market_overview.php> (accessed 16 September 2010).

CARD. "Toward the Social Protection Strategy for the Poor and Vulnerable in Cambodia". Background Paper for the Cambodia Development Cooperation Forum III. Phnom Penh, June 2010.

CARD, World Food Programme and World Bank. "Safety Nets in Cambodia: Concept Note and Inventory". Presented during the National Forum on Food Security and Nutrition under the theme of Social Safety Nets in Cambodia, July 2009.

Carrère, C., V. Strauss-Kahn, and O. Cadot. "Export Diversification: What's Behind the Hump?" CEPR Discussion Paper No. DP6590. London: Centre for Economic Policy Research, 2007.

Cervantes-Godoy, D. and J. Dewbre. *Economic Importance of Agriculture for Poverty Reduction*. OECD Food, Agriculture and Fisheries Working Paper No. 23. Paris: OECD, 2010.

Christiaensen, L. and L. Demery. *Down to Earth Agriculture and Poverty Reduction in Africa*. Washington, D.C.: World Bank, 2007.

Commodity Online. "Cambodia Rice Surplus to Hit 3.1 Million Tonnes in 2010". Available at <www.commodityonline.com/.../Cambodia-rice-surplus-to-hit-31-mln-tons-in-2010-26956-3-1.html> (accessed 12 October 2010).

Deininger, K. and Binswanger, H. "The Evolution of the World Bank's Land Policy". *World Bank Research Observer*, vol. 14, no. 2 (1999): 247–76.

Department for International Development. *Agriculture, Growth and Poverty Reduction*. DFID Working Paper. London: DFID, 2004.

Dyer, E. "Research Shows Trust in Property Sector Low". *Phnom Penh Post*, 5 April 2010.

FAO-Global Information and Early Warning System. "Country Brief on Cambodia", updated 23 October 2009. Available at <http://www.fao.org/giews/countrybrief/country.jsp?code=KHM> (accessed 15 February 2010).

————. "Country Brief on Cambodia", updated 2 September 2010. Available at <http://www.fao.org/giews/countrybrief/country.jsp?code=KHM> (accessed 12 October 2010).

Feder, G. and A. Nishio. "The Benefit of Land Registration and Titling: Economic and Social Perspectives". *Land Use Policy* 15 (1998): 25–43.

Follmer, M. "Unchecked Water Pumping around Angkor Wat Threatens Temple Complex". Available at <http://www.takepart.com/node/202370/actions> (accessed 14 October 2010).

Guimbert, S. "Emerging Industries". Presentation during the 2010 Cambodia Outlook Conference. Phnom Penh, 17 March 2010.

Hausmann, R. and B. Klinger. *The Structure of the Product Space and the Evolution of Comparative Advantage*. CID Working Paper No. 146. Cambridge: CID Harvard University, 2007.

IMF, Primary Commodity Price Database. Available at <http://www.imf.org/external/np/res/commod/index.asp> (accessed 12 October 2010).

Jalilian, H., S. Chan, G. Reyes, C.H. Saing, D. Pon, and D. Pon. *Global Financial Crisis Discussion Paper Series 3: Cambodia*. London: ODI, 2009.

Jalilian, H. and G. Reyes. *Global Financial Crisis Discussion Paper Series 4: Cambodia*. London: ODI, 2010.

Jalilian, H., G. Reyes, and P. Lun P. "Cambodia's Food Security in the Face of the Food and Economic Shocks". Unpublished, 2010a.

————. "Double Blow to the Poor: Cambodia's Food Security in the Face of the Food and Economic Shocks". *CDRI Annual Development Review* 2009–2010. Phnom Penh: CDRI, 2010b.

Lewis, B. "US Bill Targets Kingdom over Uighur Case". Available at <http://khmerization.blogspot.com/2010/05/us-bill-targets-kingdom-over-uighur.html> (accessed 19 September 2010).

Ligon, E. and E. Sadoulet. "Estimating the Effects of Aggregate Agricultural Growth on the Distribution of Expenditures". Background paper for the *World Development Report 2008*. Washington, D.C.: World Bank, 2008.

Lipton, M. *Land Reform in Developing Countries: Property Rights and Property Wrongs*. London: Routledge, 2009.

Malaysian Rubber Board. "Natural Rubber Prices and Charts" (Monthly and Yearly Average). Available at <http://www3.lgm.gov.my/mre/YearlyAvg.aspx> (accessed 12 October 2010).

May, K. "Opening of Bourse Delayed to Next Year". *Phnom Penh Post*, 14 July 2010.

Meas, S. and S. Finch. "Law on Foreign Property Passed". *Phnom Penh Post*, 6 April 2010.

Ministry of Economics and Finance. "Recent Macroeconomic Performance". Available at <http://www.mef.gov.kh/> (accessed 4 January 2010).

————. *Economic and Monetary Statistics Issues*. Phnom Penh: MoEF, various years.

————. *Monthly Bulletin of Statistics*. Phnom Penh: MoEF, various years.

Ministry of Tourism. "Report on the Situation of the Tourism Sector 2008/2009" (text in Khmer.) Phnom Penh: Cambodia, 2009.

National Bank of Cambodia. *Annual Report 2009*. Phnom Penh: NBC, 2010.

Naudé, W. and R. Rossouw. "Export Diversification and Specialisation in Africa". UNU-WIDER Research Paper No. 2008/93. Helsinki: United Nations University — World Institute for Development Economic Research, 2008.

Pratruangkrai, P. "Rice Trade Liberalisation under AFTA Poses Challenges". *The Nation*, 2 March 2010a.

————. "Government May Opt for Foreign Paddy Rice to Boost Exports". *The Nation*, 30 August 2010b.

Prebisch, R. "The Economic Development of Latin America and Its Principal Problems". Reprinted in *Economic Bulletin for Latin America*, vol. 7, no. 1 (1962): 1–22.

Singer, H.W. "U.S. Foreign Investment in Underdeveloped Areas: The Distribution of Gains Between Investing and Borrowing Countries". *American Economic Review, Papers and Proceedings* 40 (1950): 473–85.

Soeun, S. "Government Warns Developers to Apply for Licences". *Phnom Penh Post*, 10 March 2010.

Wingqvist, G.O. "Cambodia Environmental and Climate Change". Policy Brief. Gothenburg: University of Gothenburg, 2009.

World Bank. *Sustaining Rapid Growth in a Challenging Environment (Cambodia Country Economic Memorandum)*. Washington, D.C.: World Bank, 2009.

————. *East Asia and Pacific Economic Update Volume 2: Robust Recovery, Rising Risks*. Washington, D.C.: World Bank, 2010.

World Bank-International Finance Corporation. "Second Investment Climate Assessment". Prepared by the WB and IFC for the RGC, 2009.

INDEX

CPSIA information can be obtained at www.ICGtesting.com
Printed in the USA
BVOW04*1028080714

358479BV00019B/620/P